PENGUIN BOOKS

A WOMAN'S GUIDE TO LAW SCHOOL

Linda Hirshman is a professor at Brandeis University. After graduating from the University of Chicago Law School, she practiced for thirteen years, and presented three cases to the Supreme Court. She has taught law at Chicago-Kent in Chicago and has been a visiting professor elsewhere, most recently at the University of Iowa Law School. She is the co-author of *Hard Bargains: The Politics of Sex* (1998), and numerous law review articles, magazine articles, and opinion pieces, including "Sex and Money: Is Law School a Dead End Street for Women?" which appeared in the *Northwestern Law Review* and "Law Schools Where Women Succeed," published in *Glamour* magazine.

A Woman's Guide to Law SCHOOL

Linda Hirshman

PENGUIN BOOKS

PENGUIN BOOKS
Published by the Penguin Group
Penguin Putnam Inc., 375 Hudson Street,
New York, New York 10014, U.S.A.
Penguin Books Ltd, 27 Wrights Lane,
London W8 5TZ, England
Penguin Books Australia Ltd, Ringwood,
Victoria, Australia
Penguin Books Canada Ltd, 10 Alcorn Avenue,
Toronto, Ontario, Canada M4V 3B2
Penguin Books (N.Z.) Ltd, 182–190 Wairau Road,
Auckland 10, New Zealand

Penguin Books Ltd, Registered Offices:
Harmondsworth, Middlesex, England

First published in Penguin Books 1999

1   3   5   7   9   10   8   6   4   2

LIBRARY OF CONGRESS CATALOGING IN PUBLICATION DATA
Hirshman, Linda R.
A woman's guide to law school/Linda Hirshman.
p.   cm.
Includes index.
ISBN 0 14 02.6437 X
1. Law schools—United States.   2. Law—Study and teaching—United
States.   3. Women law students—United States.   I. Title.
KF283.H57   1999
340′.071′173—dc21   98-51363

Printed in the United States of America
Set in Bembo
Designed by Susan Hood

Dedication

I was in the middle of law school the year President Lyndon Johnson appointed Thurgood Marshall to the United States Supreme Court. Although there were fewer than ten women in my law school class, I believed in the law as an institution to redeem the world for people on the bottom as well as to protect the interests of those on top. Not even the worst story of sexual harassment and disrespect that I heard while researching this book has shaken that belief. As Justice Marshall said at the end of his life, "I did what I could with what I had." All over the country, tens of thousands of women law students, faculty, and practitioners are doing the same thing. This book is for them.

Contents

Acknowledgments

Everything I know I learned from some woman—or man—of goodwill somewhere in the legal education system. Thanks to the scores of students who set aside hours of their time to talk to me, who called as they remembered more information, and who passed me from hand to hand throughout their communities, in the interest of making this book better for you, the next generation of women to come. Some of the women I spoke to had very disturbing tales to tell. Others seemed able to navigate the white water of law school with ease. Although I repeatedly asked people to recommend students who had succeeded and seemed satisfied with their law school experiences, even such very successful students had grave reservations about the institution. *But to a person, they were all glad they had gone!*

Thanks to my colleagues on the faculty, who shared their stories and directed me to others. Too many of them had to speak in hushed voices, like dissident Chinese students after the massacre in Tiananmen Square, fearful that the little ambition and security they still had would be snatched away if I told their stories of harassment, marginalization, and discrimination ("If you tell this story, I'll never get out of here," one of my sources said, looking anxiously around the apparently peaceful school cafeteria where we met). In a disturbing number of cases, they asked me not to use their names or even to tell their stories if the stories could be traced to them. I have honored those requests, but every fact in this book is backed up by data and interview notes in my files. Although I use pseudonyms or refer to the students by their roles (the "editor in chief"), each of the students I talked to is a real person. I did not alter their stories. You don't need to read their names to recognize they are speaking the truth.

I also attempted to interview women faculty who have expressed great satisfaction with their lives in the law school world. Barbara Black, former dean at Columbia, spoke to me with irresistible enthusiasm about the intellectual excitement surrounding the world of feminist theory she had helped create at Columbia. Some enthusiasts of law school did not accept my invitations to be interviewed for this book. Professor Suzanna Sherry, of the University of Minnesota Law School, who had pooh-poohed the existence of lesser lives for women in law in the *Washington Post* ("There are unrepentant bigots in every profession"), would not return my phone calls or letters about the status of women at her institution. Professor Maxine ("Marc") Arkin, of Fordham Law School, quoted in the conservative *City Journal* criticizing her female students ("If you call on them, you're imposing hierarchy; if you don't call on them, you're overlooking them"), would not speak more than a few sentences to me. If law school life at Minnesota and Fordham is really so great for women, as Sherry and Arkin assert, this book is the poorer for their silence.

Thanks to Flip Brophy, who couldn't believe there wasn't already a *Woman's Guide to Law School* and worked hard to make it happen, to Wendy Wolf, the editor who never lost her sense of balance, even when all about her (me) were losing theirs, and, as always, to David, a just man in an unjust world.

Acknowledgments

AUTHOR'S NOTE

Although I have been associated with many institutions over the fifteen years of my academic career, and have had various experiences at those institutions, the findings and conclusions in this book rest entirely on the statistics and other factual evidence gathered in my research and on the anecdotal evidence freely offered by the students and faculty interviewed. Sometimes law schools that provided me personally with opportunities for which I can never fully express my gratitude did not come out well as the numbers came in; other law schools manifesting the most callous indifference to my virtues sometimes present a picture of extreme friendliness to women; sometimes my experience on the scene and the evidence I found produced a consistent picture of women-friendliness or hostility.

A Woman's Guide to Law School

Why a Woman's Guide to Law School?

THREE YEARS OF private law school costs upwards of $75,000 in tuition and living expenses. A very nice suit is no more than $750. It turns out that men and women don't fit into law school in exactly the same way any more than they fit into the suit the same way. You'd try on a $750 suit before you bought it, especially one that was originally designed for a man! This book was written to enable you to do the same thing with the much more important decision about law school.

What's a smart girl like you doing considering or attending law school? Maybe you haven't been able to decide what to do when you get out of college, and you think law school will let you keep putting the decision off. Maybe you've been working as a teacher or a nurse, and you're tired of laboring long hours for lousy pay. Maybe one of your parents was a lawyer, or you've always been a great arguer at the dinner table. What are the chances that law school will give you what you want? Should you be going to law school at all? This introduction and chapters 2 and 3 should help you decide.

If you do decide to go ahead, there's lots of guidance out there already—magazine publishers' guides to law school, student guides, the catalogs from the schools themselves. Why a *woman's* guide to law school? Here's how the enormously confident and successful female editor in chief of a selective and prestigious state university law review put it: "There's no question that women have to work twice as hard to get half the respect." Lani Guinier, the woman President Clinton put up for civil rights chief and then a professor at the University of Pennsylvania Law School (she's now at Harvard), found that first-year men at Penn were three times more likely to make the top 10 percent of their class than women were. In the fall of '97, the all-female Mills College in California had a three-day conference to address the problems of women in law schools.

This is a pretty sad picture. If Ms. Editor's story were the whole story, or if all law schools were the same, women would have no choice but to work twice as hard and expect to be dismissed and condescended to, by teachers and students alike. But Ms. Editor isn't telling the whole story. She herself says she's had some wonderful experiences in law school. And she did make it to the very top of the law school heap. Despite the rash of publicity surrounding Guinier's study, there is a debate among scholars about how big the gap in achievement really is. We have some numbers in chapter 5 to help you decide. This book is about how Ms. Editor succeeded and how to raise the odds that you'll make it, too. You'll also hear about women's very different points of view about what success means.

For a woman to make it in the law school world, she needs some smart strategies and some good, solid information. I'm going to begin at the point where your thoughts turn to law school, perhaps at the beginning of your junior year in college, perhaps after a few years of working or even after another whole career, whether of wage work or full-time homemaking. You and I will examine the decision to go to law school, its pros and cons, and whom to talk to before you spend another penny, even to register for the Law School Admission Test (the LSAT). I'll steer you to where you need to go to prepare for the test and the other things that go into constructing an appealing application.

Probably nothing affects the law school experience for women as much as the school they choose. The schools are very different. In recent years, lots of people have examined the experience of women in law school and ranked the various schools, but not according to how likely women are to succeed there. I looked at 158 of the accredited law schools during the year 1997, gathering data on how many women teach there, what percentage of the classes of '96 and '97 are female, and how many of the women in those classes are on law review, and then I ranked the schools by status and then according to how well women were doing on all those measures. The heart of this book is the ranking I give to the law schools for their value to women. My research has revealed that at every level of status and cost, even among schools with identical median LSAT scores, women rise higher at some schools than others. And fall lower at most.

Compare, at the top of the status ladder, NYU School of Law, with an academic faculty 20 percent women, with the 15 percent female faculty at the equally prestigious Harvard Law School; NYU's student-edited law review was 52 percent female in 1995–96, while Harvard had only 32 percent women on law review. Compare, in the next status ranking down, the University of Washington School of Law's 26 percent female academic faculty and 45 percent female law review with Northwestern School of Law's 21 percent women academic faculty and 27 percent females on 1995–96 law review. Don't miss chapter 5.

In addition to gathering the statistics available from the public record (most law schools wouldn't answer questions about their female students or faculty), I've conducted scores of interviews with women law students around the country and gathered the growing body of research on the position of women in law schools to paint a detailed picture of law school life. After you have a rough idea where you might be admitted to law school, and after you've located your prospective schools on the women-friendly ranking, those stories tell *you* what else *you* want to ask about the particular institutions you're considering.

All the women interviewed agreed that the first year of law

school, where the "Socratic" teaching method involves the professors calling on them whether they like it or not, was the most difficult for them. The first year also weighs most heavily on their career opportunities during and immediately after law school and on their self-esteem for a long time after that. As a University of Chicago professor told his first-year class, "Most of the goodies around here go to twenty percent of the class, who emerge in the first year. The other eighty percent spend the next two years licking their psychic wounds." It's a dirty little secret of law school life that if you do well the first year, you won't have to succeed in as tough a situation again for years. Read chapters 6 and 7.

Many women were surprised by how hard the first year was on them. Studies at all Ohio schools, the law schools in Chicago, a national set of testimonial hearings, reports from Stanford—all reflect the disproportionate male participation in the first-year classroom. One University of Minnesota student summed it up: "The first three weeks of class I raised my hand every day and after a while I felt extremely pretentious and now there are only men who raise their hands in class." Many of the women I interviewed compare law school to a "game" and one that men seem mysteriously to know how to play and want to play.

Not talking in class has severe costs, like not having the professors know you when you need them to write you letters of recommendation for jobs. Making the game seem mysterious is just part of the game! If you know how the game is played, maybe you'll be more willing to join in. I'm going to tell you what goes on in the first-year classes, so you can prepare yourself for it. We don't want you to be one of the women students who never talks after the first three weeks. After all, as that old ad for the lottery put it, you can't win if you don't play.

Most students of any sex agree that exams are the hardest part of the first year. There are better and worse ways to prepare for your first-year exams. Although women do a little less well in law school than men do, rather than focus on that small disparity, I interviewed women law students who got the best grades you could wish for to share their secrets. You'll also see what role the commercial aids you can buy will play to help you understand the mysterious body of knowledge the Socratic method of law teaching seems to make so obscure.

Grades, especially the first-year grades, play the largest role in how useful law schools are to many of their students. Students who make it into the top half, and particularly the top quarter, of their class in law school have more job offers from firms that pay bigger bucks and, even if they don't want to go the big-firm route, have other opportunities, like prestigious judicial clerkships or academic posts, where their less-favored classmates don't stand a chance. Making law review, or getting to be a staff member of the student-edited journal, used to be just a reflection of first-year grades, and the opportunities went to law review members. Recently, however, the selection criteria have been modified to allow students to try out using a combination of grades and a writing competition, or even writing alone. If you haven't made it into the thin sliver of your class eligible for law review on grades alone (and some schools don't take anyone on grades alone), read chapter 8 to learn how to shoehorn yourself onto law review through the other channels or to win the writing competition, if your school makes everyone surmount both hurdles. If you don't have the top grades, being one of the group making law review is still a lot better than just being in the undifferentiated 80 percent that professor described.

At the beginning of the second year, the focus turns to getting a job in your newly chosen profession, and there women and men seem to follow somewhat different tracks, with many women forgoing the high pay/high status world of private practice. But if you do wish to pursue the firm track, chapter 9 explains strategies for the interviewing process.

On the subject of jobs, you *can* go to any place in the law from any school, but if you must buck the general expectations of your law school, it's just going to make your experience more of an uphill battle. More Wall Street practitioners come from Columbia than from Fordham and more public interest lawyers from CUNY Queens than from Columbia. Women already have to "work twice as hard for half the respect," according to our editor in chief. Why make it even harder on yourself?

To my surprise, many of the women I interviewed did not want to talk in class, edit the law review, or work for a Wall Street firm. They wanted to be left alone in class rather than have to defend their answers in a high-pressure exchange, to have time for socializing rather than edit the law review, and to work in public interest jobs, as union-side labor lawyers, or in firms that don't require "more than forty hours" a week. One student described her law degree as a credential in the marriage market, which demonstrated she was smart enough to produce genetically desirable children for some traditional male who she hoped would liberate her from working at all. Although they were often silent about their disaffection from the striving world of legal education, these women are acting out a kind of personal civil disobedience in the law school world. In chapter 10, I will discuss their ways of coping with what they perceive to be a hostile world and suggest ways in which they can use their disagreement with the existing law school order as an opportunity for change, rather than just experiencing it as alienation and resentment, marginalizing themselves in their new world.

Why Do Women Want to Go to Law School?

Let's begin before the beginning. One recent study reports that a really big indicator of women's success in law school is why they went in the first place. As you will see, law school is not for everyone. Before you commit any more resources to the undertaking than the price of this book, let's look closely at whether you should go at all.

THE IDEAL CANDIDATE

When former lieutenant Carol Counselor, High Status law school class of '90-something, was an officer in the armed services, the soldiers in her squad got into trouble a lot. The military assigned lawyers to defend them, but the military lawyers weren't zealous enough to suit Carol. "To help my soldiers," she says, "I would have to look up the regulations. I often learned I was the only one who actually looked them up. Including their lawyers. When the soldiers were in trouble, I always took more of an interest in them than I had to."

Even before she went to law school, Carol was on the right track for what lay ahead. Representing her soldiers when the military police—the government—came after them is a model of what lawyers do. People are good at what lawyers do when they are zealous about their jobs—part of that zeal involves taking the legal system seriously, and taking the legal system seriously includes going and "looking up the regulations."

After leaving the military, Carol enrolled in law school, where she ranked at the top of her class. She soon figured out that, like 70 percent of all women lawyers (and 74 percent of men), she will likely be employed in the private practice of law. (The National Association of Law Placement reports 58 percent of men and 52 percent of women starting in firms, along with assorted clerkships, etc. The 70 percent number is long-term.) Although she is looking forward to clerking for a judge for a year after graduation, she's also glad that as late as her third year at High Status U she can interview with corporate firms and nail down a secure, high-paying job in the future.

Representing people with regard to their government's laws, and taking the job seriously, whether at a small firm, a big firm, or in solo practice, is what most lawyers do. That's what law school is best at teaching. If Carol's story sounds appealing to you, you probably belong in law school.

THE DOUBTING CANDIDATE

Another Carol, Carol Too, wasn't too sure about law school. Carol Too was a liberal arts major at a prestigious state college. Because her dad's a lawyer, the possibility of law school was always around. But she wasn't sure it was a good idea, because "everyone goes to law school, and I knew the law school experience was hard, so if I wasn't sure, then I decided to take some time off." Carol Too got a job in a law-related field, working for a lawyer in a non-professional role. When the lawyer was appointed to the elite federal appeals court, she followed him there. In his chambers, she met the most brilliant of law graduates, who vie with one another for the prestigious judicial clerkships. Every day they talked about the issues in the cases the judge would be having to hear and decide.

Her exposure to the give-and-take of the legal world convinced her that she would find law school worth the effort. When she got there a few years after college, she "liked it, even my first year." (But even Carol Too found the classroom a surprise.) If you like the rigor and competition of debating issues, even fairly obscure issues like whether or not people have actually committed themselves to a contract or what constitutes "custody" such that potential criminals are entitled to be apprised of their rights, then law school is probably for you, too.

What Is the "Law" in Law School?

Chances are most of you don't know whether you'd like to practice law or not or even what it involves. Unlike the Carols, if you're lucky and drove carefully, you probably never needed a lawyer before you thought about becoming one yourself. Unless someone in your family is a lawyer, you don't know much about the practice of law.

For our purposes, law is the way government regulates people's activities. Criminal law, like the laws against murder and theft, prohibits what may be done, period. The police watch for people who try to kill each other or rob banks, and, if they catch such people, someone like the district attorney prosecutes the offenders on behalf of all members of society. Civil law, like the law against negligent driving, also tells people what the government wants them to do but is usually enforced only when someone affected by the illegal conduct complains. So the law prohibits people from driving carelessly, such as looking at their car phone instead of at the road, but the government, in the form of the judiciary, usually steps in only when the careless driver hits someone. If the victim brings the driver before the court system in what we call a "personal injury" suit, the government may punish him or her by making them pay the victim money.

Civil law also tells people what kinds of arrangements they can make between them and expects the government to step in and make them keep their promises or at least pay a penalty for breaking them. We call legally enforceable private arrangements "contracts," and, from the small agreement you made to pay back your student loans to the biggest merger of Turner Network Television with Time Warner Communications, the government will only enforce private contracts if they meet the legal requirements for contracting that the law sets out.

In modern times, governments have begun to act through "regulatory" laws, which tell people what to do and are enforced by the government without a complaining party, sort of like criminal laws, but which usually carry monetary penalties or orders to obey like civil law. The law requiring automobile manufacturers to put seat belts in cars is an example of a regulatory law.

Law is the business of government, which explains why about half of the nation's legislators are lawyers and why so many of the residents in and around Washington, D.C., or most state capitols are lawyers. They're looking after their clients' business at the place where the laws are made, in part, by trying to influence them in advance.

Every private lawyer, from the lawyer for the bank writing up your student loan agreement to the partner in a Wall Street firm putting together the billion-dollar merger, is doing his job, because people need to know three things about law. First, what does the government require? For instance, the bank will probably need to ask if the government will prosecute its loan officers if they try to extract 100 percent interest from you for your student loan, a practice called "usury." So the bank hires a bank lawyer to tell them how much interest the government will allow them to charge. Second, how do they convince the government that what they're doing or did is okay? Someone suspected of murder may find himself attracting what he feels is an unhealthy amount of attention from the police. Unless he's going to hop into his Ford Bronco and run away, he's going to need a lawyer to convince a jury that he is not guilty. Finally, people are always dreaming up new things to do, and they need a good estimate of how the government will respond to their new ideas. Maybe there's never been a media merger as big as Turner and Time Warner. The federal government regulates TV in certain ways. Will the government allow two such media giants to merge or will they apply the laws on the books to prohibit the merger? I bet there were a lot of lawyers around when Ted Turner decided it was time to merge with Time Warner. Many new ideas involve making novel arrangements with others that the government will enforce if one party tries to break their word. How can they make an agreement that reflects what they want and that the government will enforce?

Many critics of the law school curriculum decry the emphasis on learning what the government will or will not allow, as if life were as simple as yes or no. They report that women have a harder time thinking in these off/on ways and emphasize that when people—or institutions—come into conflict or desire to cooperate, there are many ways that a lawyer can resolve the conflict into cooperation or enable the cooperation without conflict. If these critics had their way, the "law" in law school would include these strategies for mediating conflicting desires and needs, as well as simply deciding them. Here and there people of this persuasion are having an effect on what is the "law" in law school, using arguments of gender as well as broader arguments about the well-being of society, although this position is by no means common.

What Is the "School" in Law School?

Most legal education is intended to teach you these three things about the law. If you decide to go to law school, you will learn a sample of what the law requires or will enforce, like that there is a law against killing your spouse or that some kinds of agreements have to be in writing. Courses in the substance of law include criminal law, contracts, property, wills and estates, and tax. Second, law school teaches you something of how to convince the government that your client is doing what the government wants, like Johnnie Cochran convincing the jury that O. J. Simpson did not kill his wife. Courses in this process include civil procedure, criminal procedure, evidence, and trial advocacy.

Third, law school teaches you how to figure out from what government did in the past what government is likely to do in a new case. This third piece of legal education is often called "legal reasoning," or "legal process" and is usually a part of each of the substantive classes (and sometimes the subject of a special class all its own). For example, the class in contracts will use existing contract law to teach you what it takes to make a valid contract (the substance). The contracts professor will also ask you to figure out from the existing law of contracts what a court might do when confronted with a new situation. For example, existing contract law of infancy might require a party to be eighteen in order to conclude a valid contract. Obviously, the law developed to protect very young children, and their families, from being stuck with purchases they weren't old enough to decide about—or pay for— by unscrupulous merchants. Think of how unfair it would be if someone could bind a thirteen-year-old to pay for a thousand-dollar stereo he or she just "couldn't resist" at the mall when their parent was not around. A law professor might ask you to figure out whether the law of infancy applies to void a contract for a stereo signed by a mature thirteen-year-old with a mental age of nineteen.★

Law schools present this "legal" thought process as if it were new or unique to the law, but reasoning from old premises to new cases is as old as the Greek philosopher Socrates (which is the du-

---

★ The answer is probably that the contract is not binding, because the law presumes a lack of seasoned judgment at thirteen and does not look behind the chronological age. More of this later!

bious reason first-year teaching is called "Socratic"). The only difference is that most undergraduate educations are devoted to transmitting a body of knowledge, like the law schools transmit the substance of law, rather than teaching undergraduates about the process of reasoning to new cases. So most new law students experience learning "legal reasoning" as new. Many law school guides emphasize the importance of a knack for playing mind games; for example, can you see how the principles behind the contract rule might apply to the puzzling problem of the rare, mentally capable youngster? Women often find such games sterile and too abstract, but are eager and talented problem solvers in day-to-day life. I will have more to say about how to use the bent for problem solving to learn the lessons of legal reasoning and the Socratic method when we get to chapter 6, "The Dreaded First Year."

Curiosity is a great asset in law—and law school. UCLA's second-year student Diane Information, for instance, looked up magazine articles about law schools and catalogs at the public library. "I love libraries," she says. "I just like to know stuff." Since law school teaches how to make arguments from old cases to new ones, if you're a good arguer and would like to know how to persuade the government to do what your clients want, you should also do well in law school. A second-year UCLA student, Ms. Persistence, boasted to me that she never had a class in her undergraduate years at a large state school she didn't get into. "If there was a class I wanted, I just went and saw the professor every day until they let me in." Unlike most students in California's public university system, Persistence graduated early, completing her undergraduate education in three and a half years. When the time came for job interviews at UCLA School of Law, Persistence saw all the firms she was entitled to under UCLA's interviewing system and shanghaied the other interviewers in the hallways or at their lunch breaks. When she settled on a prestigious San Francisco firm, she turned away loads of other offers.

Since law ultimately rests on nonlegal assumptions about what makes a good society (for instance, we want people to be able to buy and sell things without subjecting everyone to a psychiatric evaluation, so we just draw a bright line at eighteen for capacity to contract in most cases), if you have an analytic bent, and love to figure out what a rule really means and therefore to be able to predict what the government is likely to do in a new situation, you're a good candidate for law school. UCLA moot court finalist Ms. Policy says, "Why not say something wrong in class? Maybe in being wrong you can say something valuable and maybe figure out a policy reason why your answer is really right." Remember our contracts problem of the mentally mature thirteen-year-old? The courts would probably refuse to consider the buyer's mental maturity, because very few people want sellers to sell stereos to youngsters, who are usually immature and impulsive, and then try to stick them with the purchase by demanding a test of each teenager's mental age when the teenager comes to his or her senses. As a policy matter, the lawmakers have decided to protect the majority of impulsive teenagers with a hard-and-fast rule, even if it means that a few stereo merchants are going to have to take the stereos back from the handful of youths who are mentally old enough to make decisions of that magnitude. The really hard problem is whether the courts will enforce a contract in a closer case, say by a sixteen-year-old who actively misled the seller into thinking he was older. Policy would think this was fun to try to figure out.

Show Me the Money

One thing that will help you feel comfortable in your law school education regardless of your curiosity, argumentativeness, or problem-solving inclinations is if you like money. If you aspire to earn a very good living, like women who have worked at crummy jobs for a few years after college, you will tend to be more goal-oriented about law school. Ms. Older, age forty-seven and living in a law school dormitory, went to law school for one reason:

"California public employees haven't seen a wage increase in years." A student at Minnesota said, "I couldn't make a living in my undergraduate subject."

The National Association of Law Placement reports that in 1994, lawyers in private practice averaged starting salaries of $50,000, although the Princeton Review correctly notes that a few high numbers probably raised the average. Nonetheless, a majority of starting lawyers made more than $40,000. In 1993, a survey of women practitioners in Colorado, far from the highest-end legal market in the United States, revealed a salary range from $30,806 for a lawyer with one to three years' experience to $102,500 at more than twenty years out of school. The Colorado numbers reflected substantial disparity between men's and women's compensation; still, Colorado's women lawyers made a lot more money than someone with a history B.A. can make driving a cab. And salaries have gone way up since 1993.

If you're in it for the money, you won't see law school as defining you as a person. If you get into a more prestigious law school, even if you don't have great grades there, the status of your degree will give you a shot at a good job in practice. UCLA's intrepid arguer went from making the minimum wage slinging hash the summer before her first year in law school to making $1,300 a week the next summer at an L.A. law firm. At the lower-status law schools, the students of both genders are often the first generation of their families to get a higher education, and even a modest middle-class life seems good to them.

You Don't Have to Practice What You Learn

But even if law school's for you, you still must decide if you are a good candidate for the private practice of law. As my favorite client, the president of a local bus drivers' union in California, described a good job, "You stay warm in the winter and cool in the summer and you stay clean." Practicing law usually meets that standard.

There are two things about practicing law that many of the women I talked to find unattractive. First, you may have to work very long hours. Second, you may have to represent really icky people. A recent survey of eight large New York firms revealed that 41 percent of women associates worked between forty-one and fifty hours each week and another 41 percent worked fifty hours or more. Averaging fifty hours at the office every week doesn't leave a lot of time for sleeping, dressing, eating, commuting, running errands, and having a social life. UCLA's Ms. Persistence, for instance, simply eliminated from the firms she would work for during the all-important "tryout" summer between the second and third years a very well-known San Francisco firm that required its first-year associates to bill 2,400 hours a year. To bill 2,400 hours, you must bill forty-eight hours a week, assuming two weeks of vacation, and to bill forty-eight hours, you must be in the office much more. She didn't want to spend fifty or sixty hours a week at the office.

Then there are the clients. Remember the tobacco executives who each stood up in Congress a couple of years ago and swore that cigarettes were not addictive? Every single one of them had a lawyer, probably more than one. Many legal matters involve a more powerful player and a less powerful one or someone trying to accomplish his own goals regardless of the cost to society. Polluters have lawyers, people who want to fire their African American and female employees have lawyers. Criminals have lawyers. Many of the women I interviewed hoped to avoid making a career as the lawyer who helps people increase their power over hapless subordinates by going into the jobs called "public interest." But a lot of the clients in public interest jobs, like the criminals public defenders represent, aren't all that appealing either.

I actively tried to meet women who were destined for their 70 percent majority jobs in private practice, but I still saw a lot of female law students trying to find places in the world of public interest or government. As of 1991, the Law School Admission Council found that, regardless of what fate held in store for them, only 45 percent of women first-year students aspired to private practice or business. An almost equal number hoped for government or public interest work. By contrast, the same study found almost 60 percent of men looking to private practice or business and only 32 percent thinking of the public sector.

Ms. Union, a third-year student at an Ivy League school, for example, never wanted to be a traditional private practitioner. She has taken a job in private practice, but in a firm representing mostly organized labor (called a "union side" labor law firm), which she perceives as a public interest job because even organized workers on the whole are less powerful than their employers. Through her law school's public interest center, NYU's Ms. Interest found a public interest internship with a Prisoners' Legal Services Project and a summer job with the Justice Department to her liking. At Minnesota, Ms. Rights, a first-year student with an interest in international human rights, specifically went to law school because so many of the issues she cared about were tied up with law, like international conventions and immigration law. Half my interview subjects at UCLA were anticipating working with such institutions as the office of the public defender (public defenders still represent criminals, by the way) or the California public counsel.

It's Hard to Be a Lefty—Especially in Law School

Although some so-called public interest jobs like Ms. Union's union side labor job are technically in the private practice, most are not. If you do not expect to practice law in a firm or a business, you will be a distinct minority in law school. Being a minority is generally not a big advantage in any society. So most law students hoping to do public interest work are swimming upstream. Even if there were no such thing as gender discrimination or favoritism in law school, not wanting to go into private practice is sort of like being left-handed—you will seem a little different, and most services are not going to be oriented to your special needs. Women are also a minority of law students—as of 1994–95, women were a minority at 88 percent of American law schools. A woman law student who is also a law student who doesn't expect to enter the private practice of law is a minority of a minority.

Not surprisingly, many of the women I spoke to in this minority/minority felt unsatisfied with their experience. One public-interest-bound lawyer described herself as feeling very out of place at Columbia, because, she said, her classmates were all going into corporate law, and she felt the law school did not enable students easily to find work in other areas. She recommends that instead of just blindly picking a law school, a woman with public interest aspirations ask the admissions office what careers the graduates choose and specifically about public interest law, like being a public defender or working in public policy.

The American Bar Association's *Official Guide to Approved Law Schools* contains an entry, "Type of Employment," which reveals the initial placement of the most recent graduating class from each law school. Only a few of the schools (Northeastern, CUNY Queens, St. Thomas, Northern Illinois) reflect a "public interest" placement of more than 5 percent in the ABA guide, although the number goes up to more than 20 percent if you add in "government employment," which conceals a lot of jobs traditionally regarded as "public interest." Another way to tell how supportive a law school will be for a public interest career is to ask if your prospective law school is one of the over seventy law schools that belong to a public interest consortium started through NYU. It is important to note that only one of the dozens of public interest–oriented women I talked to regretted going to law school. They think they can make law school work for them. They just recommend that new students like them try to find the friendliest place within an unfriendly system.

That being said, I would be less than honest if I didn't tell you that there are big costs to passing up the high-paid, high-status jobs. First, money is definitely an asset in our society. One of my interviewees said she didn't need a lot of money—"only enough to buy a nice house in San Francisco," one of the most expensive housing markets in the country. And in a market-oriented society like America, money buys much more than material things. It buys security, power, and, later in life, after the sixty-hour weeks, some leisure. I wonder how many of the idealistic public interest students I interviewed are actually thinking their boyfriends or husbands will fill the money bill, although they'd be reluctant to admit it. In an effort to avoid going into debt that would force her into a high-paying firm job, a midwestern school's Ms. Daughter found a man to support her—her father! But she had to pick a law school her father would pay for (the school is his alma mater), and she found it less than ideal (see chapter 4, "How to Pick a Compatible Law School"). Having someone else pay your way can have a lot of hidden costs.

Those Who Don't, Teach

A handful of my subjects went to law school with an eye to teaching law, or later developed an interest in teaching in order to avoid the conflict between the fifty-hour weeks at a New York firm and a poorly paying public interest job. State University's Ms. Editor started out to law school because she was interested in discrimination and sexual harassment law. She worked for attorneys who usually represent the women claimants in such suits. After two years of law school, Editor, like at least half of the female law review editors I spoke to, hoped to stay in the academic world. Interestingly, law school turns out not to be such a great preparation for teaching. Since law school classes are so much bigger than most academic Ph.D. programs, they turn out far more candidates for teaching than there are places. Accordingly, an increasing number of the desirable entry-level academic law school jobs (as opposed to jobs in the practice clinic or teaching legal writing) require both a law degree and a Ph.D. in something like economics. As Pamela Gann, the well-respected dean of Duke's School of Law, put it in the *National Law Journal* a year ago:

There are too many look-alikes with the same excellent credentials. Increasingly, legal education is becoming interdisciplinary, and those who want to get ahead of the competition would do well to have an advanced degree in a related field, such as economics or public policy.

Two of the three aspiring academics I interviewed had figured this out and were in joint programs, both in sociology. Another would-be teacher was increasingly coming to grips with the reality and was thinking of settling for a less prestigious teaching post.

Whatever

A lot of you are probably thinking of law school because you can't think of anything better to do, or you think you can make better wages than the pink collar or generic humanities jobs you're holding. Ms. Daughter's tuition-paying dad always said being a lawyer means you can do anything. The *Pre-Law Companion*, published by the Princeton Review, a company that specializes in test preparation, says that "a large percentage of top business executives are lawyers." But most chief executive officers of American corporations are not lawyers: they are, surprise, engineers; after that, the largest percentage went to business school. Once in law school, Ms. Daughter learned that legal education and practice are actually quite specialized. The specialized education and practice are difficult, intense, and extremely competitive. Viewing the competition from comfortably beyond the finish line, Ms. Editor observed that "the people who go to law school as a general, vague, 'viable career option' are far more miserable and shocked by the intensity of law school than the people who know they're going for a highly competitive, technical education."

Some women go to law school because they believe that a law degree would add legitimacy to their opinions and beliefs. One of the women I interviewed had managed a bunch of liberal political campaigns, and she was frustrated with her lack of impact. Such women observe that lawyers seem to command a lot of respect when they speak, and these women were tired of being ignored when they tried to make their opinions and beliefs felt. To some extent, they were correct. Lawyers get attention. Partly that is because they occasionally have a lot of money, and people with a lot of money often get a lot of attention. For the most part, lawyers get attention because they know some technical information that is occasionally desperately important. You may remember Barry Scheck, the previously unknown DNA-expert defense lawyer on O. J.'s "dream team," who discredited the evidence that it was O. J.'s blood around his ex-wife's murder scene.

Scheck commanded the undivided attention of the nation for that brief time, and he still makes TV appearances now and then. But the reason the nation was riveted on Barry Scheck for a few days in 1995 was not that he possesses unusual moral insight, political savvy, social graces, or opinions worth having. He just knew a lot about DNA evidence and the art of cross-examination, which, if you were O. J. Simpson, was desperately important at that moment. It did not, however, entitle Scheck to hold the floor at cocktail parties or political conventions. (Indeed, Scheck's later performance at the disastrous Boston nanny murder trial led me to believe that his strategic judgment wasn't all that terrific either.) So women who go to law school to obtain a credential to legitimate their opinions on subjects other than the technicalities of legal education are probably going to be disappointed.

Moreover, in a world of lawyers, a law degree does little to add heft to a woman's voice. As Stanford Law School professor Deborah Rhode put it, law school faculty meetings too often resemble that cartoon of a room full of surprised-looking men staring at a single woman. "Good point, Mary," the man in charge is saying. "Now we'll just all wait for a man to make it."

There Are Almost No Born Lawyers

Clarence Darrow. President Abe Lincoln. Justice Ruth Bader Ginsburg. Law can be a good job and a good life.

Teddy Roosevelt. Charles Dickens. Ambassador Pamela Harriman. You can have a good life if you didn't finish law school (or even start). Even the most dedicated and successful lawyers probably wanted to be firefighters or rock singers when they were young. Now that you know what the possibilities are, you can make a good decision.

Part of growing up is learning to live with your decision. The good news is that almost none of the more than one hundred women I interviewed for this book said that they were sorry they had gone to law school. You are going to do even better than they did, because the rest of this book is designed to help you have a good experience, once the big decision is made.

What Law Schools Where Women Succeed Are Like

IN CHAPTER 4, "How to Pick a Compatible Law School," I rank 158 law schools in America according to various indicators of women's success there. You will notice that law schools where women succeed have lots of things in common, like being public institutions and having satisfied students of both sexes, and you'll see that law schools where women fail have lots of things in common, too, like being mostly in the South or in the city of Chicago and having students who sound kind of grumpy.

Although this is the first book to look nationally and name names, the matter of women and law school has attracted a *lot* of attention. After studying the matter at Penn, newly appointed Harvard professor Lani Guinier wrote a whole book about what she thinks is wrong with all legal education. But other than the Penn numbers, most of the thinking was just speculation. Given law schools' reluctance to share data about how their women do, before this book there was no way of isolating where women succeed and examining what was going on there. Now that we have national data on where women make law review, we have a rough measure of women's success. And so we know where to go for information—to the success schools. This chapter is going to look at what a couple of success schools are doing that's different.

This matters to you as future law students for three reasons. One, you will see that good schools for women are good for people of both genders and good for training lawyers. So you won't feel like a whiner if you ask the school to give you what you need (for your $30,000 or $40,000 in tuition money). Second, you will find out what to ask for at your schools of choice. This guide is of necessity limited in the amount of information I can give you about 158 different schools. And law review is only a very rough measure of how well women succeed. In this chapter, we will see some of the ways in which institutions make themselves hospitable for women regardless of the women's ambitions regarding law review. So whatever your individual thoughts on law review, this chapter will help you to know what to ask for when you focus on your particular school. I think you're in for some surprises.

Finally, if you care about other women and want to do a little something to make a better world, you'll learn what you should be seeking at your law school. After all, most congressmen, mayors, presidents, and so on, are lawyers. If law students learn to expect women to be successful fellow and sister citizens and are educated in a respectful law school environment, maybe they'll run the world a little better for women as a result.

This chapter takes a closer look at two success schools, NYU, the second most women-friendly of the elite schools in Status Group #1, and Arizona State University, the most women-friendly of the middle range of schools in Status Group #4. We also take a look at two less successful schools, George Mason, one of the least women-friendly, and McGeorge, where women didn't make law review much, which is a surprise in the failure category, because McGeorge is not located in the Old South.

For this chapter, I also looked at the literature about how social institutions other than law schools react to a change in the racial or gender composition of their members.* I was amazed to learn—and maybe you will be, too—how accurately the literature about racial and gender diversity predicts where women will succeed and fail in law school. Briefly, the literature asserts that there are four responses to the appearance of newcomers in an institution. First, Exclusion, in which outsiders are completely shut out. The famous white male canon of Western literature is an example of Exclusion. The second stage is Quantitative Diversity, in which women or the excluded group are brought into the institution without any intent or desire to change anything else about the place. Cigar-smoking tax lawyers in skirts are an example of the Quantitative Diversity of many law firms.

Sometimes, Quantitative Diversity requires "retooling the newcomers," so they can be assimilated or "fit in." I want to confess right here that this book is in part an effort to retool women to succeed according to the unreconstructed norms of formerly exclusive institutions of legal education. Some retooling is both difficult and necessary.

The retooling is necessary, because, regardless of gender, going to law school of necessity requires some retooling of all incoming students. All law students must acquire new learning habits, because they must learn how to argue from an existing law or set of case decisions to a new outcome. Remember the case of the sixteen-year-old who deliberately misled the merchant we dis-

---

* This analysis is largely drawn from Sarah Berger, Angela Olivia Burton, Peggy Cooper Davis, Elizabeth Ehrenfest Steinglass, and Robert Levy, "Hey! There's Ladies Here!," 73 *NYU L. Rev.* 142 (1998), which in turn rests on Marilyn R. Schuster and Susan R. Van Dyne, "Stages of Curriculum Transformation," in *Women's Place in the Academy: Transforming the Liberal Arts Curriculum* (Marilyn R. Schuster and Susan R. Van Dyne, eds., 1985), Peggy McIntosh, *Interactive Phases of Curricular Revision: A Feminist Perspective* (Wellesley College Center for Research on Women, Working Paper No. 124 [1983]) and David A. Thomas and Robin J. Ely, "Making Differences Matter: A New Paradigm for Managing Diversity," *Harv. Bus. Rev.* Sept.–Oct. 1996.

cussed in chapter 1? If the law the legislature passed doesn't specifically address the problem, lawyers are going to have to convince judges to interpret the law in favor of their client, whether the youngster who's trying to escape his contract or the merchant who's trying to enforce it. Because the political history of the English-speaking democracies requires most law to be the product of elected legislatures, if the law is unclear, mostly unelected judges can't just free-associate about what they'd like the law to be. Accordingly, law students must learn how to make arguments to push the interpretation of existing statutes in the direction of their clients' positions, in order to achieve the outcomes their clients desire from judges who are ultimately answerable to the democratically elected legislators.

The retooling also exists because the common law system we inherited from our English settlers, which lacks even the fig leaf of legislative authorship of statutes, actually allows judges to make law themselves. This presents judges in a democracy with an even harder problem. The common law system solves this problem similarly to the way it solves the problem of having unelected judges tell us what the statutes mean. It pretends the judges are just extending preexisting doctrines. Accordingly, law students in our common law system are going to have to work even harder than in statutory systems to learn how to imagine cases stopping short or going beyond their existing rationales and facts. If, for example, you are faced with a case involving a sale to someone under eighteen, you are going to have to learn to reason by analogy ("Is this more like the rare mature thirteen-year-old, or the mature, deliberately misrepresenting sixteen-year-old?") And you will be subjected to Socratic dialogue to inculcate the habits of pressing your assumptions to the limit. If you contend that mental age should count, your teacher may ask, "If we're going to consider mental age every time we're concerned with age, how long would it take to sell a beer?" You will be asked to demonstrate your ability to reason by analogy and defend your ideas on issue-spotting examinations ("An underage but very smart sixteen-year-old college freshman approaches a computer salesman"). Very few colleges use those teaching methods. Some retooling for law school is unavoidable.

Sometimes, Berger et al. note, the newcomers take on the task of trying to fit in. Where the retooling is necessary, this is an appropriate response. The problem is that women seem to be having a harder time retooling for law school than men are. Scholars speculate that this is because women are more relational, more consultative, less confident in public argument, and so forth, so their retooling job for a culture of distinction drawing, Socratic arguing, and issue-spotting is bigger. At some level, it doesn't matter whether this female stereotype is true or not. Sociologist Claude Steele has produced remarkable evidence that when behaviors stereotypically associated with an excluded group are disfavored, the group members experience *stereotype threat*. Stereotype threat means they internalize their low status and expect themselves to fail. Anticipating failure, they fail at higher rates than necessary. If the law school can't value the traits of relationalism, consultativeness, conciliation, and thoughtfulness, then women are stuck. They must do all the hard work of retooling the guys do, plus correct for their disfavored traits if they have them, and labor under a burden of stereotype threat whether they have those female traits or not!

We will see that law schools can value such traits as building on other people's statements, taking time to think before claiming a share of the collective attention of the class, cooperative problem solving, patient research, careful writing, thoughtful analysis, and skillful listening, and would benefit from doing so. So a piece of the burden of retooling that women bear is unnecessary. Nonetheless, to the extent that the legal system requires the contrary traits of arguing risky or imaginative points, thinking on your feet alone, and analyzing from your clients' interests exclusively, etc., women must retool.

The third response is to establish Perspectives on Exclusion and Perspectives on Difference. We will hear the stories of the women at dozens of law schools. By telling these stories, this book will identify such sources of exclusion as lack of confidence and the naturalizing of social or learned behaviors. My favorite is the story of the male law student who brought into the classroom a lot of information he learned clerking in a law firm. When one of his male classmates asked him how he knew so much, the know-it-all admitted he had seen a lot of cases in his clerking job. When a woman asked the same question, the classroom big mouth said the law came "naturally" to him.

I'd like to go one better than just describing stereotype threat and identify why the lack of confidence extracts a price. It will help the excluded group, because it makes the stereotype threat visible, hopefully discouraging women from internalizing their inferior status. I also seek to realize Perspectives on Difference by identifying bad differences—I will argue that it's bad for women to be unwilling to take the risks associated with participating in the law review writing contest, for example. And I will emphasize examples of good differences—for example, female cooperativeness led to the establishment of a class outline network open to anyone who wished to participate to replace the exclusive Old Boy outline network at the University of Arizona.

Finally, the community may come to the point of integrating the newcomers in part by adopting the good differences, what Berger et al. call "Qualitative Integration." In this chapter and, interestingly, in the chapter on an institution beyond law school— the law firm—we will see how all the firms we spoke to and the schools where women succeed have integrated the differences rightly or wrongly associated with women, differences such as listening, mediating, community building, and collective problem solving that the newcomers bring, to the apparent advantage of all the people involved. Coincidentally, this integration minimizes the effect of stereotype threat.

Bottom line of institutions that have reached Qualitative Integration? Women do better. Let's see the process at work in real schools.

Two Law Schools Where Women Succeed: NYU and Arizona State

Although NYU has been approved by the American Bar Association since 1930, in an important sense it is as new as Arizona State University, which celebrated its thirtieth anniversary recently. For reasons of history, NYU had come into ownership of a pasta manufacturer, the Mueller Macaroni Company. When the law school sold its pasta holdings in 1977, NYU became one of the richest law schools in the country. Like any of the newly rich, the school responded by building itself a fancy new home along with a bunch of other buildings—libraries, dormitory, etc. That's when the fun began.

NYU's second important act of self-creation was the appointment, in 1987, of the irrepressible John Sexton, a dean described in the *New York Times* recently as a rare combination of priest, scholar, and Music Man. Sexton's appointment came at a critical time in the history of the institution as a player in the status race.

For about a generation, law schools have been competing for status based on the "scholarship" of their faculty. No one exactly knows how this development came about, in an educational institution originally intended to train people in the methods and content of legal doctrine to enable them to engage in the professional practice of law. (Law schools coexisted on an equal footing for a long time with "reading" law as an apprentice in a law office. The Harvard philosophy department they were not.)

The likeliest culprit in this "scholarship" business is Yale, which, a perpetual second to Harvard in the corporate-lawyers-trained-and-employed department, some time in the sixties began to evolve an image as an intellectual bastion, with people on the faculty writing about—and then teaching—courses in law and literature and the like. The University of Chicago produced a bunch of men devoted to analyzing law as an economic system designed to produce efficient outcomes, and then everybody picked their favorite nonlegal discipline to pursue. Reacting to the incursion of outside disciplines, traditional legal scholars produced theoretical analyses rooted in the development of legal doctrine. Fine distinctions and at least a superficial familiarity with disciplines like economics became central to prestigious law teaching. Interpreting, rather than learning, the law became the vogue. Writing up interpretations rather than training students in the range of practical skills necessary for them to take their places in the corporate world became the avenue to successful academic careers. Since lawyers seem to be natural creators of hierarchy, they quickly established a pecking order of prestigious publications, led, not surprisingly, by the *Yale Law Journal*, and the race was on.

NYU had lagged significantly behind in the emphasis it put on "scholarship" in this sense. However, as the heritage of its scrappy past, NYU had two very avant-garde programs—the Root-Tilden Public Interest Fellowships and a very large, very well regarded legal clinic, for teaching students by actually working on cases—and those mostly practical programs absorbed a lot of the resources and interest of the institution. Right about the time Sexton was being considered for dean, famed criminal lawyer Anthony Amsterdam conceived of a third, non-scholarship program, the "lawyering program," wherein first-year students spend several credit hours per term in small groups, in real and simulated client interviews, counseling, negotiations, and advocacy, both formal and informal.

At this crossroads, Sexton was the scholars' candidate. In the decade of his stewardship, he has boasted of luring scholars from Yale itself and going head-to-head with Harvard over the hottest prospects in the legal academy. However, despite his extraordinary energy and education, he was himself not all that noted a scholar, and this probably turned out to be a blessing in disguise. In addition to hiring all these philosophers and doctrinal theorists, Sexton also presided over the expansion of the lawyering program, with its insatiable demands for faculty staffing and the establishment of a colloquium designed to analyze the process of lawyering. Six years ago, Steven Kalban, the executive director of NYU's Public Interest Law Center, started the Public Interest Law Colloquium, which now boasts eighty-five to ninety member schools, to try to build students' access to public interest programs. Through programs in loan forgiveness, public interest scholarships, and $3,000 summer stipends, NYU brings resources to bear to enable its students to pursue public interest careers.

The most remarkable thing about the NYU program is that public interest is not marginal at NYU. The Root-Tilden fellowships, which provide tuition in exchange for a commitment to public interest, are among the most prestigious in the school. The "Roots," as they are called, are selected from a huge pool of applicants by a committee of former Roots, faculty, present students, and federal judges, and often the application process is a fast track to the prestigious clerkships students at the elite schools so cherish. In 1996, 80 percent of Roots had clerkships with federal judges, while only 17 percent of the overall student body did.

Although many of the Roots are women, Kalban would not concede to a pink ghetto: "To say it's a woman thing is to degrade it. NYU expects [students will] be doing public service during your years at the firm. We're not second-class citizens here." Kalban credits Sexton: "The first thing the dean talks to the students about in orientation is the responsibility to incorporate public interest in your career."

Why do these programs help women to succeed? Women express themselves as interested in public interest careers in much greater numbers than do men. As it turns out, at least for the class of 1995, only a tiny percentage of NYU grads were actually working public interest jobs, although we know a lot of the Roots were clerking for judges. Perhaps, even without much actual product, the simple regard for public interest work, stereotypically associated with women students, removed the stereotype threat a little.

Second, women are stereotypically associated with a wider range of capacities than the "dreaded first year" calls forth, at least in most places. At NYU, the lawyering program, by honoring and eliciting capacities for careful listening, for human community forming, for cooperative working, is prominently situated in the required first-year curriculum. Lawyering occupies only a few of the hours of NYU's required first-year curriculum, and lawyering is only pass/fail, so it wouldn't raise the grades of the first-year women and alone account for their superior performance in making law review. But here, again, women are offered a world in which they are expected to succeed right in the middle of the dreaded first year. And they do succeed. The connection is up to you to decide. Remember, even at places where nothing is done to ease the process of retooling, one study reports that women only lag behind men an imperceptible amount at the average and one grade in eight courses at the median. Maybe the amount of respect activities traditionally associated with women get at NYU is just enough to boost their confidence and enable them to retool as a man would do.

I don't want to overstate the case. Lots of the women at NYU have complaints similar to women elsewhere. They complain that the classes are too big, and only the big mouths get known, and only the known get clerkship recommendations. They started a group, the 2Xers, to look into problems of gender after Lani Guinier blew the whistle at Penn. NYU is not heaven. But it's obviously doing some things right.

Started in 1967 when the boom in lawyers just began, Arizona State University law school is a very young law school. Not only is ASU the top school for women in its status hierarchy, Group #4, it's one of the top over all.

A confession. I live part of the year outside Phoenix, where Arizona State is located. I'm a westerner. Indeed, I'm the quintessential westerner, because I was born in Cleveland, Ohio. When I came to Arizona, I got a fresh start. After all, the state wasn't even seventy-five years old itself.

As at NYU, the women I interviewed at ASU differed widely on what they thought. In an anonymous student survey, several of them expressed the usual discomfort with speaking in the big classes because of fear of "people wait[ing] for you to make an ass of yourself" or feeling the professors are using them or "stand[ing] up there like God" "with absolutely no interest in what women think." They also articulated a powerful anger with their male classmates—"guys talk and say almost nothing . . . these men never shut up . . . even the class bully gets reinforcement from the professors," and lots, lots more. As we will see in chapter 4, ASU had a big problem with an alleged sexual harassment incident a couple of years ago, and last year students protested the return from leave of the accused teacher.

But others are extremely happy there. One first-year student, a woman with an interest in Indian law, thought the entire law school experience was individual, estimated that the women participated in the same numbers as the men, and perceived the professors as extremely receptive. Even one first-year teacher generally classified as the Kingsfield of ASU didn't scare Ms. Indian Law. "He's smart and funny and knowledgeable," she said. "I learned a lot."

Ms. Law's attitude was especially convincing, because when I interviewed her she had only achieved respectable first-semester grades, so she didn't have the common bias of people to love an institution that has valued them highly. Moreover, she had left her prior field due to gender bias, and she was trained in a specialty dealing with human behavior in groups. So, as she quickly assured me, she was the last person to miss gender bias or stereotype behavior or stereotype threat, if it was there.

As a big western state school, ASU is more representative of the success schools than NYU is. Women outperform themselves at the University of Washington, at UCLA, at the University of California at Davis, at Oregon; even at the state school of conservative Mormon Utah, the University of Utah. Yet, as different as Tempe, Arizona, is from Greenwich Village, lots of things are the same.

Students and faculty at both places report a powerful norm of cooperativeness and a downgrading of competitiveness. The faculty at ASU contended in interviews that there's a "culture here that's passed on," a "cooperative atmosphere." The atmosphere at ASU gets going at orientation before the students start. Speculating about why ASU's women succeed so well, faculty mentioned in passing that orientation had included a psychologist. Although the faculty weren't sure it mattered, one of the women students I interviewed mentioned it immediately. "One of the first people I saw was a psychologist!" she said, in some amazement. "The psychologist told us we were in a class full of 'top ten percent' students and that 'P=JD,' which means pass equals juris doctor." The student continued, "At exam time you could hear the students going around chanting 'P=JD, P=JD.' " Such input can't help alleviating the burden of the first-year competition for grades. The student services department at ASU helps the students with everything from counseling to loans to extensions of due dates. The woman who ran student services for years reputedly knew the name of every student within weeks after their arrival.

Both places had very caring deans. Sexton was the subject of much praise, from many places on the political spectrum. The immediate former dean at ASU, Richard Morgan, came in for praise as someone who deliberately placed women faculty in the first-year classes.

Perhaps not coincidentally, ASU, like NYU, has a program in the first year that powerfully rewards the traits stereotypically associated with women. At ASU, the program is moot court. Moot court is the training in appellate argument and consists generally of an assigned legal problem that the students must brief and argue in "teams" of "lawyers," each team representing one side of the issue. Moot court is part of legal writing at ASU, and like lawyering, is essentially pass/fail and not part of the GPA, although the students who make it to the finals get to argue before real local lawyers and judges. After the students complete their closing briefs and arguments for the moot court part of legal writing, they can submit their final briefs and arguments for an optional competition.

The year following the competition, the three winners are placed on the school's moot court teams, which compete in the three national moot court competitions—the general national moot court competition, the First Amendment competition, and the Environmental Moot Court Competition. At the present moment, the entire moot court program at ASU is run by women students.

There are very few women on either faculty—only 21 percent at ASU and 20 percent at NYU. ASU makes up for its failure to hire women faculty in part by concentrating the women in the first-year classes. Of the six women on the faculty, all but one teach in the first year. Since ASU is so small (student body 463 altogether), there are only two sections in the first-year class. These two statistics, taken together, mean that most students at ASU have at least one and usually more than one female first-year teacher. Making such good use of a small number of female faculty members doesn't help the many qualified women looking for jobs in law teaching, but it sure may affect the students.

As a state school in a big city, ASU does manifest one characteristic that NYU lacks: It's an opportunity school for very well qualified women who would otherwise not get to go to law school. The availability of in-state tuition and location in a population center where they would find work or where their husbands or mates have work mean that women can shoehorn law school in. I can't cite statistics, but if you think about your lives and the lives of the women you know, you will realize that women, more than men, have to shoehorn in their educational and career ambitions among a host of other commitments. For long-standing social reasons, women move to where their men's work is, not vice versa. Instead of going to where Harvard is, women have to find a law school where they happen to be living. Because of these social reasons, although women go to college in large numbers, women are also less likely to claim familial resources or go deeply into debt to go to graduate school. They just have to manage law school financially somehow.

Accordingly, state schools in cities where women can already live their roles as wives and breadwinners play the role they have historically played in America: helping otherwise qualified people in the society to raise their sights. If these women were men, they wouldn't be at ASU; they'd be at Berkeley or Duke or Vanderbilt or the University of Illinois, all schools with much higher status ranking. But they have to live in Phoenix. So they go to ASU.

I had figured this all out when, by chance, my interviewing

schedule presented me with a flesh-and-blood example of this phenomenon, an older ex-M.B.A. and second-year law student I'll call Juliet. Juliet, eastern born and bred, got a B.A. from a prestigious Ivy League college, an M.B.A. from a respectable grad school, but then followed her husband to a southern state as he pursued his career. She got a job she hated working for a corporation with a bad woman problem, and then followed her husband again when he moved to Phoenix, in pursuit of his career. If Juliet hadn't met her Romeo, it seems pretty clear she would never have moved to the South, never worked for a company that was a holdover from an earlier era of American life, never gone to Phoenix, and never gone to ASU law school.

As it was, Juliet was destined to star there. With an LSAT of 167, she was well over the median at ASU. Indeed, chances are she could have gone to Stanford. By the end of her first year, she was in the top 10 percent of her class, had made law review, and was on the award-winning environmental moot court championship team. The wide-open West also seemed incredibly welcoming to Juliet after her stint in the South. She described law school as a veritable haven of gender equality after her last experience and, like Ms. Indian Law, said she would surely recognize discrimination after her experiences in the M.B.A. program and at work. "The women here really speak up," she said, and "there's no hostility from the professors."

As someone in the top 10 percent of her class, Juliet had no problem at all getting a job at one of the most prestigious firms in Phoenix, all of which interview at ASU. When asked about women's success, she identified some of the same factors the faculty had. While she had had "only" two women professors the first year, "the two were fabulous persons," and Juliet also noted that the assistant dean (and professor) Hannah Arterian was "a fabulous role model." Juliet articulated the beneficial effect of the heavily female moot court competition, expressing gleeful satisfaction with the warm and trusting cooperative relationships that had developed among the women in her all-women team. Since moot court teams argue as a team, of course, characteristics stereotypically female and thus the source of stereotype threat in most circumstances are beneficial. So where moot court is important, women benefit. In Juliet's case, they went on to win the nationals.

She also thought that being a little older helped her succeed. If she could advise you readers of only one thing, she said, she'd tell you to wait a few years before going to school. Juliet and Ms. Indian Law both told me something that almost summed up completely the atmosphere for women at ASU: They said that in 1998 the Women's Law Student Association was voted the best student organization on the whole campus.

Two Law Schools Where Women Don't Succeed As Well: George Mason and McGeorge

Does history matter? ASU is only thirty years old; NYU reinvented itself in the seventies and eighties. Seven of the top fifteen success schools are in western states. Chris Littleton, the well-loved feminist law teacher at UCLA (rank fourth out of sixteen in its status group; success rate for women 101 percent) thinks that women do well at UCLA because it's just too new to have the historic sexist baggage of older schools in its status group.

None of the guidebooks tell you, but George Mason University School of Law (rank third out of three in Status Group #6) was founded by a conservative Christian group in Virginia as the old International School of Law in 1972. Facing some difficulty getting accreditation and coming to the realization that all its graduates weren't going to be evangelical Christians, the school began broadening its hiring practices in the seventies and also acquired a very valuable piece of property in Arlington, Virginia. Meanwhile, George Mason, a Virginia state school in Fairfax, had been looking for a law school, and a deal was struck.

George Mason Law School didn't really come onto the map until it hired the law and economics entrepreneur Henry Manne as dean in 1986, just before full accreditation. Manne, a New Orleans native, who had been converted to a strict economic analysis of law at the University of Chicago in the sixties, had been making his way up the academic ladder for decades, first at Miami, then Emory, and so forth. Law and economics emphasizes that the law should aim at making the most economically productive social arrangements, with an assumption that productivity usually results from everyone being a free individual acting as competitively as possible. Government should be as small as possible, law should do as little as possible, and individuals should be as free as possible. As a political matter, this approach results in great freedom for the most powerful players, and it has garnered great support from traditionally conservative thinkers and funders. Everywhere Manne went, he took his Law and Economics Institute, funded by conservative foundations such as the Olin Foundation. (We will see more on the Olin Foundation and its role in law school in chapter 4, "How to Pick a Compatible Law School.")

When Manne became dean, he fired or bought out most of the faculty and hired a lot of law- and economics-oriented academics. He made Quantitative Methods, a course in economics, accounting, and statistics, required, and established four specialty tracks: Regulatory Law, for practice before agencies that regulate business, International Business, Litigation, which is explicitly "not a clinical training program," and Intellectual Property, for engineers or other science types who want to become patent lawyers. Manne took the law review away from the student editors and insisted that grades be uninflated and workload high.

Although faculty interviewees insisted that there was no sectarian holdover from the school's Christian conservative founding, one professor noted that the school does employ twenty-four law and economics scholars out of its twenty-seven academic faculty, and such intellectual diversity as exists comes almost exclusively from the inclusion of all types of law and economics scholars. Even among the economics types, however, there are, one faculty member says, no Marxists, and no followers of Harvard welfare economist and recent Nobel Prize winner Amartya Sen; among noneconomics scholars, there are "no crits [leftist critical legal scholars], no traditional feminist scholars." After Manne came, he hired two failed Reagan Supreme Court nominees, Robert Bork and Douglas Ginsburg. Manne's law and economics summer institute drew fire from the left-oriented Alliance for Justice, because it takes federal judges to very fancy resorts and pays all their bills, amounting sometimes to thousands of dollars, all under the aegis of teaching them how to analyze problems to produce what the law and economics people consider economically desirable results.

The Olin Foundation countered that the George Mason courses expose judges to several different economic theories, including some that the Alliance would find congenial, and the attendees are "perfectly capable of drawing their own conclusions."

George Mason has very few women on its faculty; current women teachers speculate that the word of mouth on George Mason's orientation may be a factor, regardless of how true it is. There are usually no women teaching in the first year, except for the traditionally marginal legal writing teachers and an occasional section of criminal law. Last year, Manne was succeeded as dean by a law and economics scholar, Mark Grady, formerly from Northwestern.

Although Status Group #6 is small, because only three schools had median LSATs of 158 for the class of '98, George Mason is not only last of three in Group #6, it would be second to last in each of the larger status groups around it; in Group #5, Tulane is lower, and in Group #7, only South Carolina is lower. George Mason has a part-time program, which is not formally included in the calculations of rank, but even counting its part-time program, George Mason would still be in roughly the same place.

When asked to speculate on the reasons for GM's women's limited success, my source reported that in some classes, there are a handful of women at the very top, but then it drops off rapidly in the next fifteen or so ranks, with women emerging again at a B+ level.

The reason is not clear. As we will see, one common complaint from women at schools where women don't succeed as well is that the constitutional law teachers imply that women must forgo their support for abortion rights or other more female-oriented interpretations of the Fourteenth Amendment as a measure of their tough-mindedness. But sources at GM deny that that's a problem: "The con law guy is one of the more liberal on the faculty." A lot of the teachers give multiple choice exams; one of my sources speculated that George Mason's women may succeed in lesser numbers because women are more reluctant to guess than men are.

With less than the average number of female students for the years we looked at, George Mason might actually still be in the exclusionary phase of the stages of institutional diversity. However, the numbers of women students seem to go up and down over the years reported in the ABA guide, so exclusion seems too simple an answer. Instead, I suspect, George Mason is willing to take newcomers, but only if they willingly replicate the formerly exclusive norm. In an interview a few years ago, Dean Manne unwittingly gave a graphic description of the Quantitative Diversity approach. When Manne came to GM in 1986, he found two young women faculty members whom he thought had potential but had gotten "off on the wrong track" before his arrival. Accordingly, he offered them the following deal: You can stay at George Mason, but you have to go to the university and get a master's degree in economics. Both took him up on it, he reported a few years later, and both pursued economics Ph.D.'s.

I spoke to one Ph.D., Margaret Brinig, who reported that she was grateful for having done the study; she said Manne pushed her to do a lot of very careful scholarly work. The happy picture of a fuzzy female thinker liberated by retooling to a male norm was somewhat blurred by the fact that Brinig is a single mother whose ex-husband was very involved with the children and tied to the D.C. area, so she had to stay in George Mason's geographical location regardless of how she liked it. She reported herself as having no one to talk to at George Mason and told me she had to go to other schools in the area to find someone else who was working along the lines she was pursuing. In a pattern that surfaced again and again among retooling females, she even manifested a kind of civil disobedience to Manne's regime, using her economic learning to look for "where law and economics breaks down." (Think about it: How would you expect most women to fare in a system like law and economics, dedicated to liberating the competitive energies of the strongest players?) However, to Manne's credit, she was apparently not punished for her rebellion! (Brinig has since departed for the friendlier University of Iowa.)

The law and economics types at George Mason probably wouldn't be surprised to learn that a substantial number of their student body go there for the economically rational reason that it's the only law school with cheap public school tuition close to Washington, D.C. As Ms. Strategist, a second-year student at George Mason told me, "Most are here because of the cheap in-state tuition. As a matter of pure economics, if you're living in D.C., the outcome can be in excess of forty thousand dollars."

Ms. Strategist absolutely denied that the dominant conservative culture of law and economics affected her in any way. "The student body is not as conservative as the school's reputation," she asserted, and "most students are pragmatic—working—they go to school and leave. We're not afraid to tell them [conservatives] what we think—when they were discussing the VMI case [a recent Supreme Court decision holding the state of Virginia could not maintain a male-only military college], we were all over them."

When asked about her own nonachievement of law review—and the proportional underrepresentation of women on law review—Strategist asserted that the older students and the women students weren't interested in law review. Why not? "Because I'm not going for a firm job. Jobs that come are oriented toward twenty-three-year-old law review types" whom she characterized as "anal retentive" such as "a guy I know who got all A's." Ms. Strategist, an architect and engineer by background, was hoping for a bureaucratic job with a corporation or a government agency. She hadn't looked for a summer job, planning to spend the summer moving into the new house she and her husband had just bought, but thought she'd spotted a couple of interesting-sounding long-term prospects on the Internet.

It's hard to feel sorry for Ms. Strategist—she's getting what she's paying for, a cheap notch on her résumé and a possible escape from what she describes as the intolerably sexist world of big-ticket engineering. But it's hard to resist comparing her to ASU's Juliet, also trapped in a big city and also lured by the good bargain of a law degree for the price of in-state tuition. If the ASU analysis is right, George Mason's women should be overqualified and starring. But they're not. And our Strategist is certainly not getting what the "anal retentive all-A's" guys are getting. When asked for evidence of his law school's rise in the hierarchy and increased presence on the national scene of legal education a couple of years ago, Dean Manne didn't point to the legions of female bureaucrats desultorily working in government jobs. He said, "Call up any big law firm in Washington, D.C., and ask them if they're hiring my students."

The people at McGeorge School of Law of the University of the Pacific were really surprised when I apprised them that their women didn't score particularly well by the standard of making law review. (The percentage of women who made the national senior honor society, Order of the Coif, in 1995 at McGeorge was also extremely low, among the lowest in all the Coif chapters.) The law review has a "gender blind selection process," for second-year staffers, a professor told me, which works as follows: First, law review selects the top student in each of the three day sections and the top two students in the evening section and the top seven overall on grades alone (for a total of nine to eleven slots), with the remaining slots filled by a writing competition among students in the top 40 percent of the class.

Like George Mason, McGeorge was a freestanding law school. Affiliated with the Stockton-based University of the Pacific in 1966, McGeorge was accredited in 1969. For twenty-four years, until 1991, McGeorge was largely the product of the will and imagination of its longtime dean, Gordon Schaber, a successful Democratic politician and California state judge. The law library bears Schaber's name. Under Schaber's tutelage, McGeorge sought out a niche as a law school heavily oriented to training trial lawyers, featuring its technologically advanced "courtroom of the future." Schaber hired, a current faculty member told me, "his friends and people in firms, an Old Boy network, a WASP network." In the mid-1970s, he reported that "there were no Jews on the faculty." That began to change, as McGeorge entered the "scholarship" game in the seventies.

There were also few women on the faculty, but that remains the case; at 18 percent academic females, McGeorge has one of the least female faculties in the country. When asked about the lack of females, a faculty member informed me that "this is not a faculty that *ardently* favors affirmative action. There is no faculty-wide sense that gender is high on the list of factors. *Race* is considered a more serious concern, especially the presence of Hispanics."

Despite its association with a Democratic politician, my source continued, many people express the opinion that McGeorge is a conservative society. There is a little-noticed but substantial Mormon population in San Joaquin County, my faculty source told me, and way back, McGeorge was regarded as a Mormon pipeline school. If you couldn't get into Brigham Young, also last in its status category, McGeorge was a second choice.

Like the faculty members I interviewed, I was a little surprised at McGeorge's poor success rate for women. But with few women on the faculty, and no obvious programs like NYU's lawyering or ASU's emphasis on team-based moot court, and with a reputedly onerous required grading curve, perhaps I shouldn't have been surprised. The anonymous student survey in the Princeton Review's law school guide, *1997 Best Law Schools*, turned up two more hints of the situation at McGeorge: "gender bias" was explicitly included in the "misses" portion of the "Hits and Misses," and so was "lack of diversity among faculty." Perhaps things will be better for classes after the classes of '95, '96, and '97, which provided my data. After study by a faculty/student committee, McGeorge has revised its grading scale, and the law review adviser informs me he thinks the numbers for the class of 2000, which just became eligible for law review, are more like fifty-fifty.

Conclusion

In law school, as in other aspects of life, small distinctions can make big differences. If our closer look at some exemplary law schools is any example, it doesn't take much to empower women to compete with their male classmates. Change starts at the top: Is the dean a sympathetic character? If differences have value, valuing them reduces stereotype threat. Are there important aspects of the first-year curriculum that value carefully researched, patiently planned, collective presentations? Or is it mostly multiple choice tests or the equivalent, three-hour closed-book issue-spotting contests? Is the school a winner-take-all society with all the goodies going to the top 20 percent and the other 80 percent "licking their psychic wounds"? Or does P=JD? Ask these questions when you apply, when you interview, when you visit. And don't take my word for women's success. Many law schools have done internal studies like mine and like Guinier's detailed study. They just aren't passing them around. Maybe you could ask for a copy before you write that first big check.

You Go, Girl:
A Winning Application

WOMEN APPLYING TO law school are in a rare position of competitive advantage. Women go to college in greater numbers than men do. In 1995, 53 percent of the full-time college population was female. What's more, women do better at college than men do. So (big surprise) women graduate from college in greater numbers than men do.

Women also have the competitive advantage of having higher grades. Women who applied to start law school in the fall of 1995 had an undergraduate grade point average of 3.15, compared to men's 3.06. They outperformed men in 1994 and 1993, too. Women got better grades than men subject by subject, so we're not talking about women studying basket weaving and men nuclear engineering. Not only that, but women applied to law schools substantially beyond their reach, based on their grades and test scores, and women were accepted to law schools where they could not have been predicted to be accepted!

That's the good news. On the other side, however, even though more women than men graduate from college, more men apply to law school. A lot more. In 1995, 54 percent of law school applicants were men, and 46 percent were women. The underrepresentation of women in the applicant pool is puzzling. One of the purposes of this book is to remove some of the fear and mystery from law school, so that women who would genuinely benefit from a legal education will be encouraged to apply.

Moreover, women are admitted to law schools at a slightly lower rate than men are, so that the 46 percent female applicant group in 1995 produced law school classes only 44 percent female. In 1997, the entering class went up to 46 percent female, so the increased number of female applicants has increased the integration of American law schools more quickly recently. A study showed that women are accepted at more selective law schools than they "deserve" based on their grades. But regardless of why women haven't crossed the 50 percent mark, as they have, for instance, in medical school enrollment, many women report that they do not feel empowered by their 40-something percent presence in law school. We will explore whether this is because under 50 percent means you are a minority regardless of how large or whether there are other, less easily measured, explanations.

Why don't more college women apply to law school? The answer is a mystery, especially since a nationwide survey of college freshmen consistently reveals that a lot of women college students aspire to go to law school when they start out. All the press about how nasty it is can't help. In the late 1970s, just as women began graduating from American colleges and universities in numbers equal to male rates, the book, movie, and TV show *The Paper Chase* appeared, starring the overbearing Professor Kingsfield, and telling the story of the terrible experiences law students have, especially with the first year. When the moment comes to decide, *The Paper Chase* picture of law school is suddenly more than just a funny story.

Also, the stories about how women don't do as well on the Law School Admission Test may be discouraging some. As we have seen, Claude Steele's "stereotype threat" predicts that people who are stereotyped as underachievers underachieve, not because they're dumber, but because they lack self-confidence. Lacking self-confidence, they may not even try to take the test. If you're out there thinking you won't try for law school because you might not do well on the LSAT, *stop thinking that way.*

Women may see law school as a bad financial investment. Many law students borrow some or all of the money it costs to go to law school. As we saw in chapter 1, all surveys of lawyers' earnings show that men lawyers earn quite a bit more than women do. Law schools don't charge women lower tuition, however, so law school looks like a better investment for men than for women. A couple of the women I interviewed for this book spoke quite straightforwardly about the economic reasons for their decisions, for instance, to go to Northwestern, which offered them big scholarships, rather than Harvard, which did not.

Finally, consider a recent survey of college students at the very tony Williams College. This study turned up the interesting statistic that Williams women expect to marry (91 percent) and have two or more children. When they have their two children, they expect to reduce their working hours outside the home to twenty-two hours per week. Although many firms tout their flexible-time and part-time options, as the Princeton Review's prelaw guide put it: "Flexible Work Arrangements are a lot like New Year's Resolutions. Everyone makes them but no one ever does anything about them." Law firms make their money by billing clients for lawyers' time, so you can imagine how popular part-timers are with the people who make the promotion decisions. By contrast, the male students at Williams College did not expect to reduce their hours. Even the women only hoped their guys would cut back about three hours a week, while they themselves would spend eighteen weekly hours in the nursery. People who expect to spend a substantial part of their adult life in unpaid child care positions are understandably hesitant about investing in their own higher education.

That decision is a self-fulfilling prophecy. If you don't get further education, you will likely earn less than the baby's father even before the baby comes, so it will look reasonable for you to be the one to stay home. If you stay home, study after study has shown that your lifetime earnings never catch up, and your pension won't be worth much. Almost 50 percent of marriages in America end in divorce. If you're really unlucky, you'll end up old and poor. Maybe those Williams College girls should think again.

Fear of humiliation, fear of financial loss, expectations of being able to rely on a male breadwinner. These are not good reasons for you high-scoring female college graduates to pass on law school. This book is going to help you do well on the LSAT and pick a law school that does not have a reputation for humiliating women. Furthermore, after you read chapter 6 ("The Dreaded First Year"), you're going to know how the "Paper Chase" game is played, and it won't be so scary as it's made out. Although it is a sad truth that women lawyers make less money than male lawyers do, short of a sex change, you can't become a male lawyer. Your choice is between the quite good living the profession offers and the best job you can get with skills that cost less to acquire than a law degree. We've already seen how superior law is to making a living as a sociology major. If you can make it in business school, God bless. Otherwise . . . you go, girl.

Here's how. Write, call, or register on-line to take the Law School Admission Test and, while you're doing it, write or register on-line for the Law School Data Assembly Service. You're going to need the LSDAS to process your transcripts and stuff for almost all accredited American law schools, so let's just keep it simple. Here's how to sign up:

Reggie, the Law School Admission Services on-line registration service, is found at http://www.lsac.org. The telephone number to register for the test is: (215) 968-1001, 8:30 A.M. to 8:00 P.M. ET, September–March, and 8:30 A.M. to 4:45 P.M. ET, April–August.

OR

Call (215) 968-1001 and ask for the LSAT/LSDAS registration and information book, which contains a form and an envelope and elaborate instructions for registration for everything.

OR

You can even write Law Services, at Law Services, Box 2000, 661 Penn Street, Newtown, PA 18940-0998, and ask them to send you the registration and information book, if you happen to be on the moon or someplace where there are no telephones and no Internet.

The Law Services people are all set up to process you through every imaginable variation in the application process, including a learning-disabled Sabbath observer taking the test for the third time. You don't need me for that; just call Law Services and get the ball rolling.

All the guidebooks tell you to get an early start. They're right. Almost all law schools send out applications for the upcoming year in August, about a year before admission. That's way too late! You should start the process at least as early as one and one half years before the earliest possible admission. This would be very early December of your junior year in college, if you're planning to go directly to law school from college. Get on-line or call the Law School Admission Council for the materials and the *Official Guide to Law Schools*.

You will need your Christmas vacation to use the prep books to start cramming for the admission test. You'll need your spring semester to take courses that reflect commitment to a course of study or that will yield good marks to show an upward trend in grades or, hopefully, both. You can use the summer between junior and senior years to fatten up your work résumé in ways we will explore in this chapter and do something for important recommenders as well as do the specific work for the autumn LSAT. Some people take the LSAT as early as June, which pushes all the dates back. Most law schools use rolling admissions, taking promising applications as they come in after a start date around October. The class looks a lot emptier to admissions officers in October than it does in January. When would you like to have your application reviewed?

What They Really Do with Your Application

The application consists of four important parts: (1) the index number, which is composed of your undergraduate grade point average and your LSAT score, (2) your formal life story, including work history, (3) your essay, and (4) your references. Some law schools have an interview procedure that may generate a fifth column in your application, and some even still allow local alumni to do the interview work.

Law schools have different ways of administering the admissions process—some, including a big state institution whose admissions director talked to me with admirable frankness, have a process to sort the applications strictly by the index number, eliminating the candidates whose number is hopelessly below the law school's standards and accepting candidates whose number is well within the law school's ambitious aspirations for itself.

At state institutions, this sorting is done commonly by an administrator, because so little judgment is involved, and frequently this sorting eliminates or accepts as many as half the applicants. When the pile is reduced to the applicants in the gray area, occasionally accompanied by a file that eludes summary determination because of very unusual characteristics pro or con, the process is often taken up by an admissions committee that includes faculty as well as staff. Some committees even include a student or two. (Some other schools, however, assign the dean of admissions, rarely a faculty member, and their staff to do the whole job.) The committee divides the files, sometimes assigning them to an individual member, sometimes expecting each file to be read by more than one member, but usually expecting each member to dispose of scores of them each month, up or down. Only the files that an individual or subcommittee can't decide about come to the full committee.

At other schools, all the applications are divided between the administrators and committee members, and each file is expected to be read in its totality, not just categorized on the index number first. This variant of the admissions procedure has been dwindling in response to the large number of applications since the law school boom in the 1970s. In those schools that still look at everyone's whole application, or in determining the fate of the marginal applicants, admissions officials generally report that other factors, such as the selectiveness of the undergraduate institution or the degree of grade inflation they can sniff out, as well as the life story, essays, interview, and recommendations, weigh in.

A Quick and Dirty Way to Get into Law School

Because most sorting at a lot of schools is done at the beginning, index phase of the process, the fastest way to get into law school is to have really good undergraduate grades and make a high score on the standardized Law School Admission Test (LSAT), or at least to do so well that if you add them both up, you get a high index number. If you have a high index number, you will most likely be put in the desirable category of "presumptive admit." The lucky presumptive admits will likely be admitted right away. At our rather typical state law school, this category accounted for half the students admitted! Of course, at the other end, there are the automatic rejects, again essentially on grades and test scores alone.

Just in case you're harboring some illusion that law schools care about your community service or your immortal soul, you should know that the Law School Admission Test is scored so it's easy for the number to be added to the normal undergraduate grade point average and divided by two to construct a total index number. The required writing sample, on the other hand, is ungraded. If admissions officers were going to be concentrating on your (ungraded) writing sample, why would they want to make this scoring business so easy for themselves? As it works, if you had a 3.50 undergraduate score and an LSAT of 170, you'd wind up with an index of 3.5; LSAT 170 and 3.0 average generates an index of 3.25. Notice that unless the law school tinkers with the formula, as some do, three or four years of undergraduate effort and the three hours of LSAT are weighed the same! Moreover, one of my more LSAT-oriented colleagues at a prestigious West Coast school has told me that his admissions people create their own number, which weighs the LSAT even more heavily than 50 percent, because they believe it's the best predictor of law school performance. (Because women do less well than men do on the LSAT on average, note that this procedure, rightly or wrongly, has the effect of disadvantaging women.)

So a really clever strategy might be to pick a pretty easy college and an easy college major to jack up your grades and then to devote yourself to preparing for the LSAT with as much effort as you put into doing your college work. There are two drawbacks to this approach. First, law school admissions officials *say* that they look at the status of the undergraduate institution and major; one admissions dean even said he worked his opinion of the college into the formula, favoring colleges whose graduates had in past years turned out to be good law students at their school. Even the index-oriented school I interviewed admitted that college quality was "one of several concerns," although they could not spend the time to "make fine distinctions" among the hundreds of applicants.

Those of you who think you're getting away with something by beating on your college professors to raise your grades should know that the Law School Admission Services tells the admissions officers about where there's been grade inflation by reporting the grade point averages for all applicants to law school from a particular institution. Since it's unlikely everyone applying is a straight-A student under some uninflated standard, if your school sends a pile of seniors to apply with straight A's, the admissions officers are going to suspect that an A might not be worth as much there as at a more hierarchical school. One admissions expert I talked to reported that his school engaged in an extremely elaborate original data-gathering scheme to find out where the grade inflation was, to avoid being fooled by it in admissions.

Second, most law school applicants major in subjects not known for their extreme difficulty, like social sciences and humanities, although more women than men major in social sciences, like history, sociology, and education, than humanities, like classics, philosophy, and foreign languages. So choosing a high-grading college and majoring in something easy is probably not a foolproof strategy.

The argument against devoting yourself to preparing for the LSAT is that it's hard to judge how much difference preparing for the LSAT makes in your scores. I'm going to recommend that you do the preparation. If we even guess that lots of preparation will jack up your LSAT scores, it would be worth doing, considering the emphasis law schools place on the LSAT. As a matter of pure cost/benefit analysis, it pays to cram for the LSAT.

Despite the problems with the pure grades and scores approach, it is still true that the fastest way into law school is to do everything humanly possible to extract a high score from the unforgiving Law School Admission Test and the second fastest way is to bust your ass in college. Women, who often learn from the culture that they can get a lot of what they want by charm or good looks, have said they think law schools care about social characteristics or look for some sort of "well-rounded" profile. Remember, half the students at the pretty desirable law school I looked at got in without anyone in the admissions process even knowing whether they were (or were not) the social chairman of their sorority or tutored underprivileged children.

The exceptions to the grades and scores rule are: (1) if you fall into the gray area at a law school you're interested in or (2) if you apply to a handful of extremely selective law schools who have more top-scoring students than they can accept or (3) if you happen to pick one of the dwindling number of law schools who read the whole file. In these three areas, there are some possibilities for creating a more well-rounded image, which we will talk about in a minute (see "Fudging," later in this chapter). But first things first.

The LSAT Tilts Admissions Toward White Men, But We're Not Going to Let That Stop Us

The LSAT has been scrutinized very closely for a reason having nothing to do with women and law school: According to the Law School Admission Council, people of color have lower mean test scores than whites do. Indeed, a study from the LSAC reports that much of the difference between men's scores and women's scores on the LSAT disappears if you compare white men and white women; because more minority women than men apply to law school, their typically lower mean scores bring the women's scores down. Accordingly, a great deal of time and effort has been spent to see whether the LSAT is actually predictive, because otherwise it's nothing more than a socially damaging barrier cleverly designed to keep the law schools mostly white and male, like adding points for having facial hair or having an ancestor who came to America on the *Mayflower*. The LSAT may also function indirectly to keep law school mostly male, despite women's dominance in college graduation rates, because fear of not doing well on the LSAT may discourage women from applying at all.

The first thing you need to know is that women's scores are only a tiny bit lower than men's are on average—and at every point along the way. Not surprisingly, women's first-year grades are only a little less good than men's are, once admitted. The bad news is that a small difference can mean a lot: One law school guide reported rejections of several candidates with a 150 LSAT score who would have gotten in had their scores been a trivially improved 155. Men supposedly care about small differences in measurement; women should start to care, too.

A recent, as yet unpublished, study of law students' performance done at UCLA reveals that for the 5,800 students at thirty-some American law schools examined, LSAT scores are the single most powerful predictor of first-semester grade performance. UCLA turned up the fact that there is a practically significant difference between how women score and how men score in first-year grades, but that the difference disappears if you compare men and women of equal LSAT scores. In other words, since women do slightly less well than men do on the LSAT, and since LSAT scores predict first-semester grades, women do slightly less well than men do on first-semester grades. So the argument over the predictive value of the LSAT actually slides into an argument about the value of the testing methods that produce the LSAT *and* the first-year grades. Do we need to train lawyers to exhibit the skills and characteristics that the LSAT and the first-semester teaching process are designed to reward? Even though women do a little less well at that process?

One way to answer that question is to pursue the relationship between LSAT/first semester grades and success in the rest of the profession. My data reflect that LSAT scores don't heavily predict whether students make law review. As we glimpsed in chapter 2, and we will see in detail in chapter 5 ("The Femscore: How to Pick a Law School Where Women Succeed"), even among law schools with identical median LSATs, there are schools where women succeeded in making law review in 1996 and 1997 in large numbers and those where they substantially underperformed in making law review. Unless the women's LSATs at the success schools like NYU and ASU were much higher than their male classmates' LSATs, there is a discrepancy between UCLA's conclusion that LSATs mostly predict performance and my findings that women make law review in excess of their class presence at ASU and NYU. Similarly, unless women's LSATs at schools like George Mason and McGeorge are much lower than their male classmates' LSATs, LSATs also would not powerfully explain the failure to make law review there.

Some of this discrepancy may be explained by the narrowness of the UCLA survey (only thirty schools), but more of the explanation lies in the fact that first-semester grades are only one factor in the competition for law review. Since many of the slots on law review are claimed by people who have the research and writing skills to prevail in the writing competitions that are commonly required or who have the determination to compete even if their grades alone were not enough to qualify them, it is fair to say that except insofar as LSATs predict first-semester grades, LSATs don't heavily predict ability to make and perform on law review.

In fact, neither UCLA nor the Law School Admission Council claims that the LSAT predicts ability to make law review or the whole three years of performance in law school, although, naturally, doing less well the first year would affect the three year *average*. Since predicting three years of performance would be a much more powerful argument for keeping the test than predicting one year of performance, the fact the testers don't make that claim would seem to indicate that they don't have data to support it. (Remember, UCLA only looked at first-semester grades.) And they are certainly not reporting that the LSAT predicts performance in the profession.

Probably a better indicator of how the LSAT relates to the legal profession is the relationship between LSAT scores and graduation and LSAT scores and bar passage. The Law School Admission Council studied racial minorities admitted to law school when their index (LSAT and UGPA) would not have indicated they were eligible at all, and concludes that those lower-scoring candidates passed the bar at only a slightly lower rate than the higher-scoring candidates would have done. So, on balance, the LSAT probably keeps law school more male and more white, while not being very useful beyond first-year grades. Against these drawbacks, the chief defenders of the standardized tests are the test givers themselves and people who like to believe that intelligence is all genetic, so the people on top of the ladder now naturally deserve to be there.

This does not mean that minority women should be discouraged. The LSAC's *Thinking About Law School: A Minority Guide*, contains a good chapter on these issues. There is a substantial movement afoot to reduce or eliminate the use of the LSAT for law school admissions. Until that day arrives, however, women of all races and ethnicities need to worry about how to do as well as possible on it.

An Overview of the LSAT

The Law School Admission Test is a three-hour test consisting of five parts and a writing sample. (The writing sample is not graded, just sent to the admissions people.) The other five parts consist of four real parts (one section of reading comprehension, one of analytical reasoning, and two sections of logical reasoning) and a "wild card" section to help the test makers develop future tests. You will know you have a wild card section when you see an extra version of one of the sections, two reading comprehensions, for example, but you won't know which of the two sections is real during the test.

Reading Comprehension for the LSAT

Reading comprehension is the most familiar subject for people with a humanities or social science education; it's what you've been doing—or did—for four years, reading in English to extract information in an efficient way. You're doing it right now, in fact. The reading comprehension the LSAT tests is a little different from normal in that it is sort of intended to test the level of your distrust rather than your capacity to extract information from a trusted source. In most college courses, you assume that the material your teacher has selected for you is reliable and important. Accordingly, you read it hoping to grasp as much of what it says as possible. In the adversary system, people often use words in order to persuade and even manipulate the reader; as the University of Chicago Law School's resident philosopher Martha Nussbaum (who is not a lawyer) reminded me in an interview, lawyers, as Socrates was accused of doing, learn to "make the lesser argument appear the greater." (In the end, of course, Socrates's fellow citizens rewarded him with a cup of poison.) So the reading "comprehension" section of the LSAT actually tests the extent to which you can resist being fooled by sneaky reading material.

Does it matter if the test taker is a male or a female in the exercise I've just described? Well, one respectable school of psychology asserts that, for cultural or natural reasons, women are more interested in maintaining relationships and accomplishing ends than in one-upping one another, so thinking like an adversary may not come as easily to women. Furthermore, women use words to maintain relationships, so treating words, of all things, as untrustworthy may also be harder for women. Nonetheless, the LSAT asks women and men alike to do this.

Here's how it works.

Sample Prep Questions for Reading Comprehension

Most passages have a primary idea to get across. The test will often ask you to choose among five candidates for the main idea. For example, here's the paragraph you just read about the uniqueness of the LSAT exercise.

Reading comprehension is the most familiar subject for people with a humanities or social science education; it's what you've been doing—or did—for four years, reading in English to extract information in an efficient way. You're doing it right now, in fact. The reading comprehension the LSAT tests is a little different from normal in that it is sort of intended to test the level of your distrust rather than your capacity to extract information from a trusted source. In most college courses, you assume that the material your teacher has selected for you is reliable and important. Accordingly, you read it hoping to grasp as much of what it says as possible. In the adversary system, people often use words in order to persuade and even manipulate the reader; as the University of Chicago Law School's resident philosopher, Martha Nussbaum (who is not a lawyer) reminded me the other day, lawyers, as Socrates was accused of doing, learn to "make the lesser argument appear the greater." (In the end, of course, Socrates's fellow citizens rewarded him with a cup of poison.) So the reading "comprehension" section of the LSAT actually tests the extent to which you can resist being fooled by sneaky reading material.

The LSAT would ask:

Question 1: *Which of the following best captures the main idea of the passage?*
(A) The LSAT ought to test whether you can resist being fooled by what you read.
(B) Adversary systems rely on fooling people.
(C) The adversary system of the legal profession is different from other human relationships.
(D) The LSAT reading comprehension is different from the trusting reading you learned in college.
(E) The LSAT tests how well you will understand law school reading assignments.

The correct answer is (D). (A) overreaches; I said nothing about the rightness or wrongness of the method the LSAT uses, just described what it did. (B) is partially correct, but is a small fact used to build the main point. (C) is too broad; the reading is about the test, not about the profession in general. (E) is both too broad and too narrow; it's not clear exactly how the test relates to law school reading assignments, so the statement is too broad, and the passage is making a larger point than just the relationship between law school and the test. The passage is discussing the relationship between law school/LSAT-type reading and the college reading you're used to, so the statement is also too narrow.

By asking you what the main idea of the passage is, the test is really asking you to be alert to statements that overreach and claim for the passage more than it is fairly saying and to distinguish between the building blocks of a conclusion and the conclusion itself.

The reading comprehension also may ask a narrower question

about the passage. For instance, such a question may ask the following:

Question 2: *The passage states that the adversary system:*
(A) Makes the best arguments it can with the available material.
(B) Makes weak arguments appear strong.
(C) Requires people not to trust one another.
(D) Assumes that you read to extract information.
(E) Explains why people dislike lawyers.

The correct answer is (A). Although the passage seems to say (B) that the system makes weak arguments strong, that is an exaggeration, and is further weakened by the fact that it is a comparison to the death of Socrates, not a direct description. (C), Requires people not to trust each other, is too broad, and (D), Assumes that you read to extract information, is an assumption in the passage, just not one having to do with the adversary system. (E), Explains why people dislike lawyers, is also an inference, not a statement in the passage. So (A) is the best answer.

If the question asked about inferences, as they often do, they are looking to see if you can smoke out what the author is counting on you to believe, rather than what she has to say explicitly and defend. So:

Question 3: *It can be inferred from the passage that lawyers use words to manipulate, because:*
(A) They are naturally untrusting and untrustworthy.
(B) They make more money that way.
(C) They learned in law school to be sneaky.
(D) The adversary system directs them to do so.
(E) They are unconsciously emulating Socrates.

Remember, in an inference question, none of the answers appears explicitly in the text. The author is counting on you to supply the missing link between what is said and the conclusion the question is suggesting, in this case that lawyers use words to manipulate. (D) is the answer. The passage says that in the adversary system, people use words to manipulate. The author is expecting you to infer that there is something about the adversary system that makes this happen. This is a hard question, because each of these inferences is in some way rooted in the text, except (B), more money, which can be eliminated immediately. But (A), (C), and (E) are all further away from the line of argument "adversary, therefore manipulative" than (D). (A) really appears nowhere in the text, except in the far-fetched argument that the LSAT tests for the ability to withhold trust, (C) requires two jumps—from sneaky to adversarial system and from adversary system to legal education, and (E) is a little too close to humor to be a legitimate answer in the deadly serious structure of the LSAT.

Other reading comprehension questions ask you to identify the structure of the argument in the passage or the author's "attitude." For example, the LSAT may ask whether the argument gives a bunch of examples and then draws a conclusion from them, the method known as inductive reasoning, or whether the conclusion is stated first, followed by examples, or whether other structures of argument are used. These questions are not asking for the content of the passage, but asking you to identify the technique the writer uses to carry you, the reader, along with his or her argument process. In the passage on reading comprehension, I gave an account of something, why reading comprehension is different for the LSAT, followed by a reason for it, because the adversary system produces untrustworthy writings, and then drew a conclusion about how testing for untrustworthiness might be unfamiliar to the average college student. So the structure is account, explanation, conclusion.

On attitude questions, the LSAT asks you to imagine the writer as a person and figure out his degree of adversarial commitment to the statements he is making. Is the writer telling the story as a committed advocate, to make you believe? Is the writer telling it because the writer is critical of the material? Is the writer not only critical, but optimistic that the situation the writer is describing will change? My attitude toward the reading comprehension section of the LSAT is neutral to critical of the system (if nothing else told you that, the little remark about Socrates being poisoned would be a hint) but doubtful that it can be replaced. So you would choose critical but skeptical over, say, committed or optimistic.

Lessons from the Reading Comprehension Examples

These few examples are not a substitute for test preparation, of which more in a minute. I put them before you to teach you a specific lesson. In the legal system, words are a tool in a system of persuasion, not a neutral reflection of the world or a way to establish and maintain human harmony. A bunch of words together usually has a main idea, a couple of smaller ideas that the writer is using to support the main idea, a couple more unspoken ideas, or inferences, that the author is counting on you to bring to the party, an order of presentation intended to persuade you, and an attitude he or she wants you to adopt, like indignation or, at the other end, passionate support. When you get a legal document, you soon learn to read it, looking for these five things: main idea, supporting ideas, inferences, structure, and attitude. Can you break down written material in these ways? This is what the LSAT is testing for.

Even though this mind-set might be harder for some women, I have a mental exercise to help you practice. Just open a piece of written work and pretend it's some guy you just had sex with telling you he'll call you. In the morning.

Analytical Reasoning

This section sets forth a set of rules and asks you to test how real situations stack up against the rules imposed. In that sense, like the skeptical reading in the reading comprehension, the test is related to what law school teaches and ultimately to some of what lawyers do.

Remember the example from chapter 1 of the law that requires a contracting party to be eighteen years old? What if a college freshman friend of yours came to you and said he had contracted to buy an expensive computer from a senior in his dorm, and he now didn't want to pay for it. (Maybe IBM had just come out with a new generation of computers, rendering the computer he just bought obsolete.) Turns out, your young friend is one of those prodigies who went to college early, so he was just sixteen when he contracted for the computer. You would be called on to advise your friend on whether he could get out of his contract. You would first ask about the law of contract. You might learn that the general law of contract only enforces contracts between adults of eighteen or older. You would then ask questions of the situation designed to find out what *must be true* for a party to be able to escape the contract. What must be true of the facts of your case? A reading of the terms of the law of contract tells you that, for contract law to operate on his side, it must be true that your friend is really younger than eighteen.

Then you would ask questions designed to find out what cannot be true. You might find a case that held that contracts will be enforced even against underage contractors, like a sixteen-year-old, if the person seeking to get out of the contract misrepresented his age. If so, you will know that under the law of contract as interpreted by the courts, it cannot be that a person who deliberately tried to fool his contract partner gets to repudiate his contracts. As a matter of fact, it cannot be true that your friend tried to pass himself off as a mature man about campus, or he's stuck.

Finally, you would ask questions to find out what the law and cases might allow your client to do and still get off. Is it possible that someone who just lived in a college dorm, which would indicate odds are that he's eighteen, but didn't actively pretend to be eighteen, might get off? It's possible, because he didn't make statements misleading enough to compel enforcement of the contract nor forthright enough to make enforcement an open-and-shut case. Or it's not possible for your client to get off, because the opinion holding the misrepresenting sixteen-year-old to his contract says, "Anyone found in a place where people of adult age normally gather is implying he's an adult." Then you wouldn't bother asking your client what he said to the computer seller because it wouldn't be possible that his statements would matter.

Rather than present you with real legal opinions, from which you might figure out what must be the case for the law to apply, what cannot be the case, and where the wiggle room is, the LSAT tries to abstract from this process and test how quickly you can figure out three things from a description of a *physical* situation: what must be true (what's necessary), what cannot be true (what's impossible), and what might be true (what's possible). The LSAT uses two methods to test this: asking you to put one set of things in order (simple order) or asking you to keep track of two kinds of order (harder order). Then it presents you with different suggested orders and asks what orders must be true, what orders cannot be true, and what orders may be true.

Let's start with the simple order. It doesn't matter whether the order is over time, like asking you to figure out the order in which people became partners of a law firm, or over space, like asking you who sits near whom at a table, or is an artificial order like who scores higher than whom on the exam. It's all about order; more importantly, it's all about necessary orders, impossible orders, and possible orders. You may find that it helps you to answer by making a little diagram of years or a seating chart, but you'll learn the details of that when you take the prep courses or when you practice from the test prep books that are all over the bookstores. As far as I can tell, women and men prepare for the analytical reasoning section of the LSAT pretty much the same way. The only barrier particular to women, if there is any, is that women may be less willing to just leap in and do something that looks so unconnected to anything they've ever known. That's why I'm showing you what the test givers are really doing.

Sample Test Prep for Analytical Reasoning

Example 1

Weather analysts took temperatures from six Arizona cities on a series of days. No two cities were the same temperature on the same day. Yuma, Arizona, is always the hottest city. Phoenix was hotter than Flagstaff each time. Tucson was hotter than Prescott every time. Winslow was somewhere between Flagstaff and Prescott every time.

Note that this is an open-ended set of facts. You could make yourself a little diagram to fill in as the questions about this fact pattern roll by, which would look like this:

Known:

1) Yuma.
2) Not Prescott or Flagstaff.

Variable, but

1) Phoenix always above Flagstaff.
2) Tucson always above Prescott and
3) Flagstaff never next to Prescott.
4) Winslow always between Flagstaff and Prescott.

In a multiple choice situation, this gives you a fast way to identify any answer with Yuma below first place or Prescott in second place as impossible (and therefore wrong, unless the test is asking you to identify the unacceptable answer). The test continues. . . .

Question 1: *If Phoenix is the third hottest city on a particular day, then what must be true of the temperatures on that day?*
(A) Prescott was the second hottest.
(B) Flagstaff was the second hottest.
(C) Prescott was the fourth hottest.
(D) Winslow was the fifth hottest.
(E) Flagstaff was the sixth hottest.

I'm going to show you how to figure it out before I tell you the answer, because that's what happens on a test, right? Here's a fast way to figure it out. We are asking what *must* be true (what is necessary) of a set of facts. Technically, a fast first thing to do is to look for a lie about the one city you know must be on top, Yuma, and eliminate that choice, and which comes in handy if you run out of time and have to guess, because it cuts down on the number of choices you have in front of you when the moment comes to guess. But the test givers aren't usually that generous. So after you've quickly looked at the choices to eliminate any that have Yuma below the top, you have to look for the next easiest elimination. In this problem, Prescott and Flagstaff can never be second, because Tucson must always be hotter than Prescott and Phoenix must always be hotter than Flagstaff, so, Yuma, always being first, must occupy the only spot above second, so you can eliminate (A), which puts Prescott at second place and (B), which puts Flagstaff at second place.

That's all you can do without using the new facts. There, the testers have fixed Phoenix, too, setting it firmly in third place. This tells you to look at the overall fact pattern for what it says about Phoenix's relationship with any other city, and you will find that it tells you Phoenix was hotter than Flagstaff. So if Phoenix is third, Flagstaff must be fourth, fifth, or sixth. The order now looks like: 1. Yuma 2. Not Prescott 3. Phoenix 4. Flagstaff? 5. Flagstaff? 6. Flagstaff? *The only new information is about Flagstaff, so it stands to reason that the testers now expect us to focus on Flagstaff.* Now you ask yourself what we know about Flagstaff, which we have now sort of pinned down. We know that Winslow is always between Flagstaff and Prescott. The only place next to Flagstaff with room on the other side is fifth place. If we put Winslow in sixth place, nothing is after sixth place, and if we put Winslow in fourth place, it will have Flagstaff on one side (okay), but where will its other bracket city, Prescott, have to be? Second. Now we know Prescott can never be second. So Winslow must be in fifth place, and the answer is (D). Note that this problem is answered without ever solving whether it's Flagstaff, Winslow, Prescott or Prescott,

Winslow, Flagstaff (C and E). Either of those orders is possible, but the question didn't ask what's possible; it asked what *must* always be true.

Next the testers usually ask you to figure out what's possible. Here's what that looks like:

Question 2: *Which of the following temperature readings might have happened on a given day [hottest to coldest]?*
(A) Yuma, Flagstaff, Phoenix, Winslow, Tucson, Prescott.
(B) Yuma, Phoenix, Flagstaff, Winslow, Prescott, Tucson.
(C) Yuma, Phoenix, Winslow, Flagstaff, Tucson, Prescott.
(D) Phoenix, Yuma, Prescott, Winslow, Flagstaff, Tucson.
(E) Yuma, Phoenix, Tucson, Prescott, Winslow, Flagstaff.

In a question about what's possible, even one mistake eliminates the choice (remember the "deliberately misrepresented his age" aspect of the rulings on competency to contract?), so you don't have to figure out what the order is, which is hard and would take too long. Just test each choice for any mistake. We know from the problem that the simplest fact is that Yuma is always first. Look at the choices to see if Yuma is ever not first. Oh, boy! In (D), Phoenix is first. That eliminates (D) as a possibility; scratch it out. Prescott is never second, but the testers haven't given us that option, so that knowledge isn't useful in this particular question. Flagstaff is never second, so that eliminates (A).

Next, pick any relationship from the facts. Tucson must be hotter than Prescott. That eliminated (B), where they have Prescott hotter than Tucson. Then ask whether, in the remaining choices, Winslow is always between Flagstaff and Prescott. In (C), Tucson, rather than Winslow, is between Flagstaff and Prescott, which eliminates (C), so the answer is (E). Since any mistake eliminates a choice in a possibility question, possibility questions are often easier, so if you are short of time, you might try to do those first.

Third, the test may ask what cannot be true (impossible). Here, all the choices but one will be right, so the technique again is to look for any single mistake and there's your answer. This is even easier than the possibility question.

Question 3: *Which order cannot describe the temperature in Arizona on any given day?*
(A) Yuma, Phoenix, Flagstaff, Winslow, Tucson, Prescott.
(B) Yuma, Phoenix, Tucson, Winslow, Flagstaff, Prescott.
(C) Yuma, Phoenix, Tucson, Flagstaff, Winslow, Prescott.
(D) Yuma, Tucson, Prescott, Winslow, Phoenix, Flagstaff.
(E) Yuma, Tucson, Phoenix, Flagstaff, Winslow, Prescott.

Is Yuma ever not first? Nope. Darn. Is Flagstaff ever hotter than Phoenix? Nope. Ah, they're making it a little harder. Is Prescott or Flagstaff ever second? No, again. Double darn. Is Tucson ever below Prescott? No, again. Is Flagstaff ever next to Prescott? (Leaving no room for Winslow in between?) Yep, in (B), Flagstaff is next to Prescott. Can't be. It's the only one that's clearly wrong, so (B) is the answer.

The who sits next to whom problems (people at a negotiation, never people at a dinner party!) work the same way. Just look for what's forbidden, and where they add a new fact, use that as quickly as possible.

The test givers often make the problem more complex by involving more than one variable—multiple colors, different spaces, etc. Since this isn't a test prep guidebook (you will go to one of the professional prep companies for that), I will leave the rest of the exotic variations up to them. As far as I can tell, as a mechanical matter, women and men must prepare for the analytical reasoning section of the LSAT in pretty much the same way.

The Lessons from Analytical Reasoning

All analytical reasoning problems proceed step by step from the facts you know to what you know about their relationship to other facts to the answer. Ergo,

1) It pays to start out by writing down quickly the facts you know in an easily visible format. If there are only two variables, like cities and temperatures, I just make a list. If there are more, like years and modems and hookups, I like a grid format that allows me to see a lot of facts and possible facts at once and move them around as I learn more. Use a pencil to make the grid quickly at the beginning and then just erase or mark the grid as new data become available to you.

2) Don't read forward until you've organized. Read the basic problem and make your list or grid. Then look at the first question and note if what they're asking for *must* be true, *is possibly* true, or *can't* be true. No point to blowing the answer because you misread the question. The list or grid from the first set of facts will hold for all the questions the testers ask from the fact pattern. If a problem doesn't add anything more, just compare each answer to what the grid or list tells you at that point and the answer should emerge.

3) If a problem adds a new fact, I usually ask the easy questions anyway, like Is Yuma ever out of place?, to eliminate or identify obvious answers. Then I turn to the new fact and put it in place and then I go back and ask where the new fact is mentioned in the old fact pattern. Usually, the new fact allows you to take a relationship left sort of open in the basic fact pattern, like Phoenix is always hotter than Flagstaff (which doesn't tell you which number Phoenix is), and make that relational information firmer.

Logical Reasoning

The test contains more sections of logical reasoning than any other. The "logic" of the LSAT is a distant cousin of the logic you may have learned, for example, in a logic course in college, but, like the reading comprehension, it *is* designed to test your ability to see an argument coming at you, identify what its parts are, and see its weaknesses and strengths. Here, again, the exercise is simply one of cautious reading; recognize every sentence as an attempt to make you

You Go, Girl: A Winning Application

believe something and don't give the author any more credit for truth than is absolutely necessary. Like the reading comprehension, logical reasoning often asks you to identify the main line of argument, infer something from the argument, or identify the structure of the argument. LR also asks you to identify the best argument against the passage and to identify flaws in the argument explicitly.

Sample Test Prep for Logical Reasoning

A logical reasoning passage might read as follows:

> Something must be done about our weather prediction system here in Tennessee. It rained two inches in an hour yesterday with little warning. If the rain had been snow, we would have been buried under two feet of snow and we would have had little warning of the blizzard.

The logical reasoning testers might ask several questions from a fact pattern like this, although LR usually involves a different fact pattern for each question. For example:

Question 1: *Which of the following, if true, would be the most serious objection to the argument?*
(A) Many people would rather be warned in error than not warned when threatened.
(B) Actually, if the rain had been snow, the snow might have risen to two and a half feet, not two feet.
(C) If the air had been cold enough for snow, the moisture the air could hold would have been much less.
(D) When it snows in Tennessee, it usually catches people more unprepared than rain does.
(E) People would prefer to be surprised by rain than to be caught unprepared when it snows.

The best objection is (C). This is so because the whole argument rests on the assumption that a rainstorm, a common occurrence of little threat, and a bad blizzard are interchangeable. But this is nonsense; the natural facts that produce rainstorms and snowstorms are not interchangeable. (A) is irrelevant to the argument, or at best weakly supports it. (B) is also irrelevant. The small degree of blizzard is trivial once bad snow conditions are reached. (D) and (E) actually support the call for better predictions.

Question 2: *Which of the following best describes the logical structure of the argument?*
(A) A statement of a specific event followed by a statement of a general rule.
(B) A statement of a general rule followed by an instance of a specific event.
(C) A statement of a specific event followed by a statement of a general rule followed by a specific event.
(D) A statement of a conclusion supported by an historical event followed by a prediction.
(E) A statement of a conclusion supported by a specific event.

The correct answer is (D). First the writer gives a conclusion (weather prediction should be better), then an example of the questionable state of affairs that's not terrible in itself (rained without prediction) followed by a prediction of worse ("If the rain had been snow . . .").

Question 3: *What is the structural weakness of such an argument?*
(A) The historical event does not manifest the general conclusion.
(B) The historical event does not predict the predicted event.
(C) The predicted event does not support the general conclusion.
(D) The two events contradict one another.
(E) The historical event is too specific to support the general conclusion.

This is a little harder, because the rain/snow argument is pretty weak, even though we hear it on the weather report all the time. The best answer to identify the weakness of the argument is (B), because it takes a pretty sophisticated theory to tell us whether rainstorms are like snowstorms, whereas common sense could support the leap from bad predicting to unpredicted rainstorm (A), and common sense could support the leap from bad predicting to unpredicted snowstorm (C), the two events are not obviously contradictory, we just don't know (D), and an unpredicted rainstorm is some evidence for the general conclusion of bad predicting (E).

The Lessons from Logical Reasoning

The hardest thing about logical reasoning is carefully reading the passage. An example from the LSAT a few years ago turned on whether people who quit smoking do so because they're aware of the dangers of smoking or because they become aware of the dangers of smoking *from government warnings*. The passage criticized the ineffectiveness of government warnings. When asked to choose an argument that rebutted the passage, many people chose the answer that noted people had stopped smoking because they were aware of the danger, missing the fact that the proffered answer—awareness—didn't necessarily stem from government warnings. The folks at the LSAC had the good grace to classify the question as difficult. Less than half the test takers answered it correctly. Including me.

There Is No Quick Way to Game the LSAT

Your faithful guide took the better part of a week to do the problems and figure out the structure of the LSAT sufficiently to write the preceding sections. One third—forty pages—of the ARCO guide, *Getting into Law School Today*, is devoted to samples from and an analysis of the LSAT.

The LSAT is not like learning how to ride a bike, which most girls do. It's like learning how to catch a baseball properly, which not enough girls are taught to do. You *could* guess at how to catch a small object coming right at you at a high speed. But as millions of guys know, you will be better off if you let other people teach you how to play and drill you until you're fast. Why do you think all those Little League parents are out there on suburban evenings tossing the ball and tossing the ball and tossing the ball?

There are three ways to get good at playing the LSAT. Cheap, pretty expensive, and really expensive. The cheap way is to buy the test prep books. There are a gazillion books. If you're very cheap, you can hang around the places where college seniors live in late fall and buy their test prep books for a song after they take the test and certainly after they get their scores. The cheapest books for the amount of drill are the LSAC's own books, which contain exams from past years with explanations. For $16, you can buy the *LSAT: Triple Prep Plus with Explanations*. Commercial guides include *Cracking the System: The LSAT* from the Princeton Review, *Cramcourse for the LSAT and LSAT Supercourse* (ARCO), *Inside the LSAT* (Peterson's Guides), and *How to Prepare for the LSAT* (Barron's). Kaplan's *LSAT: Powerful Strategies to Help You Score Higher*, at $34.95, includes only one prep test with answers.

Taking Kaplan as an example of commercial prep materials, commercial materials, however expensive, are written by real human beings who have spent a fair amount of time trying to figure out how the test works, so you can bring strategies to bear on recognizing and solving the problems quickly. The official LSAT guide sounds as if it were written by a bunch of pompous blowhards. For example, in explaining one of the problems in logical reasoning, the LSAT guide presents an entirely new argument it claims is parallel to the problem and then gives you the following helpful advice:

Notice that there are several differences between this argument and the one in the passage. The second premise has no "NOT" in (A), and the entities in question are arranged differently in the two arguments: in the first premise, "radishes" corresponds to "Paulsville" and "peppers" corresponds to "Longtown," but in the second premise, "radishes" corresponds to "Salisbury," and "spinach" corresponds to "Paulsville," while in the third premise, "spinach" corresponds to "Salisbury," and in the conclusion, "peppers" corresponds to "Longtown."

Kaplan gives you "The Kaplan Five Step Method for Logic Games":

1) Get an overview
2) Visualize and map out the Game

and so forth. The answers are broken down into simple steps of reasoning, one after the other. Explaining a seating problem, for example, Kaplan says, "Question 5, in its exploration of who can or cannot sit across from whom, explicitly places two people in chairs and allows you to do likewise with a third. Specifically, if Stanley is in Chair 3, Tonga (who again has to be next to Stanley along a long side of the table) has to take the other chair along that side, Chair 2. [And then just in case you missed it, the author repeats] Stanley in 3, Tonga in 2, and Matt in 6."

What's the difference? To use the LSAT explanations, you need to be as good at the sample problems as you are for the LSAT! What's added? Just a little drill. The Kaplan explanations (and the others—Princeton, ARCO, etc.) teach you techniques to make it easier to do the problems *and* add drill. I don't have a preference among the books; if you're going to prepare from the books alone, you would probably be best off buying one of the commercial books to learn the shortcuts and then using the cheaper books from the LSAC that give you the tests from the last few years with answer sheets as practice questions to try out the tricks you've learned on a large number of questions.

Kaplan, like Princeton Review, the other national test prep company, offers a computer-based prep course, on a CD-ROM. The computer program is actually a complete application program, which tells you what materials you need to gather to apply, apprises you of deadlines, and essentially walks you through the whole process. On the test preparation side, the computer program offers a diagnostic test (to see how you are at the outset) and a final test in written form, to be answered on-screen, and the prep tests on-screen. The advantage of the computer is that the graphics are cute, it satisfies people with a taste for working on computers, and it's a little more stressful than the paper-based test prep, because a somewhat human voice shouts at you that you have limited time and the program includes distracting noises. Since the test is stressful, it probably pays to have a stressful prep course to get you used to the stress. The disadvantage of computer prep is that the LSAT so far is a paper test, so preparing on computer is one step removed from the experience, never a good thing.

Money Well Spent?

Finally, you can take a cram course for the LSAT. As of 1997, Kaplan (which is a subsidiary of the Washington Post Company) was charging $899 per student for about forty hours of in-class instruction, with the Princeton Review close behind. There are other courses available locally, including some offered by colleges, so be sure and check with the prelaw adviser or career services, as those courses are likely to be cheaper.

Kaplan and Princeton are expensive, so everyone wants to know if they work, and the conventional wisdom is that we're not sure. We're not sure, because to find out for certain if they work, we'd have to have the same person take the same test without the prep and then take it again after taking each course, and even then they'd be taking the same test twice. Of course, no one has done that. Both Princeton and Kaplan claim that they raise the scores of students in their courses five, six, or seven points. They make this claim in part based on their own internal testing, which involves comparing the score their people get on a diagnostic test at the start of the course with their score on an exit test or on the actual LSAT.

Although we don't know as much about the LSAT, Kaplan,

Princeton, and the test givers have been battling it out since the late seventies about the more mass-based Scholastic Assessment Test (formerly, Scholastic Aptitude Test; Kaplan led a crusade to change the name). After the testers pressured the Federal Trade Commission to go after Kaplan for fraud in claiming his courses could raise SAT scores, the FTC commissioned a big study that produced the finding that Kaplan's coaching did indeed raise scores! In fact, the FTC's own lawyer, who left the FTC during the study, went public when the study was announced saying that it actually supported much bolder claims for test coaching. Recently, Kaplan had Price Waterhouse do a study of the Kaplan course's effectiveness, which produced the same outcome. Even more recently, researchers from the Educational Testing Service did a study that concluded the difference coaching produces at the SAT level is trivial, and, again, the test prep companies like Kaplan and Princeton characterized the findings as inconclusive. My favorite comment on the cram courses comes from an old article by the then editor of *U.S. News & World Report*, James Fallows. Of course coaching would help, he wrote years ago. "You can tell that just by looking at the questions."

Seen against this background, the answer seems obvious: Take the course. Princeton Review was good enough to share with me the information that their internal data do not show the course helping women or men more, but here again the women may be self-selecting. The women taking the Princeton Review course for the LSAT are thinking strategically, as you're going to do, deciding that it's worth the money to increase their chances of admissions, and the select group of women who think strategically are probably going to be just as good as any group of men on an exam that tests, among other things, for the capacity to think in a very clever, self-interested way.

But I want all women law students to be clever. Let's figure it out. All students score between 120 and 180 on the test, a spread of 60. Every seven-point drop is more than 10 percent of the spread. In the 1997 *U.S. News & World Report* law school rankings, the median LSAT score at top-ranked Yale Law School was a staggering 171. That's a median, so of course not everyone scored that high, but when you are thinking of applying, your chances are of course greatest if you apply with a score as good as the median at the school or higher. If you scored seven points lower, let's say, because you didn't take the cram course and didn't get the benefit of their seven-point improvement, your median falls all the way to 164, which is median at fourteenth-ranked Northwestern. Lose another seven points (157), and you're aiming at forty-second-ranked University of Tennessee at Knoxville, or forty-sixth-ranked Case Western Reserve in Ohio. Lose another seven? At 150, you're aiming at schools in the magazine's unranked third tier of schools, ranked approximately 98–120, such as John Marshall of Illinois or Syracuse.

You are not a bad person if you didn't have a high LSAT. But presumably you're not going to law school for your moral well-being or pure intellectual stimulation, but to get a good job. According to *U.S. News & World Report*, Yale has a number-one placement success rate, while Northwestern's is only twenty-five, Tennessee is thirty-four, and Case is eighty-five. After the top fifty, the magazine stops evaluating placement success and just counts the percentage of students employed. Both John Marshall and Syracuse have employment rates of 81 percent.

I'm going to suggest something even nastier than grinding away at the Princeton Review three nights a week for six weeks in the summer before your senior year or whenever you take the LSAT. Buy the book from the course you're going to take and work your way through the book first, say in the early summer or Christmas vacation before the fall when most people take the test. Then try out the techniques on the LSAT prep tests from the past you can buy cheaply from the LSAC. Closer to the time of the test, take the course. (Don't switch from one book to a different course; you'll just get confused with the different techniques.) *Remember, in many schools, the three-hour test counts the same as the three and one half years of college that went before.*

Ms. Marginal and the Golden Parachute: Fudging

The Kaplan LSAT book opens with "Ten Things You Can Do Right Now to Boost Your Chances of Admission to Law School." Several of them, like "read this book," are not brilliantly helpful. The rest all relate to creating a market image of yourself as an applicant, weaving together a history of work, recommendations, and personal statement that can be useful, but, remember, only if your core grades and scores are in that fuzzy middle.

In fattening up a marginal application, the first thing you need to know is that most marginal applications go to a few faculty members in some fashion. At the high-middle-level law school I looked at, half the 1,800 applicants fell into the marginal group of 900. Five committees consisting of one faculty member and one student reviewed the other 900, or 180 applications per committee. The heavy presence of students in the process is unusual; at most schools, either the admissions dean who essentially makes the decisions is a present or former faculty member or the committees are all faculty. So you want to construct an application that will appeal to an imaginary law professor.

None of the gray area applications is compelling, but all are potentially acceptable or they'd have been thrown out in the first round. You might suspect that in choosing among all potentially acceptable applicants, law faculty might want to recruit a student body that resembles them as much as possible; that's certainly an important dynamic when they select their own teaching colleagues. This suspicion is almost impossible to pin down, because pure grade point and test scores determine so much of the class makeup, the political beliefs of the average law school class member are hard to find out, and there's a certain amount of self-selection and geographical selection. For example, the University of Chicago is famed for its attractiveness to conservative white men, who say they see it as the last haven of true principle in a politically correct world. So conservative applicants would self-select there. The women I interviewed at Minnesota repeatedly referred to a white bread socially conservative Midwestern student as typical, while the women at UCLA found the opposite. Both could be attributed to geography and the appeal of in-state tuition, not a conscious decision on the part of the faculty admissions people.

Strategy #1: Make Yourself Look Like the School

If you have targeted a particular law school with a clear political environment (see chapter 4, "How to Pick a Compatible Law School"), you may want to skew your image toward the *likely* commitments of the faculty reader. Thus, there are many more interestingly radical people at SUNY Buffalo than Boston University, more feminists at Stanford than Harvard, more postmodern deconstructionists at Cardozo than at Columbia, more libertarians at George Mason than Yale, more economists at Virginia than Duke, more social conservatives at Brigham Young and Notre Dame than at NYU or Berkeley. If you got one of the socially committed faculty members at one of these places on the committee that considered your application, you might benefit from constructing an image of yourself. For example, an English major whose senior thesis was about the lesbian subtext in Shakespeare's *As You Like It* and who worked at the battered women's shelter might fare better at Buffalo, Stanford, or Duke than at BU, Brigham Young, or Virginia. An engineer from Purdue whose senior thesis was about the application of economic analysis to allocation of research funds and whose summer job was at Lucent Technologies might do better at Virginia than Cardozo, and a political science major whose thesis was about the latent racism in the revival of Christian schools in the 1970's might do better at Yale than at Brigham Young.

Shaping your statement of interests to the profile the school provides in its catalogs is tricky, because the catalogs are public relations documents that the government would never allow if the schools were trying to sell you stock instead of tuition. Often many of the courses described are not currently taught, the teachers are not available, and the "programs" are little more than come-ons to attract students. If you sound too impressed with statements in the catalog, you're going to sound like a ditz, and nobody wants to admit a ditz. Before you shape your application toward a particular program or specialty at a law school, such as international law or environmental law, talk to students who are already specializing there and ask the admissions office for a listing of the current and next semester's actual course offerings. If you find the program is real, you can increase the impression that you will be a good community member by showing that your credentials particularly qualify you for what the law school offers. To avoid the risk that a particularly popular program will be harder to get into than the law school generally, express interest and admiration without limiting your appeal, unless you're sincerely only interested in going because of a particular specialty.

In the end, most faculty evaluators are looking for signs of success in the institution, not political reflections of themselves (they save that for when they hire faculty). Moreover, many admissions committee members are just technocrats teaching taxation with little concern for political or social imagery. And it's impossible to know what you're going to get. A better reason for a student to prefer a school where the politics are at least somewhat supportive is that they'll have one less battle to fight (see chapter 4, "How to Pick a Compatible Law School").

Strategy #2: Look Like a "Cowardly Liberal"

Reviewing a book about law school politics in the *New York Times* a year or so ago, the conservative federal judge Alex Kozinski described most law school faculties as consisting of irrational, anti-Semitic radicals on the one hand and, on the other hand, "cowardly liberals," who are more interested in keeping their safe jobs than fighting the radicals in their midst.

Although Kozinski doesn't mention it, the Cowardly Liberals are not interested in fighting conservatives, either. Indeed, most of the CLs actually have more in common with conservatives than radicals. Marooned somewhere around or just before the passage of the 1964 Civil Rights Act, they regard all social developments since the mid-sixties as suspect. Kozinski is right, however, to say that CLs are probably the commonest species of law professor.

The safest strategy for an image to present to the CLs that make up most law school faculty is that of a hardworking student with a commitment to the strange mixture of social impact and technical skill that the legal profession represents, and a dollop of interesting hobbies thrown in. If you have some time after you've read this book, try to get a job or at least volunteer in a program that has a fairly traditional legal core anchored around 1964: court watching rather than battering counseling, interning at Court TV, not talk TV.

If you have a skill that you can use in a legal context, that shows that you were more than just free help. So if you're a good writer, don't just volunteer at the local shelter; start a newsletter for volunteer shelter workers. If you're a computer whiz, don't just run errands at the patent law firm; ask to help on their computer-based document management program or volunteer to train the other interns on computers wherever you are. If you're an artist (not the most common skill among lawyers), prepare graphically effective jury exhibits. If you're a good public speaker, volunteer to go around to college or high school career days and tell about your experiences working at the shelter or the firm or whatever. This tells the admissions people you're going to be a good community member, which matters to people constructing a community.

If your grades are lousy, try to bring them up a lot in the time that's left, creating a "prodigal daughter" image or at least showing that you're on the right track. Stay away from pass/fail courses unless they're very far from your major and you are just interested or to show that you stretched yourself beyond your limit of ability to acquire a needed skill. If your grade point average is already compromised by a lousy grade in math or a language, take the next-level class pass/fail (if you know you won't fail) and explain in your statement that you know there are just things you need to be able to do, whether they come with a gold star to wear on your résumé or not. This shows admissions people that you can take adversity and are practical.

Most law schools are going to try to diversify their student body, whether by race, geography, age, or interest. There's not much you can do about the first three, but if you have a pattern of strong interests, it would not hurt to emphasize them. A brilliant athletic career is reputed to help applicants; I think the justice of rewarding athletes with law school is debatable, but I do recommend that you pursue a sport in any event, because the discipline may help you to stand up to the challenging first year of law school.

Is a record of feminist activism a red flag to admissions committees? This is a rational fear when applying to a law school with a suspiciously low percentage of women faculty, because women faculty present a largely male group with the possibility of activism that a woman student unmarked by an activist record does not display. Otherwise, I don't think a history of activism in women's issues is an automatic red flag to admissions committees. During the course of writing this book, I met dozens of young women in very selective law schools whose commitment to feminism and the myriad institutions of women's citizenship, from the National Organization for Women to the local battered women's shelter, was clear when they applied to law school. There is always the possibility that your application will cross the desk of one of the faculty members who has a commitment against women's success so profound that they will use their position to harm a relatively disempowered applicant. But the possibility is equally great in most places that you'll encounter someone who thinks your activism is a plus, because they remember the idealism of their youth or because it shows you're not a couch potato.

Although many people in powerful positions at law schools are resistant to women's issues in various ways, the raw injustice of discriminating against a candidate for that reason is so blatant and so inconsistent with deep-seated beliefs in freedom of thought in the academy that date back at least to the CLs' touchstone date of 1964 that the CLs should find it difficult to keep someone out because of a history of feminism. The issues of feminism that people like Kozinski are interested in tend to be disputes among faculty, like whether there is such a thing as objective truth, or whether sexuality is cultural or natural, not issues directly involved in the activism young people would be engaged in. In addition, women law students are generally so disempowered that faculty have no reason to fear them and therefore no reason to harm them by keeping them out.

Be aware, however, that the libertarian-type conservatives, like Judge Kozinski, as well as CLs, who formed their political identities in the sexually unbuttoned sixties, tend to be extremely sensitive to support for censorship of pornography or restraint of sexual harassment in the workplace, which many of them view as the equivalent to the end of Western civilization. So if you've been involved in Women Against Pornography, for instance, maybe a little censorship begins at home.

Letters from the Rich and Famous

The same analysis for shaping your application applies, of course, to the recommendations. All the guides say that the recommendations should be from people who have reason to know about the characteristics law schools care about: are you very smart, hardworking, imaginative, tenacious, and generous with your time and assets? The people who can know this are mostly your teachers, employers, and coworkers. Famous people, especially those met at the White House where your rich parents took you for coffee, or when they were guests on the MTV show where you were getting coffee, do not count.

On the other hand, if you believe people poured money into the 1996 political campaign on both sides out of love of democracy, you will also believe that it doesn't matter whom you know.

You Go, Girl: A Winning Application

One of my favorite law students, Ms. Marginal, wanted so badly to go to a status law school that she called everyone, including a family friend whose husband went to law school with a dean, to make calls for her. She did get in, although I'd like to think it was more because the admissions office recognized her great tenacity than because the husband of a friend of the family went to Yale with the dean! So if you know a big donor or a famous judge and they can write you a sincere letter about one or more of the characteristics listed above, or call, I'm not going to discourage you from doing it. Of course, the smartest way to parlay a well-connected acquaintance is to do something for them in the way of work or service so they can write you an honest-to-God recommendation.

Most law schools allow you to submit a personal statement. Some limit the statement in various ways, mostly length (a page or two), and some ask for a particular topic or approach. The admissions officer I interviewed in an open-ended way mentioned the personal statement last in the list of "other things" the admissions committee looks for. The ARCO guide reports that many officers identified it as the most important part, but qualifies that immediately with "after the GPA and LSAT." I have a hard time imagining that a system so grounded in the GPA would look at an essay rather than at where the applicant went to college and what she studied there next. What I think is going on is that the admissions people have two levels of information: the "hard" data like GPA and college status and major comprise one category of information and then they turn to the second (and usually last) level of data—the statement, recommendations, unpaid or part-time employment. When they say the statement is important, it's usually because it's an efficient way to form an impression of all the rest of the candidate's qualifications. So the first thing to do in a personal statement is to use it as a vehicle to tell the admissions people about the strongest thing in your history that should motivate them to admit you.

We know that admissions committees want to admit people who will succeed at their institutions. Accordingly, they look for intelligence, hard work, a reasonable explanation for interest in the legal profession, tenacity, good time allocation, political skills, and communal commitment. Many aspects of a life can reflect these: a very hard major of study or training, a record of working at jobs along with going to school, a slow but steady climb up a ladder of organizational or academic hierarchy, positions of organizational leadership. Many do not: a story of channel surfing in the college curriculum, of hobbies taken up and dropped, of parentally supported leisure and frivolity like drinking or tourism, of grunt work and default to law school after a stint driving a cab. The good personal statements described in all the guidebooks have the following things in common: They always pick a story from the person's history that reflects intelligence, hard work, tenacity, skill, and sometimes legal interest, political ability, and communal interest.

So, what have you done that enables you to portray yourself that way? Clara Counselor's story of looking up the law for the men in her unit in the military is hands down the best personal essay I've heard. But for those of you with somewhat less heroic histories, Clara Too's story would make a good personal statement. Here's how it would sound:

My dad was a lawyer, and I wanted to be like him. But when I went to Washington, I wasn't so excited to go to law school, because everyone goes to law school. Although I took the LSAT my senior year, law school is expensive and hard, so it's a serious enough decision to justify taking time off to think about it. While I was off, I signed up to work for a partner at a big law firm. Just as I started, he was appointed to be a federal judge, and he took me with him to his chambers. When I met his brilliant and interesting law clerks and I saw him and them debate the issues he faced as a federal judge, I became convinced that my original ambition was right.

Too's academic credentials already demonstrated her intelligence, but consider what this story adds: It tells the reader she exercises sober judgment, is serious about things that deserve serious analysis, has a generous inclination to help people, is interested in the world of law and was attracted to it because it is an intellectual challenge, which she wasn't just inferring from the catalog; she learned it in the hothouse atmosphere of a federal judge's chambers. No wonder she got in everywhere she applied. Including Harvard.

The second lesson about the personal statement is also the punch line of the joke about the tourist who stopped a long-haired, artsy-looking fellow on the street for directions to Carnegie Hall. Tourist: "Pardon me, sir, but do you know how to get to Carnegie Hall?" Answer: "Practice, practice, practice." The ARCO guide tells a story of a student spending forty hours on his personal statement; Kaplan tells you to allow at least three months to write it, doing a draft and then letting some weeks go by. Better advice was never given. If you turn in your personal statement hot off the computer, unless you have a perfect LSAT, you're a ditz and you shouldn't be going to law school anyway.

As you struggle to bring your personal statement into line with the elementary rules of good writing, which, for some of you, will be a first, don't make particularly female mistakes either. *Don't talk about your personal or emotional life, family, sexual or parenting relationships.* Clara Too told us nothing of how her father reacted to her struggles with the decision to go to law school. *Don't think the reader is interested in you because you're you.* No one ever described inner feelings better than the playwright John Guare: They are "banal, sordid and of interest only to myself." *Don't use words as a substitute for substance. Don't boast.* Notice that Clara Too didn't tell us how well she did on the LSAT. *Don't pretend to talk like a lawyer* (remember how stupid those cops sounded on the stand in the O. J. Simpson trial; they have been taught since time out of mind to try to sound like the legal system they enforce). Clara Too's story has a respectful distance even from the new law graduates who worked in the judge's chambers. *Don't tell how you're going to save the planet.* Note that Clara's story says nothing about how she's going to use her legal education to change the law and provide assistants for every judge in America, laudable as this goal would be. The only change I'd make is to give it a more interesting first line.

Strategy #3: Just Be There

At the beginning of this chapter, I mentioned the importance of an early start. Even if you're not going right to law school after college, it pays to start thinking about the picture you present before all your college courses are chosen and the grades in. Regardless of when in your life path you apply, you're better off statistically with your application in the stream early in the fall before you want to enroll than later. The LSAC official guide has all the addresses and phone numbers, most law schools have Web pages, and the LSAC sells a CD-ROM with all the applications on it.

The Waiting List Game

All the guidebooks say to get an early start, but there's also an important strategy that people don't know about—the late start. I know a woman lawyer in her fifties who is about to retire from her job as general counsel of a major American corporation with enough money from stock options, pensions, etc., to spend the rest of her life at the beach. When she got out of college in 1966, she screwed around for a year. Her LSAT score and college grades were good but not great, and she hadn't applied anywhere. She showed up in Chicago a couple of days before the fall quarter began at the prestigious University of Chicago Law School in 1967, and popped in to the dean of admissions, a wild and crazy guy named Nicholas Fee, with tuition (I think at that time it was $3,000) in her purse. Why not? Fee put another chair at the end of the row of students in the first-year class, added $3,000 in tuition money to the budget of the law school, and three years later, she graduated somewhere in the middle of her class. Thirty years later, she's about to end a successful career and go live somewhere

in the South of France. What do you call the person who graduates last in medical school? Doctor!!

The odds are not with you on my friend's strategy, but it does
illustrate the value of pure unadulterated chutzpah or nerve.
Which brings me to the subject of the waiting list and the related
subject of the transfer. Most law schools have a waiting list, where
they put applicants they'd be glad to have but who definitely
come in second compared to the ones they've already accepted.
Until they know how many of their first-choice group have accepted, they want to keep the second list to pick from. If you're
accepted at a less desirable school and on the waiting list where
you'd rather go, you're going to have to put down the not insub-
stantial deposit where you're accepted and sit tight. Ms. Thin Skin
was accepted at a good school and asked to wait at her first
choice. Although she was ultimately accepted, she decided to attend the lesser school. "If they don't want me," she said, "I won't
be happy there." After graduating, she spent several years striving
to put herself in the place where opportunities were as good as
they would have been if she hadn't been so thin-skinned. Law
school is not about love.

If you're on the waiting list, one thing law schools are looking
for is how sincere you are about going there if they take you. This
is where I think some influence may actually work, because you
know you're minimally qualified and very few schools go to the
enormous trouble of *ranking* the waiting list. As we know, the in-
comparable Ms. Marginal was on the waiting list at her first-
choice school when she resorted to calling her friend's husband to
phone the dean. If you know people on the faculty or influential
alumni and they can put in a word without being obnoxious, this
seems like the time. Other strategies for getting off the waiting list
include writing the admissions office to tell them of your accom-
plishments while waiting, like a really great spring semester senior
year or a work achievement that makes your work-based personal
statement more compelling. If you can, you might try the last-
ditch strategy of just showing up on opening day in case someone
broke a leg.

Finally, you can always apply to transfer. If you get into choice two and you do brilliantly your first year, there isn't a first-choice school in the country that won't consider a transfer. Why shouldn't they? Now they're not speculating on how you will do in law school; you have a proven record. Your existing school will probably try to keep you, and this is a great time to negotiate for more scholarship money, but don't stay out of love. Remember, in law school, love means. . . . And don't be proud. What do they call someone who graduates after only two years at Harvard Law School? A Harvard grad.

Law school is funny. Sometimes people with really great grades from college don't do as well their first year and others do a lot better than expected. Ms. Marginal only got in off the waiting list. But her first-year grades were so good she got onto the prestigious law journal at her school without even having to go through the writing contest. As she said when interviewed, "I've probably got the lowest grades of anyone who graded onto the law review." What do they call someone who just squeaked onto the law review? Law review editor.

How to Pick a Compatible Law School

POLITICIANS MAKE LAWS and law is political. Law school is no exception to the presence of politics. As we glimpsed in chapter 2 and as you will see in chapter 5 ("The Femscore: How to Pick a Law School Where Women Succeed"), the political beliefs that predominate in any given law school can have a strong influence on women's experiences. You may decide, as one of my interviewees at a politically incompatible law school admitted, "to go to the best law school I got into." If you do, this chapter lays out some of the strategies women have followed to succeed at incompatible law schools.

If It's Tasteless and Odorless, It's Probably Politics

First, be aware that politics plays an important role in many law schools. It's not a coincidence that all the political talk shows and op-ed pages have been heavy with law professors in the last few years. In the seventies, a law professor, Thomas Emerson of Yale, did the heavy lifting on the arguments in favor of the Equal Rights Amendment. One of the con law teachers at Chicago,

Professor Philip Kurland, made the arguments about integrated bathrooms that were ultimately used to defeat the ERA. In 1998, Professor Jonathan Turley, of George Washington Law School in D.C., was a TV fixture, arguing that each of Bill Clinton's legal defenses was groundless special pleading. A GW colleague of Turley's, Professor Jeffrey Rosen, is a leader in the movement to undo the protections against sexual harassment. When she was still at Harvard, law professor Susan Estrich of the University of Southern California managed Michael Dukakis's presidential campaign. Although politics tend to be hottest at more elite institutions, where the teachers and the students really regard themselves as in training for national political leadership, most law schools have some political "feel" to them.

Second, you need to know what the dominant political agenda is at the schools you're considering. (I say "dominant" because most law schools tolerate a range of political positions wider than the range of the faculty we saw at, say, George Mason. However, even if not representative of a majority of the faculty or students, one overall political/legal position usually dominates the majority of interactions.) I don't just mean whether the dean voted Democratic or Republican in the last election or whether the constitutional law teachers think the abortion rights decision was a terrible mistake, although these are indicators of the dominant norm at most places.

Even if it seems as if you've found a relatively apolitical place, political questions are inherent in every aspect of the law school curriculum, not just in the obvious ways like your professors appearing on talk TV or what's taught in constitutional law classes on desegregating schools or protecting abortion rights. For example, tax law can be very political. You probably know that the last couple of years have witnessed a debate over the taxation of capital gains, like the profit on stock investments, which is in part a political decision about how wealth should be distributed. Recently, Congress changed the tax law. What you may not know is that for a generation before Congress acted, the issue of whether capital gains, which mostly go to people who are already wealthy, should be treated the same as income tax on wages was the subject of scholarship and teaching in tax classes at law schools around the nation. I first heard the arguments about how capital gains should be taxed in tax class in 1967!

Tort class (the law of personal injuries) can be very political. "Tort reform," for instance, seeks to change the ability of juries to levy huge punitive damages on defendants like doctors or car manufacturers, a political decision about whether a government agency should call powerful private players to account. Torts is one of the required courses in any first year of law school, and, like the tax teachers, torts professors in law schools have been taking positions on "tort reform" for decades. Law students often miss the political content of their course material. For example, one of the teachers in the required first-year torts class at the University of Minnesota Law School uses a textbook that favors tort "reform" to limit the power of the courts. But when I asked the students there if their tort class had a particular "political" point of view, they looked bewildered. They didn't know favoring tort reform was political. They'd never even heard of any other way to think about the matter. The exchange was typical:

Ms. Minnesota: "Now that I think about it, no other point of view came up; we used Richard Epstein's book [one of the leading conservative law and economics–type law professors in the country]. I'm not aware of other positions on torts. I'm sure we *had* other discussion, because it's an open, casual class that's very informal, but Farber [the torts teacher] is pretty happy with Epstein's book."

LH: "What about concepts like corrective justice [using the legal system to correct the wrong of, say, making a riskier car to save money] and moral obligation?"

Minnesota: "In crim law. We heard about it in torts, but it's not a big point."

LH: "What do you think of the political environment at the University of Minnesota Law School?"

Minnesota: "I don't know what you mean."

If It's Constitutional Law, It's Probably Politics

Although politics permeates the law school curriculum, you're not wrong to think that a lot of politics in law and in law schools is concentrated in the area of constitutional law. In America, as Alexis de Tocqueville said centuries ago, every social question sooner or later comes to the courts. Certainly, in the last half century, the core questions of wealth, race, and sex that still rend the society have all come to the courts—indeed, to the Supreme Court—in the form of constitutional questions. In 1954, the Supreme Court decided that racially segregated schools were illegal; in 1973, that certain criminal restraints on abortion violated women's rights; three years later, that campaign contributions were speech and could not be regulated; in 1995, that most affirmative action was also not allowed. So constitutional law is a class where public, political issues are front and center.

When I was a law student at the University of Chicago Law School in the sixties, I learned that *Brown v. Board of Education*, the Supreme Court's 1954 decision to desegregate the public schools, was an illegal act of overreaching by unelected judges attempting to put their personal political preferences into the words of the Founding Fathers. After all, the Constitution says nothing about "integration," only that laws must be "equal." Really smart, careful judges would never have desegregated the schools, one of the con law teachers contended.

Now, thirty years later, only a few law professors are still willing to say in public that the really smart people would realize that the Constitution permits racially segregated schools. Apparently, however, someone at the University of Chicago is still using the argument that federal judges are not elected to argue against less well-accepted social change. In an interview last fall, Ms. U of C, a second-year student at the University of Chicago, volunteered to me how the law school had taught her to think more carefully, using as her example that the law school had taught her to doubt whether the Supreme Court should have voided state laws making abortion criminal in 1973 in its landmark *Roe v. Wade* decision. After all, she informed me, the Court is unelected, and careful judges would have noticed that the Constitution is silent about abortion.

In an example from a little farther up the lakefront, when a third-year Northwestern student wrote a paper on the constitutionality of the law that funds initiatives to reduce domestic violence, she reported that she couldn't find a single con law teacher at Northwestern to lay out the view that the Violence Against Women Act was legit, as a constitutional matter. This despite the fact that the legal precedents supporting it go back to President Roosevelt's New Deal in the thirties.

Neutral Principles Sometimes Just Mean Men on Top

Criticizing the abortion decision and arguing that the Violence Against Women Act is unconstitutional could rest on a clear commitment to the constitutional mandate of a limited judiciary and a limited federal government, as Ms. U of C described it. There are, indeed, times when the health of the constitutional system must prevail, even when it produces really nasty results. The Supreme Court has narrowly taken that position in protecting people who burn the American flag, for instance, in the interests of protecting the constitutional commitment to free speech.

In the particular examples of segregated schools and criminal abortions, however, I'm skeptical. After all, racial segregation and female sexual punishment operate so strongly to the advantage of the people making the arguments! Moreover, I have a test to figure out whether someone is really committed to judicial restraint or whether they just don't like women to get abortions. The test goes as follows. The Constitution doesn't use the words "affirmative action," any more than it says "abortion." Yet, for some years people have been arguing that the Constitution forbids public law schools like the University of Texas to follow publicly generated programs of affirmative action in order to avoid turning into all-

white schools. To be consistent, someone who thinks the unelected federal judges shouldn't overturn state laws making abortion criminal should also think that the judges shouldn't overturn
the laws requiring state schools to use affirmative action to integrate their otherwise all-white schools. Because the Constitution
is silent on both matters.

This is a good test, because supporting affirmative action is not
so obviously in the interest of the white men making the arguments, so the test forces them to choose between self-interest and
constitutional purity. Applying my test for consistency, I asked Ms.
U of C whether the University of Chicago had caused her to
doubt whether an unelected Supreme Court should have struck
down the state of Texas's democratically enacted affirmative action program as they did in a 1995 case. She said the University of
Chicago Law School had not caused her to doubt whether the
Court was also wrong in undoing affirmative action. She had only
learned to doubt the wisdom of *Roe v. Wade.*

Although these are examples from a conservative point of view,
political liberals often engage in the same politically charged "legal" analysis. For example, the same liberal professors, like NYU's
Ronald Dworkin, who think the constitutional protections of free
speech will suffer mortal damage if feminists succeed in getting
pornographic speech reined in are the biggest supporters of limiting the amount of money that can be spent for political speech in
election campaigns. Dworkin's theory of the First Amendment allows the government to limit political speech but not sexual
speech, just like the Chicago theory of the Fourteenth Amendment allows states to make abortion criminal but so far hasn't
been used to defend states that mandate affirmative action.

So the third thing you need to know is that positions with a lot
of political consequences are put forward in the law school classroom as mere applications of "neutral principles" of law by people
who would not be willing to live with the full application of their
so-called theories, when white men would suffer the consequences. When positions are presented as flowing naturally from
neutral principles, it's hard for a young woman with no legal

training or experience to think up the arguments for the other side. Even Ms. U of C, a brilliantly successful law member of the *University of Chicago Law Review*, hadn't figured out that her teacher's "neutral" arguments about the rigorous limits on the Court's powers to invalidate democratically enacted abortion laws should have made him a defender of democratically enacted affirmative action. Since she hadn't figured it out, she couldn't press him on it, so she'll never know whether his arguments are so compelling that she, too, must abandon her political support for abortion rights in the interests of constitutional purity or whether his legal arguments are just a guise for his political distaste for abortion rights.

Why Men on Top Feel Heavy

Of course, all women don't believe in choice, affirmative action, or in the federal law addressing the problem of domestic violence, and all women law students probably don't believe all the same things, either. If you agree that the states should be free to criminalize abortion, that affirmative action is an unjust system that victimizes white men, and that the states are doing a good-enough job dealing with domestic violence, or that pornography is just harmless sexy pictures and the free play of sexual harassment is the foundation of a free society, learning the law in a political context that favors criminalized abortion, sexual harassment, and states rights in domestic violence matters will be compatible with your beliefs.

Almost every school also employs people of diverse positions on contested matters. Mary Becker, one of the most vocal feminist professors in America, teaches at Chicago, and, while this book was in the works, Chicago gave a part-time appointment to famed feminist theorist Catharine MacKinnon. The affirmative action "test" I use to identify authentic white male constitutional defenders was suggested to me years ago by Geoffrey Stone, formerly the dean there. But despite some diversity, being marginal to the group dominating the law school has a host of spoken and unspoken disadvantages. The people who share the dominant political view usually dominate the hiring process, so they reproduce themselves a lot. They are confidently vocal in faculty workshops and seminars, so the people on the outs feel silenced. Take, for example, George Washington Law School. Although, as we will see when we analyze the catalog, GW (worst Femscore in Status Group #3) has a very diverse set of political views included in its faculty, one source described the place as "dominated by people doing legal theory and they're intimidating the other faculty. They have a political agenda posing as an intellectual agenda. A Heritage Foundation [a very conservative think tank] agenda." Another player at GW put it more gently. That person thought the faculty workshops were okay, but stayed away from the faculty lounge, dominated by what another source described as folks conservative in orientation. The faculty, one source said, "prid[ed] themselves on not being 'liberal' like Georgetown [law school]."

Sometimes, the dominant group allies with students to criticize and challenge the marginal teachers from within the classroom. Feeling silenced, the minority-thinking teachers lose confidence in their ideas and they lose involvement in the institution. At George Washington, "a lot of people deal with this by dropping out. They spend a lot of time at other jobs [consulting, working abroad]. Doors are shut. A lot of people are not there." So they are there less and thus less available to the students who need them. As one woman at GW put it, "I can't believe it took me until my third year of law school to find someone [on the faculty] to talk to."

If you disagree with the dominant political view being advanced in the law school you attend, you may find law school to be more of a challenge than it has to be. As one star Northwestern woman student put it after extensive exposure to the political teachings there, "I wanted to know that my politics weren't *completely inconsistent with the Constitution.*"

Essentially, a politically infused law school is asking you to abandon your political beliefs in the interest of the system you're going to be a part of. The Princeton Review's *Pre-Law Companion* puts it this way: "Law students are taught to remove their 'selves' from the analytic process and apply an ostensibly objective 'legal analysis.' " But people don't just pick up political beliefs like choosing a skirt length. Usually, what people believe politically is a product of the way they were raised, how they were educated up to law school, and where they see their self-interest to lie. So in addition to worrying about whether your law professors are giving you the straight story about what the Constitution really requires (mine were sure wrong about *Brown*), another reason to be concerned about the political atmosphere of the law school you choose is that abandoning previously held political beliefs may be painful for you.

The politics of law school is particularly important for women, because issues involving gender justice are heavily contested right now, so, at incompatible law schools, women are often being asked to abandon their political beliefs on subjects particular to them as women—abortion rights, affirmative action, domestic violence, sexual harassment. In some of these areas, the interests of men as a group and women's interests are at odds. A job that goes to a woman under an affirmative action program is a job that a man doesn't get; the overwhelming majority of domestic violence incidents involves male violence against females, not the reverse; and women are the overwhelming majority of the victims of rape and sexual harassment and an undetectable percentage of the offenders under the law of rape.

So women who have to change their minds about abortion rights in order to think like lawyers are being asked to abandon not only beliefs, but also beliefs in which self-interest, and even self-love, is deeply involved. To fit in with the dominant political belief system I just described, they have to say, for instance, that they should be sent to jail if they try to escape the consequences of their sexuality through abortion. They don't ever deserve an extra chance at a job. The L.A. police are good enough for them if their husband decides to take a swing at them. University faculty should be free to hit on their students for sex. Women law students who disagree with their teachers about women's issues seem to face a tough choice: They can advocate for themselves or they can win the approval of the authority figures in their new world, but not both.

Finally, women students are asked to abandon their self-interest just as their self-esteem is under assault from the whole system of legal education. Again, from the Princeton Review: "The much trumpeted learning to think like a lawyer . . . involves a process of socialization, even indoctrination." In law school, as in the brain-washing prisoner of war programs in the Korean War, the first goal of "indoctrination" is to force the subject to let go of his whole prior sense of self.

This process is harder on females, because studies show that female students start law school with lower self-esteem than their male classmates do anyway. Then certain methods of teaching ask them to abandon everything they've previously learned as a source of opinion. Finally, where a woman's interests are at odds with the position the faculty advances, as in the abortion and domestic violence examples, the dominant political beliefs at some law schools ask them to do something even worse than disappear—to turn themselves into their own adversaries.

How to Succeed with a Man on Top

Study after study has shown that at this time in America, women are more liberal than men; they voice more liberal views and they vote much more heavily in the Democratic Party. Studies have shown that similar opinions prevail among women law students. I interviewed a dozen women at schools with well-established dominant political norms less liberal than those among American women as a group. Some of the women are on law review, and one is first in her class. They otherwise resembled a lot of you: Most had come to school from public interest jobs; about half were still intent on pursuing them when they got out. The women pursued a rich array of different strategies to "succeed" in these politically inhospitable law schools. I'm going to share them with you, because, once you see where you're admitted, regardless of the school's politics, you too may decide "to go to the best law school I got into." Here's what the women did. They resisted, they chose not to share their true beliefs, they changed their beliefs, they adopted the assumption that the law school is just a place for the neutral transmission of technical trade knowledge, and they ignored the nature of the forces arrayed against them.

THE REBEL

Michele Landis (her real name), Northwestern '98, graduated at or near the very top of her class. Given that law school is to some extent an open contest for grades, when she applied, Michele, like many women, thought if she were willing to work hard and get good grades in the existing system, she would be rewarded. So, like many of the women I interviewed, she didn't worry too much about whether the law school she chose had a woman-friendly faculty.

Michele, an unabashed feminist, was a controversial figure from the beginning, often eliciting angry attacks from her classmates. However, after she received her outstanding grades at the end of the first semester, she thought she was well on her way to a successful career. She believed that if she did well, her political differences with the mostly conservative members of the faculty would not matter. Accordingly, despite their differences of outlook, Michele selected a politically conservative law professor to supervise her ambitious individual research project.

Michele began to become alarmed about her prospects when, at the beginning of her second year, she learned that Northwestern had denied tenure to its rising young feminist star, and, worse, she heard that her adviser had written a detailed letter in the tenure process harshly critical of the feminist professor's work.

When the time came for her to apply for a judicial clerkship, the critical stepping stone to the most prestigious jobs in the legal profession, Michele needed a letter of recommendation from someone close to her research. Michele knew that although law professors will usually write some sort of clerkship letter if a student asks them, the professors use the recommendation process to write what are in essence briefs on behalf of the prized students they really want to place, so when clerkship time rolls around, anything less than an unqualified recommendation can come across as a negative. Professors are the gatekeepers.

In light of the ongoing talk about her professor's role in the tenure denial, Michele was worried enough about whether he would give her the kind of recommendation that actually gets students the highly competitive clerkships to go to his office and ask him point-blank whether, in light of their political disagreements, he could write her an unqualified recommendation. The professor responded that he could. In fact, he said he had "a draft here and it will be quite favorable and you're going to be pleased," and he detailed the favorable things he would be saying about her.

Because she had done so well in law school, Michele applied only to judges of the very prestigious federal circuit courts of appeals. She was particularly interested in Judge Stephen Reinhardt, from the Ninth Circuit, a liberal judge currently serving in the federal judiciary, and in the prestigious D.C. Circuit Court of Appeals, from which most Supreme Court Clerks are drawn. Although she was lucky enough to hear from Judge Reinhardt right away, Michele never heard from any judge on the D.C. Circuit. In fact, with one exception, Michele only heard from the most liberal of the federal judges, despite her excellent qualifications. Fortunately, Judge Reinhardt offered Michele a clerkship, which she gratefully accepted.

She was disturbed, however, because several people warned her that her file included an "odd" letter from her adviser that might damage her. When she saw the letter, she realized that he had added a paragraph to the "very favorable" letter he had promised her. In it, she says, "He went on about how I was 'quite active politically,' as a 'feminist and socialist,' and that I 'did not get along well with the law review editors last year' because of conflict over my efforts to adopt an 'affirmative action' plan for law review membership selection." He also added that she had organized meetings about "faculty appointment issues" that involved the President and Provost of the University. Michele believes that these comments were inappropriately added after the previous discussion of the letter's contents and were essentially qualifications to the letter that would be interpreted as red flags warning judges to stay away.

Luckily for Michele, Stephen Reinhardt is the last judge to be deterred by political branding. Beyond doubt, however, some judges were deterred. After learning what her adviser had said about her, she confronted him. He denied that the letter was negative, and insisted that she wasn't "damaged" by it anyway because "everyone knew that Judge Reinhardt was her top choice." "I was crying and telling him how hurt I was because I thought we had a good relationship," Michele says, "and he was sitting there mitigating my damages out loud. He never even said he was sorry. I don't believe he was sorry."

Michele confronted the law school administration about it. "I told the [Associate] Dean that here he is on this big upward mobility campaign, trying to increase Northwestern's status relative to other law schools. A part of that campaign is to place more judicial clerks. And then the administration just stands by while a so-called recommendation essentially tied a rock around the neck of the woman who was at the top of the class. How is that consistent with improving the law school's standing?" The Dean refused to intercede on Michele's behalf. She says, "I will bet the farm that this could not have happened to any man at the top of the class. Not in a million years."

GETTING MY TICKET PUNCHED

None of the women at the table in the Harold J. Green Lounge of the University of Chicago Law School was sorry she went. As she embarked upon her last year, one student said she "knew what she was getting into." She had talked to female attorneys and knew that the U of C had a reputation for conservatism and extreme rigor. Ms. U of C, who had learned to reconsider the legitimacy of the abortion decision, decided before she started, "I'm going to treat it like a job." Ms. Tough, '99, said she had actually chosen Chicago because it was male and conservative. "This is the dominant school of thought in the legal profession, and that's why I chose this school." Ms. Instrumental also had a utilitarian attitude toward the law school: "One of my family friends said, 'If you want to be a really good lawyer, you'll go to Chicago.'"

Over at Northwestern, Ms. Marginal was following a similar strategy. Like Chicago's Tough, she thought law school was probably no worse an environment than working would be (Marginal's mother is a lawyer), and, like many of the students, she sees the somewhat more liberal world of undergraduate school as the aberration in an otherwise conservative world.

Ms. Too Good for Harvard and a friend also used Northwestern for their purposes, rather than vice versa. Each of them was admitted to Harvard, and each of them turned it down to attend Northwestern instead. Although Ms. Friend said she was impressed with the atmosphere among the Northwestern students when she visited (more social, less competitive), each was heavily influenced by the money in the Wigmore scholarships Northwestern gave them to come. "I wanted to go to law school to do public interest work," Ms. Too Good said, "and when I got the Wigmore, I said, here's my opportunity. I don't have to wind up really poor and have to go to a firm. I might go to Harvard and hate it *and* wind up indebted." Top of class; off waiting list. Each of these women began the law school experience feeling that they were in the driver's seat. If anyone tried to brainwash them, he'd have to bring lots of soap.

HOLDING YOUR TONGUE

Of the six women I interviewed at Chicago, only Ms. Instrumental had ever spoken up, as Michele Landis always did, to argue on behalf of the interests of women against a teacher. She described her statements, when she felt her criminal law professor had given inadequate attention to the battered woman in a domestic violence discussion, as "this infamous outburst in crim law class." As this characterization reflects, Instrumental felt a lot of ambivalence about speaking up in opposition to her teacher and on behalf of women. Ms. Tough, who had intentionally chosen Chicago to toughen her up for the practice of law, disagreed with Ms. Instrumental. "I thought you were great," she said. "Don't you remember I came up to you after class and said so?" Instrumental did not remember Tough's private expression of support for Instrumental's public risk.

Too Good also got privately tired of hearing her teachers remind her to read the exact words of the Constitution, a generally conservative position. "I kept hearing [Constitutional law professor] Marty Redish say, 'What's in the text?' I wanted a little more of [the liberal theories of Harvard's] Larry Tribe. Rather than take Redish on directly, however, [I] just went to the library and read what Harvard had to say."

Tough always does her speaking out in this private context. In addition to "supporting" Instrumental privately, she privately "pulled one of her classmates aside and told him what he was saying was offensive." He responded, not surprisingly, that she had left him unconvinced and therefore unwilling to change his mind, but that he would stop saying the "offensive" thing *where she could hear him*. None of the other women reported any private disagreements.

Despite her silence, Instrumental felt that her core values hadn't changed. Ms. U of C disagreed. Without interrupting the technical flow of information with politics, somehow her convictions did change. "I'm more incrementalist," she said, and, you will recall, more skeptical about the activist role of the courts in protecting abortion rights.

BLAH, BLAH, BLAH

Ms. Tough did not try to convince her classmate he was wrong, just that he had offended *her*. In support of Tough's restraint, Ms. U of C reported that in the first-year theory class, Elements of the Law, when people would try to express their beliefs in the rightness or wrongness of legal doctrines, the people in the class called the discussion "blah, blah, blah." "I got mad sometimes when people got into it in class," she continued, "and there's technical information I want to get." Tough agreed. "I feel like that's not why I came to law school. Other people are good at it [blah, blah, blah], they're good at applying it. . . . There was a seminar in Current Issues in Racism and the Law," Tough (who is African American) went on, "and that's why I didn't take it." So Tough and Ms. U of C essentially treated the law school as a place to get technical information about how to succeed at a legal career and stayed away from the deeper issues like racism and the law or the policy behind the abortion decision that might require them to embrace positions in the dominant Chicago context that would be hurtful to them as individuals.

SLAP SLAP, TICKLE TICKLE

When the University of Chicago faculty voted to make an offer to the nation's premier feminist scholar, Catharine MacKinnon, the *Chronicle of Higher Education* reported that some of the conservative students objected in a series of very public E-mails, invoking the conservative alumni and involving the conservative press. This E-mail writer used fairly graphic terms to express his displeasure:

> Her [MacKinnon's] books have been a downward spiral of slack scholarship and media-baiting. . . . Kate [sic] is concerned with women's free speech rights, particularly her own. . . . MacKinnon is a disgrace, and she has no place in an office next to the likes of Epstein, Posner, and Easterbrook. . . . She, with [philosopher and classicist Martha] Nussbaum, will represent a critical mass of radical feminism festering in the stacks.

Although he was displeased with "liberal" hires of any gender, the writer singled out for attack the quality of the handful of other female faculty members:

> This quarter [Professor Martha Nussbaum] co-teaches Sexual Autonomy and the Law with [Professor Stephen] Schulhofer. Presumably Schulhofer provides the law and Nussbaum provides the Sexual Autonomy . . . [Professor] Tracy Meares (What can I say?) and [Professor] Emily Buss (. . . reasonably qualified).

When Ms. Tease (class of '98) read the signature on the E-mail, she was surprised to find it came from someone in her singing group. Another supersuccessful law student, Tease said, "The guy who generated the E-mail was the nicest guy. Everyone in the singing group just gets along." When asked whether she changed her mind about this nice guy since reading his E-mail thoughts, she responded, "I can't be totally wrong, so it's just a lot more complicated picture." When I asked her what she liked about the E-mail writer, she said, "He teases me, which works very well with me." So Tease managed to find something to like in a man who attacked every female member of their faculty. He teased her, after all.

Loving Well Is the Best Revenge

The one theme that emerged from both groups was the value of a community of like-minded people. When Northwestern denied tenure to feminist legal historian Jane Larson, her advocates among the students just stuck with their "community—the public interest group, [liberal faculty] Len Rubinowitz and Larry Marshall, the Feminists for Social Change. Just like in any law school," one of them opined, "as long as you've got your group, I think you feel okay." Ms. Tough loved her classmates, but "her husband was her support group." Instrumental and Ms. U of C thought the best thing they had going for them was their friendship with each other.

So is the glass half full or half empty? Each of the women emerged from their three years with a very prestigious and marketable law degree. Almost all of them said they had really enjoyed their law school experience. Michele did get a great clerkship. On the other hand, studies show that women come into law school with lower self-esteem, they have very mixed feelings about the experience of the Socratic method, their grades the first year are lower and therefore their access to law review is harder. It's hard to measure the effect of having to conceal—even from themselves, in some cases—how different their views are from the views that are valued in the institution. If you go to a school where the dominant views are very different from yours, you add to that difficulty the task of figuring out when the law school position is the rational, technically correct position, which legitimately requires you to change your thinking, and when it's just a bunch of people in power seeking to preserve their power over people like you. Law school requires enough learning without adding additional burdens on yourself.

Decoding a Law School Catalog

You can find out what the atmosphere in your prospective school is pretty easily. Just learn to read the catalog or the information on the school's Web site. But it takes some interpretation. After all, lawyers are taught to "make the lesser argument appear the greater." Nowhere is this truer than in a law school catalog. Even though law school is a major investment for students, law school catalogs are as reliable, for example, as home shopping catalogs, where all the models are six feet tall and weigh 120 pounds. Catalogs exist to make the law school look as good as possible to the general public and especially to the applicant pool, regardless of what's actually going on. As one Columbia student told me, "The admissions office is a sales office. The brochure sells all this multicultural stuff, and then we wind up with white male teachers and a regressive social atmosphere."

THE CASE OF COLUMBIA

Sure enough, Columbia's 1997–98 catalog claims that Columbia provides a "Legal Education for a Changing Profession and World." The word "diverse" and the synonyms for diversity—"different," "myriad," "perspectives"—appear five times in the first paragraph. Twenty-eight pictures and biographies of Columbia's finest, including representative members of its famed faculty, are displayed in a winsome way throughout the catalog. Seventeen, or 60 percent, of the twenty-eight portraits are women. Eleven are minorities. Asian Americans, African Americans, radical feminists, liberal feminists—Columbia's catalog trumpets a veritable rainbow coalition of diversity. Justices, civil rights activists, playwrights and actors—Columbia's catalog reports a cornucopia of careers.

Truth is, according to the American Bar Association, Columbia's student population in 1996 was 44 percent female, not 60 percent female. (Incidentally, the population was also 33 percent minority, not 39 percent minority, as the catalog shows.) According to Columbia's own faculty directory, its academic faculty was just under 17 percent female, way below the national average, even below the low average for the most elite schools. In addition, of the paltry ten women on Columbia's academic faculty of fifty-eight, only seven, or 12 percent, were employed without also being married to or cohabitating with men on the faculty.

As to diverse careers, according to the Bar Association, just under 70 percent of the 1995 graduating class were working in law firms six months after graduation. Another 18 percent were clerking for judges, a job usually leading to firm jobs after a year, with a small percentage leading to academic jobs. There was no category for playwrights. As for civil rights leaders, only 2.8 percent of Columbia's 1995 class were working in public interest at all.

A BLACK OR FEMALE PICTURE IS WORTH A THOUSAND BLACK OR FEMALE STUDENTS OR FACULTY

Although some schools do overrepresent women students in the pictures, there is no clear pattern of numerical overrepresentation. The University of Michigan catalog, for example, presents 45 percent female images; its student body in 1996 was 42 percent women, not a serious overage. Similarly, George Mason University, in Arlington, Virginia, presents 39 percent female images; its student body is 10 percent less female, at a low 36 percent. Mercer University in Macon, Georgia, shows 41 percent female faces, while the school is only 38 percent female. However, most schools are accurate or even underrepresent the female student presence. Florida State's catalog images are 32 percent female, while its 1996 enrollment was 45 percent female; the University of Memphis pictured 34 percent females, while enrollment was a high 49 percent. Even schools with startlingly low female enrollment underrepresented their women in the catalog, like the University of Virginia (37 percent women, 26.9 percent pictured).

However numerically accurate, the women-friendly images in the pictures often bear little resemblance to the experiences women report or to the numerical data on women's success. For example, the only picture of any student organization in the University of Chicago admissions guide is a snapshot of ten women from the Law Women's Association playing field hockey on the university green. Our statistical analysis in chapter 5 put Chicago at the bottom of the list of women's success in 1996 and 1997 among the prestigious top-status group of law schools with over 166 LSATs. As we saw, a series of savage letters and E-mails from conservative students erupted in the national press in 1997 upon the announcement of the part-time appointment of feminist faculty member Catharine MacKinnon. Unless you're a girl who just wants to have fun on the green, don't be misled by the happy faces in the catalog.

A FEMALE PART-TIMER IS WORTH A THOUSAND FEMALE TENURED PROFESSORS

The catalogs probably are most misleading in their description of the faculty. Almost without exception, the catalogs don't distinguish between academic tenured or tenure-track faculty and a host of other teaching types: clinical faculty, teachers of writing, librarians, visitors, adjuncts. Students are often very close to the people who teach them clinical practice or legal writing. In a just world, those teachers would be every bit as important to the law school as the academic tenured faculty, and, in a few places, they are. However, although some schools extend tenure to their clinical teachers or at least the director of the legal writing program or ask their academic faculty to teach legal writing, across the whole landscape of law schools, neither clinicians nor legal writing teachers generally exercise the kind of dominant influence in their schools that we discussed above. Many times, clinical courses or legal writing are taught pass/fail, and clinical courses are rarely included in the crucial first year. And, almost inevitably, there are many, many more women among the clinical, library, writing, visiting, and adjunct faculties.

As a result of these realities, although the listings aren't always misleading, by not distinguishing, an overwhelming majority of the catalogs usually overstate the influence of women faculty. In my survey of 121 law school catalogs for accuracy, seventy-five of them—or about 60 percent—list and describe female faculty who don't really matter in running the institution, pumping up the image of female faculty by including untenured skills teachers, librarians, and the like. The discrepancy can be quite great: The University of Dayton presents its faculty as 28 percent female; scrutiny reveals that the academic tenured or tenure-track faculty is only 15 percent; Franklin Pierce Law Center's female count goes down from 30 percent to 16 percent. Most of the overstatement is in the range of eight or ten points: Baylor Law School has a total of 33 percent females listed—only 25 percent of the academic tenured or tenure-track faculty is female; Cardozo dips from 29 percent to 22 percent, Cincinnati from 37 percent to 29 percent, Fordham from 30 percent to 19 percent.

Although in 40 of the 121 schools the percentage of female faculty actually goes up when you change focus from the larger group to those in the high-status academic jobs, the increase is infinitesimal (six show no change). Only a handful of the schools sent catalogs that underrepresented the percentage of females in their core faculty by more than one or two points. Even then, the difference was still much smaller than the average overstatement in the overstatement group. So, for instance, the University of Memphis listed 30 percent female of all faculty, and had 31 percent female of academic faculty, and the University of Maine showed women as 37 percent of all faculty and 38 percent of academic faculty. Since the overstatement of actual academic female faculty is common and large, and the understatement is rare and tiny, when you look at the total faculty list in a law school catalog, you can assume that it overstates the female percentage of the faculty who run the institution by a lot.

If you want to know whether you're going to be investing your tuition money in a law school that sends out an inaccurate catalog, just figure out the percentage of female faculty as they present it and then compare the percentage to the number for that school in chapter 5. If there's more than a three or four point difference, I'd read the rest of the catalog pretty critically.

A LISTING OF COURSES IN WOMEN'S INTERESTS IS WORTH A THOUSAND ACTUAL COURSE OFFERINGS

The second way the catalog may fail to represent the experience you're likely to have is in its listing of the courses offered. Brigham Young University, for example, lists in its catalog such courses as Family Law, Selected Urban Legal Problems, Domestic Relations, Law Help—Divorce Decree Enforcement, and Individual Employment Rights, but only Family Law appeared in its listing of courses for fall 1997. Louisiana State's catalog spoke of teaching Matrimonial Regimes, Employment Discrimination, Family Law Mediation, Family Law Seminar, and Matrimonial Regimes Seminar, none of which appeared on Louisiana's spring 1998 course list. Pepperdine School of Law, with only 13 percent female tenured or tenure-track academic faculty, sent out catalogs describing Advanced Family Law, Domestic Dispute Resolution, Family Law, Marriage and Family Law Seminar, Human Rights, and Employment Discrimination, but only Family Law was offered in the spring course listing.

Family Law is the least political of gender-relevant courses, because it is often no more than a pure doctrinal course to teach you the content of the law of divorce, so you can represent clients getting divorced. Mind you, Family Law can be *very* political. The change in American family law in the 1970s and 1980s to allow no-fault divorce, for example, had an enormous impact on the fate of women in American society in the ensuing twenty-five years. However, Family Law, unlike, for example, Employment Discrimination or Sex, Law, and Violence, can also be no more than a course covering the basic practice of law, rather than addressing the changing role of women in American law and life.

Minnesota professor Mary Lou Fellows alerted me to one last pitfall for the consumer. The admissions office at Minnesota often sends prospective students to meet her and Beverly Balos, her co-teacher in the course Law and Violence, if they seem interested in gender issues in the law. But Mary Lou and Bev were away on leave last year, and the course is not "institutionalized" and "not reflective of the rest of the school," so she believes if she's not there, the course will disappear.

These courses may not be of interest to you. But if you are interested in a curriculum that addresses issues of concern to women, you don't want to invest your hard-earned tuition money in a school that's like those stores that advertise milk at 15 cents a gallon but only stock three gallons of milk on the shelf. Consumer law outlawed the "loss leader" advertising gambit in most jurisdictions decades ago. And law school's a lot more money than a week's worth of groceries. Before you plunk down your thousands, ask the admissions office for an *actual printout* of the courses offered that semester and the one before.

If you're shy or don't want to be identified as a troublemaker, many law schools have a Web site, or a part of their university Web site, with course listings. Any good guidebook, like the ABA *Official Guide to Approved Law Schools*, will include a listing of the Web site with the school's other vital statistics. For instance, the University of Virginia has a Web site, www.law.virginia.edu/index.htm, which includes the fall and spring enrollment information sheets, listing the courses offered for 1997–98. Although Virginia has a 39 percent female student body, a dismal 77 percent success rate for women making law review, and only 20 percent female academic tenure or tenure-track faculty, Virginia is a big law school, and the course offerings are extensive and interesting. In 1997–98, Virginia actually offered for enrollment: the Regulation of Sexuality, an International Human Rights Clinic, Family Law and a Family Law Clinic, Civil Rights Litigation, International Human Rights Law Seminar, Family Law, Regulating the Family, Sex and Gender, and Feminist Jurisprudence.

Here is a sample of the courses offered at schools from every level of status and women-friendliness. A ★ means the course was offered. "No" in both columns means course listed in catalog but not offered in one of two successive semesters, usually fall '97 and spring '98.

		Offered	
School	Course	Fall	Spring
U Oregon	Employment Discrimination	No	No
	Family Law	★	No
	Women and the Law	No	No
U Nebraska	Legal Control of Discrimination	No	No
	Legal Control of Discrimination Seminar	No	No
	Family Law	★	No
	Gender Issues in Law	No	★
U Miami	Domestic Relations	No	No
	Family Law	No	★
	Law, Race, and Sexuality	No	No
	Women and the Law	★	No
	Domestic Violence	★	No
William Mitchell	Civil and Human Rights	No	★
	Law and Sexuality	★	No
	Employment Discrimination	★	★
	Family Law	★	★
	Feminist Jurisprudence	No	★
U Oklahoma	Family Law	No	★
	Equal Employment Opportunities	No	No
	Gender-based Discrimination	No	No

How to Pick a Compatible Law School

School	Course	Offered Fall	Offered Spring
Western New England	Discrimination Law Clinic	No	⋆
	Divorce and the Family	No	⋆
	Employment Discrimination	⋆	No
	Formation of Families	No	⋆
	Gender and the Law	⋆	No
	Parent, Child, and the State	No	⋆
U Arizona	Jurisprudence of Gender and Race	No	No
	Community Property Law	No	No
	Domestic Violence	No	No
	Domestic Violence Clinic	⋆	No
	Family Law	No	⋆
	Child Abuse	⋆	No
	Employment Law	No	⋆
Vanderbilt	Employment Discrimination	No	⋆
	Family Law	No	⋆
Hofstra	Law's Response to Reproduction	No	⋆
	Sex-based Discrimination	⋆	No
	Family Law	⋆	No
	Child, Family and State	⋆	No
	Child Abuse/Family Violence	⋆	No
U Texas	Comparative Family Law	No	No
	Sexual Orientation	No	No
	Domestic Violence Clinic	No	⋆
	Gender, Sexuality, and the Law	⋆	No
	Family Law	No	⋆
	Gender and the Law	No	⋆
	Domestic Violence and Law	⋆	⋆
Tulane	Family Law	⋆	⋆
	Gender in Laws of England	No	No
	Employment Discrimination	No	⋆
	Employment Discrimination Seminar	No	No
	Law and Gender	No	No

THE PERVASIVE PRESENCE OF THE
OLIN FOUNDATION

The catalog can also alert you to the Olin phenomenon. At the University of Chicago, for example, there is a John M. Olin Program in Law and Economics. "The aim of the program," according to the catalog, "is to advance understanding of the effects of laws, and hence to enlighten both economic theory and law reform by systematic investigation of aspects of the legal system in a framework of economic analysis." Anything could happen behind this language—for example, economic theory actually supports changing the present stay-at-home-mom-centered tax law to encourage women to engage in wage labor in order to raise the largest amount of revenue.

However, the John M. Olin Foundation, described in a recent report to the National Committee for Responsive Philanthropy as a "conservative foundation," is unlikely to support any such thing. It was the Olin Foundation that partially funded antifeminist philosophy professor Christina Hoff Sommers to write and publish *Who Stole Feminism?*, a scathing attack on contemporary feminism, including a deeply questionable analysis of the history of domestic violence law. Olin and the "Four Sisters" conservative foundations fund the conservative position on welfare reform and oppose university efforts to constrain hate speech on campus. The Olin people, being extremely clever in their giving, invest their money at places where they think they can have an impact, so Olin programs in the catalog are again an indication of what the temperature of the institution is likely to be on issues like feminism, hate speech, and women in poverty. As the *Albany Times-Union* described it recently, conservative funders like the John M. Olin Foundation and a few others provided the University of Chicago with more than ten million dollars from 1992 to 1994 "to support legal studies opposed to government regulation of all kinds."

HOW TO READ A FACULTY BIOGRAPHY

You also can extract a lot of information from the faculty biographies. Remember Judge Alex Kozinski's description of law faculties as consisting solely of radical scholars, including "critical race theorists, radical feminists and gaylegal" scholars, and "traditional liberals," who hate and fear the radicals just as the conservatives do, but are too "cowardly" to do anything about them? If Kozinski were right, you would expect to see law school faculties composed of about four equal parts: racial minorities, females, gays, and a "right wing" of cowardly white male members of the American Civil Liberties Union, circa 1964. Conservative as he is, the prospect of law schools like this understandably makes Kozinski anxious.

In fact, even a cursory look at the descriptions of most law faculties reflects that they mostly consist of heterosexual white males. Only one law school in the United States has an academic faculty that is more than half female, and only traditional black law schools have faculties that are more than one quarter racial minority. As far as I know, no law school faculty is even 10 percent gay or lesbian.

It is possible, of course, that these heterosexual white men who make up most American faculties are mostly heterosexual white male radical feminists, heterosexual white male critical race scholars, and heterosexual white male advocates of gay rights as well as old-fashioned ACLU types. After all, one of the great advocates of racial justice in the twentieth century was Jack Greenberg, a white male lawyer for the NAACP. But we know, for example, that the legal profession is at least 25 percent female, while the faculties at many schools—Harvard, Duke, Columbia, Michigan, Chicago, Georgetown, University of Georgia, Vanderbilt, Texas, University of San Francisco, Colorado, Emory, Franklin Pierce, George Mason, Hofstra, Louisiana State, and many, many more—are far under that number. It's hard to believe that schools full of Kozinski's radical, gay, and feminist white men would have found so few women entitled to teach with them.

Here's where the catalog can tell you a lot. Although some law schools catalogs, like Duke's, just tell you the teachers' degrees and areas of expertise, even a close-mouthed catalog contains a lot of information about the place. A quick count at Duke turns up the information that the Duke faculty is only around 20 percent female, a low number compared to most law schools, even elite law schools. But numbers are just the beginning of a good analysis. At Duke, for instance, some of the teachers list as areas of expertise "gender law and family law" (Katharine Bartlett), "AIDS issues" (Keith Brodie), or "application of literary theory to law" (Stanley Fish). Since important issues of gender law, AIDS, and literary theory all postdate 1964, you can assume these teachers are, if not radical, not conservative and may even be liberals of a post-1964 sort.

Moreover, some biographies give a hint of political affiliation in the form of employment in the executive branch, depending on the political party of the American president when he or she worked there. Be particularly alert to positions in the Justice Department or in important offices of the United States attorney. As anyone interested in law should know by now, it is the Justice Department, particularly the Offices of Civil Rights, Legal Counsel, and the Solicitor General, that make political/legal policy for the party in power in the executive branch of the federal government. William Rehnquist, the conservative chief justice of the United States Supreme Court, came out of the Reagan Justice Department, as did a host of other conservative judges. The long-term independent counsel appointed by a panel of Republican judges to investigate the Clinton administration is Ken Starr, who was solicitor general under Ronald Reagan. The Justice Department lawyers vet the candidates for federal judgeships.

None of the Duke faculty includes service in the Reagan Justice Department in his or her biography. However, the catalog reflects that Duke had two faculty members in high policy positions at Justice under Bill Clinton. Walter E. Dellinger III, whose expertise is in "constitutional law and civil rights," was "on leave fall, 1996, to serve as acting Solicitor General of the United States" and Professor Christopher H. Schroeder was on leave the same fall to "serve as acting assistant attorney general for the Office of Legal Counsel in the Department of Justice."

Reading further, we learn that Duke professor Madeline Morris "consulted with Senator Deconcini [a Democrat] when he drafted legislation to address the problems of sexual crime and sexual harassment in the U.S. armed forces," Professor H. Jefferson Powell, a constitutional law expert, "was a member of the litigation team that defended the Brady Gun Control Act against constitutional challenge," William Reppy founded an animal rights group, and John Weistart "published an article on gender equity in the world of commercialized college sports." Although one professor, Thomas D. Rowe, Jr., earned an appointment from William Rehnquist (to the group that drafts the rules of civil procedure), the picture on the whole is one of a faculty that is pretty liberal, politically. Of the eleven schools in Status Group #1 (LSATs 166+), Duke ranked first for women's success.

Compare this with a big D.C. school a category or two below Duke in status: George Washington. In our catalog search, GW had only a low 22 percent female faculty number and came in last in its category on women's success. The GW catalog doesn't tell you a lot in its faculty biographies: just their titles and degrees and whether they are full-time faculty or just untenured part-timers. But the information is available to you, if you know how to look.

First, the course listing in the catalog tells you who teaches what. Feminist Legal Theory is taught by someone named "Ridder." A quick look at the full-time faculty reveals that no one named Ridder is included; the Feminist Legal Theory teacher is Stephanie Ridder, a part-time "Professorial Lecturer," which usually means someone who just comes in for one course and makes most of their living practicing law or writing. Lecturers don't vote on faculty matters or participate in other aspects of faculty governance, like planning the curriculum. GW has a big faculty— eighty-four full-time and visiting faculty and administrators in the year Ms. Ridder taught Feminist Legal Theory—yet not one of them was teaching Feminist Legal Theory.

Second, look at the required first-year courses. As we have seen and as you will see in chapter 6 ("The Dreaded First Year"), the first year is the most important part of the law school experience. Get good grades there and you'll get a firm job and maybe never have to compete as hard again! Most women report the first-year experience as the aspect of law school that most heavily shaped their self-image as lawyers, something that stays with you the rest of your professional life. At GW, 80 percent of the first-year classes (other than legal writing, which is roughly pass/fail) are taught by men. If you exclude the two classes taught by a visiting female, 86 percent of the first-year classes are taught by men. Since a big class like GW's is broken into sections, a woman student at GW could go her entire first year without seeing a female teacher in a graded, first-year course there, certainly without seeing a tenured or tenure-track permanent female teacher.

The second place to look is at who's teaching con law. The con law professors are the pack leaders at most schools. As we have seen, constitutional law is the battle ground where most of the major political and legal battles have been fought since the Supreme Court sent a black man back to slavery in the *Dred Scott* case in 1857. All four con law teachers at Duke are white men. Three of the white male con law teachers at Duke have political records: one works for Bill Clinton, one argued for gun control, and one held a technical Rehnquist appointment. The fourth, William Van Alstyne, simply tells you that he was "twice named in polls of judges and lawyers as one of the most qualified persons in the country for the U.S. Supreme Court," which probably means he's one of those "cowardly liberals" Kozinski decried.

I happen to know from interviews that some of the constitutional theorists act like the alpha males at GW, but even if we didn't know about the pecking order at GW, the catalog reveals that con law is required at GW, a sure sign of its place in the status hierarchy. A quick glance at the current catalog reveals that no women are teaching first-year con law there. The basic con law teachers are Barron, Dienes, Park, and Clark. The advanced con law classes are also taught by Jeffrey Rosen, Ira Lupu, and Peter Raven-Hansen. Rosen teaches the course on the Civil War amendments, which are the primary vehicles for legal equality in America.

Who are the men of GW con law? Although the catalog doesn't tell you, in an instant on the Internet you can find out a lot of what you need to know. Just search for the school name and "law," in this case, "George Washington" and "law," and you will find their Web page at www.law.gwu.edu (as we have seen, almost all schools maintain such easy-to-find and informative Web pages now). GW lists faculty profiles including their pictures.

All seven of the current con law teachers at GW—Dienes, Barron, Park, Clark, Rosen, Lupu, and Raven-Hansen—are white men. Barron and Dienes are older—late fifties or sixties—and have the interest and expertise in the First Amendment typical of people who came of age at the time of Watergate and the Pentagon Papers. Some of Barron's interests have apparently diverted him away from the law school; he serves as legal consultant to the magazines *U.S. News & World Report, Fast Company,* and the *Atlantic.*

Barron or Dienes may have progressive commitments, but it is important to remember that an interest in free speech does not necessarily mean a progressive disposition. Free speech has changed a lot since it protected the views of the Reverend Martin Luther King, Jr., in the 1960s. Now, as the *New York Times* reported in 1998, free speech has become the rallying cry of the extreme right, from abortion clinic protesters to tobacco companies to Senate Republicans resisting campaign finance reform, while more progressive types have begun to accept some restraints on speech. The gender issue in the migration of free speech to the right is that since feminist scholar Catharine MacKinnon began challenging the production and distribution of pornography in the mid 1970s, a gender chasm has developed between 1960s-era liberals on the one hand and many feminists on the other, with traditional liberals clinging to a broad and absolute interpretation of free speech—in the words of one of the most prominent traditional liberals, New York Law School professor Nadine Strossen, "defending pornography." Accordingly, a passionate interest in "free expression" should motivate the alert student to ask some further questions.

On their face, Park and Lupu don't present particularly politicized profiles. Park is also older, with a background in a neutral-seeming subject, administrative law and university governance. Lupu is one of the leading national scholars on separation of Church and State; he wrote the brief for Americans United for Separation of Church and State, in the Supreme Court case that struck down as unconstitutional a congressional attempt to legislate some fairly ambitious protections for religious practices.

Clark and Rosen, hired in 1994 and 1996 respectively, are two of GW's rising stars. Clark's bio on the GW Web site tells a straightforward conservative story. After law school, he clerked for the famously conservative federal judge Robert Bork, whose criticism of the decisions protecting people's use of birth control kept him off the Supreme Court, and then for the most conservative of all the justices, Antonin Scalia, the sole vote in favor of segregating the Virginia Military Institute. He worked in the Office of Legal Counsel, the most political of all departments in the Reagan Justice Department, and then for Gibson, Dunn and Crutcher, one of the few big corporate law firms that regularly contributes to conservative think tanks and foundations.

Rosen presents a different picture: After law school, he clerked for liberal Abner Mikva, and he writes for publications traditionally regarded as liberal, such as the *New Republic* and the *New York Times*. Rosen teaches a course in the Civil War amendments, which abolished slavery and guaranteed the equal protection of the laws, a traditionally liberal subject. Remember, however, that the battle over the meaning of the Civil War amendments, like the First Amendment, has changed a lot since the sixties. Now, instead of being used to integrate the schools, for example, most of the Civil War amendment litigation involves using the Civil War amendments to roll back programs for integration like affirmative action, which white men have a heavy self-interest in reversing. So having a white male teaching the Civil War amendments should ring some bells. (My favorite example of professors you might think about learning from is O. J. Simpson's lawyer, Harvard professor Alan Dershowitz, who lists Domestic Relations as one of his subjects in the law school's faculty directory.)

And, indeed, Rosen has written at length in opposition, explicit or thinly veiled, to affirmative action. In articles in the purportedly "liberal" journals, he decried the efforts of affirmative action supporters to recruit women to buttress the electoral position of affirmative action, supported California's vote to ban affirmative action, and criticized President Clinton's civil rights nominee, Bill Lann Lee, for arguing in favor of affirmative action.

On issues specific to women, Rosen has led a movement, more aggressive than any corporate interest group and more conservative than almost any member of the Supreme Court, to repeal the laws against sexual harassment. In 1993, he recommended that the Supreme Court rule in favor of an employer who asked his female employee to meet him at a motel to discuss her raise and fish in his pants pockets for change, calling the behavior "mild." Not even the ultraconservative Justice Scalia agreed with that one, and the Supreme Court ruled unanimously the other way. In advance of the Supreme Court's seven-to-two rulings sustaining and expanding legal protection against harassment in 1998, Rosen suggested repealing sexual harassment law altogether, as "profoundly inconsistent with the liberal ideal" because it restrains people's speech and actions, and asked people to "rethink . . . their commitment to sexual harassment law." If we aren't willing to bump sex back into the war of all against all, he suggested recently that we make the law unenforceable by refusing to ask about it. After all, Rosen said on National Public Radio, "lying about sex is something that we're naturally tempted to do." Rosen's relentless crusade in favor of unleashing sexual harassment recently elicited a letter of protest to the *New Republic* from Katherine Silbaugh, a generally centrist professor at Boston University School of Law:

For at least five years, Jeffrey Rosen has mounted an impressive public relations campaign in favor of restricting Title VII's prohibition on sex discrimination when the claim is based on sexual harassment. We've heard enough. Substantively, Rosen has overstated the harms the law admittedly causes and, much more significantly, understated the harms the law prevents. He is certainly entitled to explicate his views, but there is another side to the sexual harassment story—one that is sensible to many working people and to many centrist jurists—and your readers deserve to hear about it.

Even on those rare occasions when the Civil War amendments are invoked in the traditional civil rights fashion, to end some vestiges of formal segregation, Rosen opposes the use of constitutional law for women, suggesting that the Supreme Court uphold the constitutionality of a gender-discriminatory provision of the immigration law and bemoaning the prospect that the Court would (as it did) compel the state-sponsored Virginia Military Institute to take girls.

If you look at everyone GW hired since 1990, say, you'll see some diversity: GW hired six women, three of whom are racial minorities, and twenty men, at least two or three of whom are racial minorities. As these numbers reflect, unlike some other schools, GW did not increase its gender integration during any of its hiring in the past seven years; the 1991–98 hires are 23 percent female, and the whole faculty is 22 percent female as of last count, about 10 percent less female than the profession, at 25 percent.

The nineties classes did include people of diverse political backgrounds—new hires Lawrence Mitchell wrote a text on progressive corporate law, and the Pulitzer-nominated *Stacked Deck: A Story of Selfishness in America*. African American Paul Butler is the author of a wildly controversial argument for jury nullification in a racist society, Michael Selmi came from the Lawyers Committee for Civil Rights and the Civil Rights Division of Justice, and a couple of other hires also clerked for liberal judges. On the other end, in addition to con law teachers Bradford Clark and Jeffrey Rosen, since 1990 GW hired Columbia's law and economics maven Richard Pierce, along with Robert Tuttle, a member of the

Christian Legal Society, which has litigated several of the antigay actions brought in the last few years. They also hired another alum of a Reagan judicial chambers, Jonathan Turley, and Gregory Maggs—who scored sort of a grand slam by working for Clarence Thomas, as well as Reagan justice Anthony Kennedy and the very conservative Joseph Sneed of the Ninth Circuit and, again, Robert Bork. Turley is a strange mix; in recent media he described himself as a liberal Democrat who voted for Ralph Nader in '96, but he's been the chief legal pundit attacking Bill Clinton throughout the Lewinsky affair and he represented the father accused of (but not found liable for) child sexual abuse in the notorious Dr. Elizabeth Morgan case.

Through interviews, I learned that none of the prestigious endowed professorships at GW are held by women, only two of the ten next most prestigious research professorships were held by women in 1997–98, and the Appointments Committee hasn't been chaired by a woman since 1989! You could have gotten a good feeling for the degree of ideological diversity on the faculty from the Web site and a strong sense of who dominates from the low percentage of diverse hires as well as who dominates the prestigious con law curriculum. Again, it's up to you. But if you don't want to learn your constitutional law from someone who believes employers have a "liberal" right to hit up their workers for sex, you might inquire about what the faculty writes, who gets the endowed chairs, and who runs appointments.

THE FEDERALIST SOCIETY

Finally, the student organizations can be a tip-off, although this is harder to find out. All law schools have organizations like the Black Law Students' Association and the Law Women. The existence of these groups says very little about the atmosphere of the school. The most self-consciously political student group in the country is the law-school-centered Federalist Society. Founded by Northwestern professor Steven Calabresi and a couple of friends at the Yale Law School fifteen years ago, the Federalist Society for Law and Public Policy Studies, as the society is officially known, was described recently in the *National Law Journal* as "a forum where the conservative and libertarian elite trade ideas and business cards and try to influence the next generation of thinkers and doers" and "a Justice Department in exile." The Federalist Society establishes relationships with judges who "participate in the society's programs and hire members as clerks."

Although the *National Law Journal* reports that the Federalist Society only includes five thousand student members, the society wields power out of all proportion to its membership. For your purposes, the Federalist Society matters, because according to Yale professor Ian Ayres, "Floating [Federalist Society] on your résumé is an important key to 'feeder' clerkships [to the Supreme Court], such as for [Ninth Circuit] Judge Alex Kozinski." Getting a clerkship with a conservative judge like Kozinski became more valuable since the Federalist Society took control of the process of credentialing federal judges away from the 370,000-member American Bar Association in 1996; in the ensuing congressional term, conservatives managed to defeat most of President Clinton's judicial nominees, including a substantial number of women judges. As a result of this development, there are fewer prestigious clerkships with judges who are not conservative, confronting ambitious law students who are not conservative with a choice between their principles and their prospects. The single largest funder of the Federalist Society is the John M. Olin Foundation.

There are chapters of the Federalist Society at most law schools, including, as its elite founders like to boast, the "top twenty," so it's hard to go to law school without encountering the society, but it pays to ask how many of the faculty are actively involved. Before you plunk your money down, you may want to know if the law school you will be attending is one of the leading centers of Federalist Society activity, including the activity of placing your conservative classmates in prestigious clerkships.

The Femscore: How to Pick a Law School Where Women Succeed

WHERE SHOULD YOU "GO"? A lot of this guide so far has been designed to empower you to get into the most prestigious, selective law school you can aspire to. Now we can to the more important question: Once you're enrolled, can you succeed there? Although we've seen that there are many issues for women in thinking about law school—nontraditional career aspirations, unresolved work/family pressures, text anxiety—nothing is as central choosing a school where *you* can succeed. That's why you want to read each catalog closely and ask good questions when you visit. Choosing a law school where women succeed doesn't guarantee a good outcome, but it certainly raises the odds. This chapter includes a ranking of 158 of the accredited American law schools, *according to how women students succeed there.*

This ranking comes from a survey and analysis I did in 1995, with these criteria in mind: I looked at the male/female numbers in the top twenty status schools using making law review as my measuring rod. I chose law review as my test, because, although law review reflects a broader population than Guinier's top 10 percent, it's a measure of success according to the terms of the law school world itself. At that time, I found that men made law review in greater numbers than their class percentage—and thus outperformed their female classmates—at thirteen of the twenty highest-status schools.

Looking at the classes of 1996 and 1997 at all the accredited law schools, the picture continues to be perilous for women. Men outperformed their female counterparts, making law review in greater numbers than their representation in the class, in approximately 60 percent of the schools I looked at. Women did less well, outperforming their numbers in the class at only 40 percent. So the bad news is women don't do as well as men at most law schools regardless of the school's status. The good news is: There are lots of exceptions to the rule.

Until Lani Guinier and others started looking at the data, everyone assumed that women and men did about the same in law school. Even after Guinier's study, people were very slow to notice that women's fates differed from one law school to another. A handful of concerned faculty or administrators looked at their own schools; the schools that publicized their findings were mostly places where women succeed, like Iowa and Stanford, and the results were mostly published in the law review literature, not a place where a lot of potential students browse around.

The rankings in this guide are mostly based on information I gathered from the public record alone, as well as my own interviews. I figured out how many academic female faculty each law school employed by interpreting their catalogs, as I described in chapter 4. Here and there, where a catalog was not informative or where I couldn't get the school to send me one, I resorted to the listing and biographies in the *American Association of Law Schools Directory of Law Teachers*. The numbers probably aren't perfect, but I did analyze the biographies to eliminate the routine overcounting of women by including low-paid impermanent or nonacademic faculty members, like writing teachers and visitors.

The percentage of female students in the full-time (usually day) classes of the 158 schools comes from *The Official Guide to Approved Law Schools* published by the American Bar Association.

Finding out what percentage of the women in those classes made law review was harder, but, I think, worth the effort. It's a dirty little secret that law school performs a very significant sorting function between the students who get most of the benefits the law schools have to offer and the rest. The line isn't drawn at making it to the middle of the class. The line is drawn a little higher than that, around the top third or fourth. And making law review is a rough but ready measure of whether women are going to make it into the privileged group. Remember the uncharacteristically frank professor at the University of Chicago who told his class: "Most of the goodies around here go to twenty percent of the class. The other eighty percent spend the next two years licking their psychic wounds." During the years I studied, the University of Chicago was not one of the schools where women made it into the privileged group very often. Although some women choose not to go on law review, regardless of whether women earned grades on average as good as men in the class, in 1996 and 1997, the men at Chicago made law review at three times the rate that the women did, leaving a lot of Chicago women "licking their psychic wounds." I thought you'd like to know that.

Although very few schools would share their students' grade point averages, fortunately, the law reviews are published documents, and they include mastheads listing their members that can be roughly broken down male and female. This rough process can't account for people with nongendered names, but, for the first time since women started attending law school in serious numbers, this book tells women law students roughly where women make law review and where they don't. If you don't think that difference matters, just skip this chapter and spend your money on a place with a nice building or sociable students.

Finally, the legal honorary society, the Order of the Coif, publishes an occasional version of its membership list, which roughly reflects the breakdown of the top 10 percent of the senior class in those schools with Coif chapters (about half of our survey). With this last piece in place, our ranking was complete.

Why You Should Know Whether Women Succeed

People who don't want to compete for your tuition dollars will say that all law students are the same and that it's whiny or special pleading for women to want to know how other women are doing at the various schools. A law student is a law student, they would say. Truth is, women as an average had grades almost as good as men did in law school.

But that's as good as it gets. I'd like you to do better than average. A year ago, the *Legal Times* newspaper carried the story of the Georgetown Law Center's reluctance when one of their female students tried to find out whether their school had the same disappointing record as Penn. Unable to get the administration to produce the data, Georgetown's Heather Marsh went to her law school library and found out that the Georgetown class of 1996 graduated with twice as many men as women in the top 10 percent and the next class was disproportionately male down to the top 30 percent. That failure occurred among women usually without children to care for or other distractions from academic life, and it occurred in one short year. And it's not just Georgetown. Women made up 44 percent of the classes of 1996 and 1997 at law schools nationwide, but they only made law review in proportion to or in excess of their numbers in the class at 66 of the 158 law schools I examined.

The Femscore Rankings

The law schools are first grouped by a rough marker of status— the median entering class LSAT from 1995 (these are the scores for the graduating class of '98). There are fifteen status groups, with several schools in each group. Group #1, the highest status group, consists of such schools as Yale and Stanford, with median LSATs for the class of '98 of 166 or higher. The second group includes schools with LSATs between 162 and 165. After that, each group represents one point lower on the LSAT scale, Group #3 at

164, Group #4 at 163, and so forth. The lowest-ranking status group includes the schools with LSATs of under 150. Within each status group, I'm going to tell you how likely women are to succeed.

Once you see your LSAT score, you will know which group is likely to include the schools where you will be admitted (assuming your college grades aren't wildly out of line with your LSATs). This ranking will enable you to select the most women-friendly school within that group of schools. If you do better or worse than you hoped in the admissions process, just look at the next group up or down.

This ranking is a change from the other major rankings, not only because this ranking focuses on women, but also because it links status and satisfaction. *U.S. News & World Report* ranks for status alone. The *National Jurist* studies student satisfaction, and the Princeton Review studies of selectivity *and* "quality of life" separate the two. Even the *National Jurist* 1995 study, the "Best Law Schools for Women," didn't rank by status. According to the *National Jurist*, North Carolina Central came out first and Harvard next to last.

We're not looking for pure pleasure or pure status. This book is trying to help you to *succeed,* which is a combination of the power of the institution plus your individual likelihood of putting the institution's power to work for you. So even though the most women-friendly law school in the country is Southern or California Western, according to our criteria, I'm not recommending that you go there if you get into Yale or even to spend your money applying there just because they are more women-friendly. As we will see in chapter 9 ("Compared to Law School, Life Is Easy: How to Succeed at Firm Job Interviews"), the power of the institution is not limited to its status, but includes the effectiveness of the placement office, its geographically privileged status with regard to desirable employers, and other factors. This chapter is designed to help you target your applications to the most women-friendly law schools with the advantages you need to launch your professional career.

The indicators of women's success for the Femscore ranking include the following:

(A) Percentage of women tenured or tenure-track academic faculty in catalogs of 1997–98.

(B) Percentage of women in the full-time student body (average of classes of 1996 and 1997).

(C) 1996–97 success rate: percentage of women on the high-status, general-subject-matter law review as a percentage of women in eligible full-time classes of 1996 and 1997.

(D) Femscore: A sum of A, B, and C, which weights C (law review success rate) most heavily.

(E) The percentage of women in the 1995 chapter of the Order of the Coif, where applicable.

(F) 1995 Coif success rate: percentage of women in 1995 Coif as percentage of average of women in law school nationally in 1995 (42 percent).

Those factors include all the data that are publicly available. And, in light of the law schools' unwillingness to reveal their students' success rates, public data were all that was available. But here's why they matter.

PERCENTAGE OF WOMEN ACADEMIC FACULTY

My 1995 study of high-status law schools turned up a startling correlation between the places where women students made law review and the places where the percentage of female academic faculty was higher than the average for such schools. Almost all the schools where women succeeded had above the 20 percent average typical of female faculties for this high-status group.

For this study of all law schools, I used the figure of 25 percent to test for correlation between women faculty and women success, because women are about 25 percent of the legal profession, so a faculty that falls below that number is presumptively suspect.

In this study of all law schools, law schools where women students succeeded again had above average numbers of female faculty. Of the sixty-six schools where women made law review at rates at or above their presence in the class (that is, at 100 percent or above), 54 percent had faculties with 25 percent or more women on them. Of the ninety-two schools where women did not score well, only 39 percent had faculties with 25 percent or more women on them.

As I said in chapter 4, in calculating the faculty numbers, I don't count anyone entirely or mostly teaching writing skills or clinical or other legal practice, because, for good or ill, law schools see themselves as providing an education for a learned profession, and academics count for more than skills in shaping or dominating most institutional cultures. Where the biographies were ambiguous about whether the person was an academic faculty with an occasional course in legal writing or a legal writing teacher with an occasional traditional academic course, I did my best to figure out what was flying. Inevitably, there will be some mistakes. Nor did I include librarians, administrators, visitors, adjuncts, or emeritus professors. Although I regret adding to the impression of second-class citizenship for the many accomplished, well-regarded, and hardworking academics in these categories, I'm focusing on the people who dominate the world you are about to enter. A lot of law school is about dominance. Many times, legal writing teachers or clinicians are not tenured or not eligible for tenure, they often don't vote on appointments, or teach mandatory first-year classes and they are almost always paid less well on average.

People have speculated for some time about whether the presence of faculty who resemble minority or excluded groups makes a difference in the students' performance, and no one has a definitive answer. More women on the faculty definitely correlates to more courses about women's interests. In the interviews for this book, many of the women students spoke about how meaningful a particular woman teacher had been for them—Chris Littleton at UCLA, Mary Becker at the University of Chicago. But many students found their women faculty to be no better or different than the men, and one well-known antifeminist came in for warm praise from one of her students for her support in the student's original research.

I'm not going to try to resolve that dispute. The numbers from the 1995 study indicated that *something* was going on, and the high correlation between female student success and large numbers of female faculty in this book about the classes of '96 and '97 at 158 accredited law schools replicates that result. My suspicion is that an institution whose academic faculty is way below the average for law schools in general is having problems with women and with new (and not so new) ideas about women's equality and law school teaching generally. After all, the profession is close to 25 percent female, so how likely is it that Harvard's faculty rate of 15 percent is just an accident? It is safe to say that the presence or absence of women on the faculty is more a sign of the underlying culture than a cause.

But if the underlying culture is hostile to women's success, the students will suffer from it, just as deserving faculty candidates do. Again, Harvard is a good example of how all these things come together. For four years Harvard has occupied the unenviable position of dead last in the Princeton Review survey of student satisfaction, not just female student satisfaction. A few years ago, a couple of the law review editors at Harvard, Craig Coben and Kenneth Fenyo, took the occasion of the annual law review banquet to distribute a savage and unprecedently personal satire of a feminist scholar from another school whose work had been published over their protest by their law review that year. The extraordinary thing about Coben and Fenyo's "prank" is that it took place one year to the day after the woman had been brutally murdered.

Harvard has a remarkable paucity of females in the prestigious tenured and tenure-track faculty, and at 40 percent, their classes of '96 and '97 were less female than any of their competitors' except the University of Virginia, and one of the lowest in the country. The 40 percent of Harvard students who were women produced only 31 percent of the law review members in the classes of 1996 and 1997, generating a success rate for Harvard women of 78 percent, where 100 percent would be equal success with the Harvard men. The 1995 *National Jurist* placed Harvard at 167 out of the 168 schools it surveyed for female success.

Although each of these pieces of data *could* be explained as unrelated to women's success, after a while, the circumstantial evidence just adds up. To put it scientifically, if it walks like a duck, it talks like a duck, and it looks like a duck, chances are pretty good that it is a duck.

PERCENTAGE OF WOMEN IN THE STUDENT BODY

The second factor in the ranking is how integrated is the student body. Women make decisions about law schools for lots of reasons, good and bad. They go where they want to live (bad), where their "intuition" tells them (geez), where their boyfriends or lovers are (worse), where good public interest programs are, and where the highest status is.

For this study of all the law schools, I have included in the factors for ranking the law schools the percentage of females in full-time programs in the classes of 1996 and 1997. In the classes of '96 and '97, women succeeded at making law review in excess of their full-time presence in the class at sixty-six schools; at just about 50 percent of those schools, there were more women students at or above the 44 percent national average.

Perhaps more important than the female student presence at success schools is the "bad news" statistic. Only 33 percent, or about one third, of the approximately ninety schools where women don't make law review in proportion to their numbers have student bodies at or above the average number of women students. Having a lot of women in the class isn't strictly correlated with success, but having fewer than usual does appear with suspicious frequency where women fail.

Like the number of women faculty, the relationship between women in the student body and success is small enough so that it could be explained away by other factors. If it matters, the percentage of women in the class should matter in the same way that the percentage of women in the powerful academic faculty matters. More women faculty, more women students. An integrated student body both reflects the culture and affects the culture. We saw in chapter 2, when we looked at thumbnail sketches of the schools where women succeed—and where they fail—that such schools often have *cultures* of success and failure and that such cultures really make a difference in how women do and that the factors in our rankings are symptoms of such differences.

WOMEN ON LAW REVIEW

All law schools ranked have some version of the general-interest law review, the student-run and edited journal that carries articles about various legal topics. In chapter 8 ("Making Law Review"), we're going to talk in more detail about law review.

Column B of the rankings reports the percentage of full-time women in the classes of 1996 and 1997, the latest date for which data was available. Column C shows the rate at which women achieved law review, when they were second- and third-year students and thus eligible for law review. If women were on law review in exact proportion to their full-time percentage of the two eligible classes, the number in Column C would be 100. Any number under 100 reflects that women are underperforming; thus the men in the class have a better chance of making law review and the women a worse chance. Any number above 100 indicates women are succeeding beyond their numerical presence in the class, and the prospects of success are better for them and better for women than for men.

Different schools have different criteria for admission to law review, but they all start at the end of the first year. Most schools take a student's first-year grades and either admit the ones with the highest grades to the staff of the law review or allow students to compete for positions through a writing contest or, most commonly, some combination of grades and writing competition. Whether women make law review can, and usually does, represent two things. First, since grades almost always play a role, a lot of women on law review can represent a school where women get good grades. Since many of the law schools refused to provide us with exact breakdowns of male grades vs. female grades at the end of the first year, I am using law review in part as a stand-in for the missing data. Second, the percentage of women on law review can be affected by the method of selection, which, in turn, gives us a hint about how much importance the institution puts on first-year grades. If the institution is insistent on only valuing the first-year exams, which resemble the LSAT in that national statistics reveal that women do a little less well on them, it is a clue that the institution may not be as friendly to women as you would wish.

But it's only a clue. Since the deans of most law schools were unwilling to respond to our survey for this women's guide, I have used the percentage of women on law review as a rough measure of women's first-year grades. This should guide you to where you should apply. But once you're accepted, if you're considering en-rolling in one of these schools whose the law review numbers in-dicate a problem in women's success, I suggest you ask the admissions people directly how their female students come out grade-wise at the end of the first year. And ask the hard questions: How did the top 10 percent break down? How did the eligible class for law review break down? Maybe when they're facing someone with a $15,000 check in her hand, the admissions offices will be a little more responsive.

The only wild card in this is that, although I counted all the fe-male names on the law reviews, I did not include in my female student count the women in part-time programs, usually night school. Over 50 of the 174 accredited law schools have more than a quarter of their students in night programs, and, for the most part, men and women in night school are eligible for law review, just like the full-time students. Since the law reviews don't distin-guish between students from day and night programs, I counted all females on law review as if they came from the full-time pro-gram.

Where there is a night program, this count is thus slightly off in the following way. If the whole eligible group—full-timers and part-timers—is less female than the full-time group alone, then the success score for that school should be higher than I show, because women would be making law review at a higher rate than for full-time students alone. If, on the contrary, the whole group of full- and part-time students is *more* female than the full-timers alone, the success score for that school should be lower than I show, because more women in the two programs means more women should be showing up in my law review count.

I ran a couple of calculations including the night students and didn't turn up much change in the ratings I got without them. There are two reasons for this. One, night students are almost always around a quarter or a third of the student body, so a difference in the gender composition of the night class would have to be very great to affect the totals, and I found that the night classes usually aren't much more than 5 or so percent more or less female than the day classes. Second, if there are more night females, the success score (Column C) goes down, but the female student body number (Column B) goes up, so the ultimate Femscore (Column D) is unlikely to change much. Conversely, if there are fewer night females, the success score goes up a little, but the student body score goes down.

Although a perfect survey would have to include night students, it's harder to figure exactly which night students are eligible for law review, because night programs mostly take four years rather than three, and different schools have different cutoffs for law review eligibility. I have included a section, "The Night Schools," on page 164, for your information, with the percentage of females who got JDs in 1996 and in the two "classes" that preceded them. If you're considering a school with a night program and you want to be sure you've got their success score exactly calculated, you can ask the admissions office which part-timers are eligible for law review, and raise the score if the night female percentage is lower than in the main chart or lower it if the night female percentage is higher than in the main chart. I doubt you'll find it makes much difference.

ORDER OF THE COIF

The Order of the Coif is a legal honorary society. Not every law school can belong to the Order of the Coif. The original member schools, like the University of Wisconsin (1908) and the University of Illinois (1902), date back to the era of self-consciousness in legal education, when law schools were beginning to regard themselves as legitimate institutions of higher learning and not just trade schools. It was in this period that the American Association of Law Schools was founded and also the American Law Institute, a prestigious body of tony lawyers, judges, and law teachers who produce restatements of law and model codes for the rest of the country to adopt.

Of the approximately 174 total accredited American law schools, only 77, or fewer than half, had Coif chapters in 1995. If you look at the rankings, you will see that the farther down the LSAT scale of selectiveness you go, the scarcer the Coif chapters become. Perversely, there are no Coif chapters at the most elite end either. Harvard and Columbia apparently always knew they were too elite to belong to an association that took other law schools, and, after an initial flirtation with democracy in 1919, Yale let its chapter go inactive.

Since Coif is not universal, I could not use it to rank all the law schools. However, membership in the Order of the Coif is an important source of information about women in law school, because only students in roughly the top 10 percent of the class get to join. So by analyzing the list of Coif members for gender clues, we can get a hint of where women succeed all the way to the top 10 percent of their class, a much more selective measure than membership on law review. Also, since Coif is pure grades, it tells us something different from law review, which is often selected on the basis of grades and various writing competitions.

The bad news is that the latest published numbers end with the class of '95, and one dean told me that the published lists are limited to the people who pay a one-time trivial admissions fee after they are elected. So some cheapskate Coif members may not be included. Since, unlike the classes of '96 and '97, which are recorded in the ABA *Official Guide to Approved Law Schools*, I do not know the exact percentage of women at any school for the class of '95, it's hard to gauge where women outperformed their percentage of the class and where they did not. So first I've given you the actual percentage of Coif members who were female in '95. If you wish, you can look at the percentage of females in the classes of '96 and '97 and compare the percentage of women who made it into Coif in the previous class.

But be careful. If a school like Georgetown has classes of '96 and '97 that are 47 percent female on average, you can probably conclude that the class of '95 was around the same percentage female. Since Georgetown's women made up 53 percent of the Coif members in the class of '95, you would normally conclude that the women at Georgetown are making it into the top 10 percent at graduation at a pretty good rate. Interestingly, Heather Marsh's research at Georgetown revealed that the success rate of '95 did not hold up in the later classes, and our data on the '96 and '97 law review rate support this pessimistic conclusion. So 1995 may have been an anomaly. The only way to know for sure is to demand information for the classes since 1995 when you apply or after you're accepted.

Another way to use the data I've gathered for you on Coif membership is to assume that the class of '95 was on the whole 42 percent female. The percentage of women in law school has been turtling up by 1 or 2 percent in the nineties, so it's probably fair to assume that most schools with classes of 44 percent or 45 percent female in '96 and '97 had graduating classes of '95 around 42 percent female. So I calculated a hypothetical "Coif success rate" like the 1996–97 law review success rate, assuming that the class of '95 was 42 percent female, and put it next to the actual percentage of women who made Coif, just to give you another idea of what the Coif number may mean. I have put that school's success rate next to its ranking in the Femscore ratings, but I did not use the Coif numbers to establish the rating, because that would discriminate between schools that have Coif chapters and those that don't, and

TABLE #1: THE FEMSCORE RANKING FOR WOMEN

Here are the rankings in order of the school's Femscore (Column D). Remember, a success rate of 100 in Column C means women are performing onto law review exactly in proportion to their percentage of the class.

★ means dean answered questionnaire.

STATUS CATEGORY #1: LSAT 166+

School	A. Female Faculty	B. Female Students	C. Female Success	D. Femscore	E. Female Coif	F. Coif Success
1. DUKE	20%	40%	128%	186%	28%	66%
2. NEW YORK UNIVERSITY	20%	44%	122%	185%	33%	78%
3. STANFORD★	22%	47%	99%	168%	45%	108%
4. COLUMBIA	17%	41%	98%	157%	No chapter	
5. BERKELEY	25%	48%	80%	154%	36%	88%
6. GEORGETOWN	26%	47%	71%	144%	53%	127%
7. U VIRGINIA★	20%	39%	77%	137%	40%	95%

	A. Female Faculty	B. Female Students	C. Female Success	D. Femscore	E. Female Coif	F. Coif Success
8. YALE	21%	42%	72%	136%	No chapter	
9. U MICHIGAN	18%	41%	74%	134%	24%	58%
10. HARVARD	15%	40%	79%	134%	No chapter	
11. U CHICAGO	19%	44%	69%	131%	35%	84%

STATUS CATEGORY #2: LSAT 162–165

School	A. Female Faculty	B. Female Students	C. Female Success	D. Femscore	E. Female Coif	F. Coif Success
1. U WASHINGTON	26%	43%	112%	181%	64%	153%
2. U MINNESOTA	24%	45%	109%	178%	54%	128%
3. U CALIFORNIA LOS ANGELES★	26%	49%	101%	176%	35%	82%
4. U GEORGIA★	15%	41%	118%	174%	32%	75%
5. U PENNSYLVANIA	23%	39%	95%	157%	38%	90%
6. VANDERBILT	19%	35%	103%	157%	32%	75%
7. WILLIAM AND MARY	27%	42%	86%	155%	41%	98%

	A. Female Faculty	B. Female Students	C. Female Success	D. Femscore	E. Female Coif	F. Coif Success
8. WASHINGTON AND LEE	16%	41%	90%	147%	18%	44%
9. FORDHAM★	23%	41%	80%	144%	39%	93%
10. BOSTON COLLEGE	23%	44%	77%	144%	28%	67%
11. U SOUTHERN CALIFORNIA	19%	42%	83%	144%	25%	60%
12. U COLORADO★	14%	42%	86%	142%	44%	105%
13. U TEXAS★	17%	41%	79%	137%	25%	60%
14. CORNELL	29%	40%	66%	135%	17%	40%
15. NOTRE DAME	20%	44%	71%	135%	No chapter	
16. NORTHWESTERN	21%	46%	56%	123%	38%	90%

STATUS CATEGORY #3: LSAT 161

School	A. Female Faculty	B. Female Students	C. Female Success	D. Femscore	E. Female Coif	F. Coif Success
1. U CALIFORNIA DAVIS	29%	49%	108%	186%	56%	34%
2. WASHINGTON U	33%	41%	105%	180%	40%	95%
3. EMORY	16%	43%	112%	171%	39%	94%
4. U ARIZONA	21%	48%	96%	164%	No chapter	

School	A. Female Faculty	B. Female Students	C. Female Success	D. Femscore	E. Female Coif	F. Coif Success
5 U ILLINOIS	26%	40%	94%	160%	56%	134%
6. BOSTON U	24%	46%	87%	156%	No chapter	
7. WAKE FOREST	26%	40%	84%	150%	No chapter	
8. GEORGE WASHINGTON	23%	44%	79%	146%	39%	93%

STATUS CATEGORY #4: LSAT 160

School	A. Female Faculty	B. Female Students	C. Female Success	D. Femscore	E. Female Coif	F. Coif Success
1. ARIZONA STATE U	21%	41%	147%	209%	54%	128%
2. U IOWA	19%	46%	108%	173%	45%	108%
3. U CALIFORNIA HASTINGS	27%	50%	88%	166%	47%	113%
4. U HOUSTON	17%	42%	93%	153%	32%	76%
5. U NORTH CAROLINA	26%	41%	82%	149%	48%	114%
6. U SAN DIEGO	14%	44%	89%	147%	46%	111%
7. BRIGHAM YOUNG	16%	31%	50%	127%	36%	86%

STATUS CATEGORY #5: LSAT 159

School	A. Female Faculty	B. Female Students	C. Female Success	D. Femscore	E. Female Coif	F. Coif Success
1. U OREGON	29%	53%	114%	195%	17%	40%
2. U UTAH	26%	43%	121%	190%	38%	92%
3. U WISCONSIN	23%	45%	118%	186%	57%	135%
4. RUTGERS NEWARK	23%	45%	115%	183%	38%	89%
5. U CONNECTICUT	23%	50%	102%	175%	No chapter	
6. VILLANOVA	17%	46%	111%	174%	No chapter	
7. U RICHMOND	19%	46%	102%	167%	No chapter	
8. LOYOLA LOS ANGELES	32%	46%	86%	164%	No chapter	
9. INDIANA U BLOOMINGTON	22%	46%	92%	160%	55%	131%
10. OHIO STATE	22%	44%	91%	156%	45%	107%
11. BAYLOR	25%	39%	90%	154%	No chapter	
12. U CINCINNATI*	29%	41%	78%	148%	62%	146%

	A. Female Faculty	B. Female Students	C. Female Success	D. Femscore	E. Female Coif	F. Coif Success
13. U FLORIDA	16%	41%	82%	139%	42%	100%
14. TULANE	22%	42%	65%	129%	53%	126%

STATUS CATEGORY #6: LSAT 158

School	A. Female Faculty	B. Female Students	C. Female Success	D. Femscore	E. Female Coif	F. Coif Success
1. U KENTUCKY★	30%	32%	117%	180%	36%	87%
2. LOYOLA CHICAGO	26%	49%	98%	173%	No chapter	
3. GEORGE MASON	14%	42%	82%	138%	No chapter	

STATUS CATEGORY #7: LSAT 157

School	A. Female Faculty	B. Female Students	C. Female Success	D. Femscore	E. Female Coif	F. Coif Success
1. U MARYLAND	26%	52%	94%	173%	48%	114%
2. U SAN FRANCISCO	15%	52%	103%	171%	No chapter	
3. CARDOZO★	22%	48%	95%	165%	No chapter	

School	A. Female Faculty	B. Female Students	C. Female Success	D. Femscore	E. Female Coif	F. Coif Success
4. AMERICAN U	26%	57%	81%	164%	No chapter	
5. CASE WESTERN RESERVE★	15%	41%	105%	162%	50%	119%
6. U HAWAII	35%	48%	75%	159%	No chapter	
7. U KANSAS	14%	40%	99%	154%	31%	75%
8. SOUTHERN METHODIST U	19%	43%	79%	141%	45%	108%
9. U SOUTH CAROLINA	9%	42%	79%	131%	27%	65%

STATUS CATEGORY #8: LSAT 156

School	A. Female Faculty	B. Female Students	C. Female Succes	D. Femscore	E. Female Coif	F. Coif Success
1. U SEATTLE★	27%	45%	132%	204%	No chapter	
2. NEW MEXICO	46%	51%	104%	202%	No chapter	
3. GEORGIA STATE	37%	51%	107%	195%	No chapter	
4. SANTA CLARA	35%	52%	105%	191%	No chapter	

School	A. Female Faculty	B. Female Students	C. Female Success	D. Femscore	E. Female Coif	F. Coif Success
5. U TENNESSEE KNOXVILLE	30%	48%	107%	185%	14%	34%
6. BROOKLYN*	32%	43%	95%	170%	No chapter	
7. PEPPERDINE	13%	51%	97%	160%	No chapter	
8. WILLAMETTE*	30%	36%	86%	152%	No chapter	
9. FLORIDA STATE	30%	46%	73%	149%	52%	124%
10. HOFSTRA	17%	42%	82%	141%	No chapter	
11. ALABAMA STATE	24%	40%	67%	131%	33%	79%
12. U MONTANA	27%	40%	47%	114%	No chapter	

STATUS CATEGORY #9: LSAT 155

School	A. Female Faculty	B. Female Students	C. Female Success	D. Femscore	E. Female Coif	F. Coif Success
1. WAYNE STATE	21%	48%	121%	190%	53%	125%
2. U DENVER	25%	48%	114%	188%	No chapter	

3. CATHOLIC	29%	46%	105%	180%	No chapter
4. DEPAUL U	32%	45%	99%	175%	57%	136%
5. U MAINE	38%	48%	84%	171%	No chapter
6. MARQUETTE	30%	40%	100%	170%	No chapter
7. SUNY BUFFALO	33%	48%	84%	165%	No chapter
8. U PITTSBURGH	31%	37%	93%	161%	36%	86%
9. U MISSOURI COLUMBIA	16%	40%	104%	160%	27%	64%
10. SOUTHERN ILLINOIS	24%	41%	95%	159%	No chapter
11. TEXAS TECH★	28%	34%	93%	155%	33%	79%
12. NORTHERN ILLINOIS	21%	41%	92%	154%	No chapter
13. CAMPBELL	6%	44%	64%	114%	No chapter

STATUS CATEGORY #10: LSAT 154

School	A. Female Faculty	B. Female Students	C. Female Success	D. Femscore	E. Female Coif	F. Coif Success
1. WEST VIRGINIA	36%	50%	87%	193%	69%	165%
2. NEW YORK LAW SCHOOL	28%	43%	110%	181%	No chapter	
3. U MEMPHIS	32%	41%	109%	182%	No chapter	
4. U MIAMI*	35%	43%	101%	180%	39%	94%
5. U NEBRASKA LINCOLN	11%	40%	128%	179%	60%	143%
6. ST JOHN'S	29%	40%	108%	177%	No chapter	
7. WILLIAM MITCHELL*	28%	48%	100%	176%	No chapter	
8. SETON HALL	32%	45%	94%	171%	No chapter	
9. HAMLINE	32%	51%	86%	169%	No chapter	
10. U VERMONT	40%	43%	84%	162%	No chapter	

	A. Female Faculty	B. Female Students	C. Female Success	D. Femscore	E. Female Coif	F. Coif Success
11. INDIANA U INDIANAPOLIS★	21%	39%	95%	155%	No chapter	
12. ST LOUIS	23%	47%	76%	146%	No chapter	
13. TEMPLE U	27%	48%	66%	140%	No chapter	
14. RUTGERS CAMDEN	19%	42%	74%	136%	No chapter	
15. MERCER★	16%	37%	65%	118%	No chapter	

STATUS CATEGORY #11: LSAT 153

School	A. Female Faculty	B. Female Students	C. Female Success	D. Femscore	E. Female Coif	F. Coif Success
1. CHICAGO-KENT	31%	49%	113%	192%	43%	102%
2. DICKINSON U	29%	50%	110%	188%	No chapter	
3. U DAYTON	15%	42%	121%	178%	No chapter	
4. U IDAHO★	18%	41%	111%	170%	No chapter	
5. U OKLAHOMA	23%	40%	104%	168%	38%	91%
6. DRAKE★	20%	40%	105%	165%	50%	119%

	A. Female Faculty	B. Female Students	C. Female Success	D. Femscore	E. Female Coif	F. Coif Success
7. U AKRON	35%	35%	90%	160%	No chapter	
8. U NORTHERN KENTUCKY	20%	41%	97%	158%	No chapter	
9. DUQUESNE	24%	44%	87%	155%	No chapter	
10. U ARKANSAS LITTLE ROCK	26%	42%	85%	149%	No chapter	
11. STETSON	19%	52%	75%	146%	No chapter	

STATUS CATEGORY #12: LSAT 152

School	A. Female Faculty	B. Female Students	C. Female Success	D. Femscore	E. Female Coif	F. Coif Success
1. U NORTH DAKOTA	41%	46%	123%	210%	57%	136%
2. ST MARYS	25%	41%	131%	198%	No chapter	
3. U MISSOURI KANSAS CITY	30%	37%	126%	193%	No chapter	
4. U ARKANSAS FAYETTEVILLE*	23%	38%	125%	186%	No chapter	
5. WASHBURN	28%	42%	107%	177%	No chapter	

School	A. Female Faculty	B. Female Students	C. Female Success	D. Femscore	E. Female Coif	F. Coif Success
6. U TOLEDO	17%	45%	114%	176%	27%	64%
7. U LOUISIANA BATON ROUGE	9%	52%	93%	154%	38%	91%
8. SUFFOLK	24%	46%	75%	146%	No chapter	No chapter
9. U MISSISSIPPI	21%	33%	78%	132%	No chapter	No chapter
10. MCGEORGE	18%	46%	62%	125%	25%	60%

STATUS CATEGORY #13: LSAT 151

School	A. Female Faculty	B. Female Students	C. Female Success	D. Femscore	E. Female Coif	F. Coif Success
1. CALIFORNIA WESTERN	37%	45%	133%	214%	No chapter	
2. U SOUTH DAKOTA	13%	36%	155%	204%	No chapter	
3. SOUTHWESTERN	26%	51%	122%	199%	No chapter	
4. HOWARD U	23%	58%	112%	193%	No chapter	
5. GOLDEN GATE	30%	54%	109%	193%	No chapter	

School	A. Female Faculty	B. Female Students	C. Female Success	D. Femscore	E. Female Coif	F. Coif Success
6. CREIGHTON	34%	43%	114%	192%	No chapter	
7. PACE U	32%	53%	104%	189%	No chapter	
8. U ALBANY	31%	48%	103%	182%	No chapter	
9. GONZAGA	33%	38%	110%	181%	No chapter	
10. SOUTH TEXAS	21%	44%	105%	170%	No chapter	
11. U TULSA★	37%	35%	89%	161%	No chapter	
12. LOYOLA NEW ORLEANS	22%	44%	93%	160%	No chapter	
13. U BALTIMORE	29%	47%	70%	146%	No chapter	
14. CUMBERLAND	15%	36%	84%	135%	No chapter	

STATUS CATEGORY #14: LSAT 150

School	A. Female Faculty	B. Female Students	C. Female Success	D. Femscore	E. Female Coif	F. Coif Success
1. JOHN MARSHALL	31%	37%	104%	173%	No chapter	
2. U SYRACUSE	31%	41%	97%	169%	24%	57%
3. VALPARAISO	24%	43%	101%	169%	No chapter	

School	A. Female Faculty	B. Female Students	C. Female Success	D. Femscore	E. Female Coif	F. Coif Success
4. WHITTIER	27%	45%	94%	167%	No chapter	
5. CLEVELAND STATE	31%	42%	86%	158%	No chapter	
6. QUINNIPIAC	36%	33%	89%	158%	No chapter	
7. DETROIT MERCY	23%	45%	66%	144%	No chapter	

STATUS CATEGORY #15: UNDER 150

School	A. Female Faculty	B. Female Students	C. Female Success	D. Femscore	E. Female Coif	F. Coif Success
1. SOUTHERN	24%	43%	164%	230%	No chapter	
2. THOMAS COOLEY	31%	34%	144%	209% (day and night commingled)	No chapter	
3. NOVA SOUTHEASTERN	24%	45%	118%	187%	No chapter	

4. TEXAS WESLEYAN	17%	34%	132%	183% (Half night students)	No chapter
5. WESTERN NEW ENGLAND	19%	48%	99%	167%	No chapter
6. CAPITAL (OHIO)★	24%	46%	84%	156% g13	No chapter
7. NEW ENGLAND★	20%	45%	79%	143%	No chapter
8. OHIO NORTHERN	12%	37%	92%	140%	No chapter

because I didn't have the exact data about how many women were in each school in the class of '95.

The Starring * Law Schools

An ★ next to the school's name means the dean made some effort to answer my questionnaires to find out how women were doing. I sent hundreds of such questionnaires, including at least one questionnaire to each dean, and letters reminding the deans I had sent the surveys and more copies when the deans informed me the surveys had "gone astray." I sent surveys to each of the chairmen of the appointments committees, which pick the new faculty, to find out whether the school was making a good-faith effort to hire more women teachers. I sent a survey of student opinion to each of the women law student associations asking them to have an officer fill out the form. You will notice that few law schools bothered to respond.

I think the willingness to answer says something about the school. Yale, for instance, responded to the dean's questionnaire in a letter from the associate dean asking me to imagine how Yale "is inundated with requests for information and [has] to draw a line, generally at the point of information that we prepare for the variety of public records." I don't know what counts as a "public record" at Yale, but you should know that *someone* from Yale does give info to *U.S. News & World Report* every year. In response to a follow-up letter, the associate dean revealed that the "Law School [sic] provides extensive information to the American Bar Association . . . by providing commonly requested information to this publication we, and other law schools, are able to disseminate it widely without having to complete numerous individual questionnaires." Several schools responded similarly, recommending that I read the ABA guide, which tells nothing about gender except the percentage of women students in each class. Apparently many people in the deans' offices around the country think that asking for information for a book about 44 percent of the law school student body is just an "individual" request, rather than a "public request" like that of *U.S. News & World Report.* Although the media is full of stories about women students wanting their schools to look at the issue, many deans apparently think requests for information about gender are not "common." And of course if data aren't kept by gender, there's no pressure to change.

If the law school deans had bothered to answer the questionnaires, we would have known whether women's grades are higher or lower than men's grades are after each year of law school for the three most recent classes. We would have known whether women enter with the same qualifications, and so should be expected to do about the same. We would have known whether women make it into the top 10 percent at the same or different rates, as Lani Guinier found out at Penn. We would have learned whether a woman student could expect to see at least one female professor in the all-important first year and whether the casebook in a representative course reflects conservative, moderate, or liberal political views. We would have learned whether the school was one of a group where rape is included in the subject matter of the course in criminal law. I have included copies of the surveys at the end of this book so you can see what you should know (see the appendix).

But don't think this is the end. You can press for answers yourself. Take a look at the questions I asked, and, when you visit or apply to law school, ask again. Ask the admissions dean how the women in last year's entering class succeeded. What percentage of them made law review, compared to their presence in the class? If the class is 40 percent female, is the top 10 percent also 40 percent female? Is the top half?

Many of the women I spoke to visited their prospective law schools, and several reported that their decision turned heavily on their "intuition" after "seeing the place," especially how pleasant the other students seemed. *This is nuts.* If you know a student or a student takes you around, ask your guide the questions on the student survey. Why should you pay thousands of dollars before you know if they've had any problem with professors hitting on the students or students harassing their female classmates into silence? Do all the first-year students have at least one woman professor in the big, required courses? Do the professors take the women's questions the same as they do the male students'? Do they turn to their female students in the crowd scene around the podium after class? Is rape treated as a serious crime in the class in criminal law, or is it not as important as the "real" crimes like theft and blackmail? This is law school—not a fraternity mixer. If the law schools blow off these questions, think again about going there.

Because there was no information for you consumers till now, there was no reason for the law schools to compete, and so they never have. An example of this came in an interview with Barbara Black, former dean at Columbia School of Law. Black, who is rightly considered a real heroine to women in law school, was dean when Columbia brought the liveliest and most diverse group of feminist legal scholars in the country to its campus, recruiting Martha Fineman from Wisconsin, who brought a whole symposium on women and the law with her when she came, as well as renowned critical race scholars Patricia Williams and Kimberle Crenshaw.

When asked whether the presence of this rare and prestigious group of feminist scholars added to Columbia's student appeal, she purported not to know or care. But when I unintentionally intimated that Columbia had a strong corporate law culture, she bristled visibly and complained that "Harvard and Yale didn't have the reputation as feeder schools for the New York law firms even though they were to the same extent that Columbia was," leaving me to conclude that she thinks that the impact of the school's reputation as a corporate feeder school is more important than its competitive reputation as a place for women.

Without direct answers, I was forced to figure out things like how many academic female faculty they did employ by interpreting their catalogs and how many women made law review by making a rough gender breakdown of the masthead and then putting the number against the number of full-time women students in the classes that were eligible. After I had calculated the numbers from the public record, I sent each dean a fourth letter, reporting the numbers and asking the school to correct them if they were wrong. For those twenty-some schools that responded,

I went over their numbers until every difference between their numbers and mine was accounted for. The numbers aren't going to be perfect, but it ill suits the law schools to complain. They had four chances to give me information themselves. Wouldn't you rather know something than nothing?

You Could Look It Up

Everybody in the business knows something about each other's law school. Four years ago, pretty much everyone knew about the Coben/Fenyo incident at Harvard. Two years ago, everyone knew that Northwestern had lost four of its six female academic faculty; one, who had spent just a year there, took one horrified look around and fled back to Cornell. We know where women mostly get hired only when the male faculty really want to hire—or keep—the guy she's sleeping with. We know where the harassers are. We know how the conservative/libertarian Federalist Society meetings function to introduce up-and-coming young conservative students, statistically mostly white and male, to established conservative judges and policy makers, and we know where the Federalist Society is very powerful. We know where public interest work is taken seriously and where it just gets lip service. As we saw in chapter 4 ("How to Pick A Compatible Law School"), this stuff matters, and a ranking that leaves out the fudge factor will be less informative than one that could take it into account.

Problem is, not even your faithful guide knows everything, and it's not really fair to have a survey that doesn't try to report on every place equally. Anyway, the numbers for female faculty, students, success in making law review, and percentage of female Coif members should reveal a pretty consistent picture of the institution without every stray bit of gossip.

But you, as Casey Stengel would say, "could look it up." I turned my computer on, went into the Nexis database, and in an hour turned up stories of some seriousness. Using the search terms "women" and "gender" and "sex" and "law school," I found stories in papers and magazines from around the country that should cause prospective students to ask hard questions about any of the schools discussed. At one very high status school, a study revealed that the women were getting far fewer of the important judicial clerkships than the men were. This was mysterious, because the women apparently had grades that were the same as those of the men who applied. As we have seen, those clerkships play a big role in making a career at the top of the legal profession. Two other schools had been sued by women faculty for wrongful denial of tenure, and both had paid, one big bucks, to keep the cases from trial. Another had just denied three women tenure and was defending itself on charges that no women at all held the prestigious named chairs there. Six schools were being sued on grounds that their male teachers had sexually harassed the students. And one was having a hiring war because some of the faculty didn't want to take on the wife of a male professor the school was trying to keep.

You can do what I did. After you identify the schools that interest you, go to the library and use the computer with the Lexis/Nexis database on it or look up the local papers on the Internet. Then search for stories about your schools. If you use Nexis, you can use my search terms. If you turn up a story, chances are the climate hasn't improved a lot. Better ask some hard questions.

TABLE #2: SIXTY-SIX FEMALE FRIENDLIES

Here are all the schools where women achieved over 100 in Column C, the success rank at making law review. You may find some characteristics in common that will help you choose a similar school in deciding where to apply and where to go.

School	Success Rate
1. DUKE	128%
2. NYU	122%

School	Success Rate
3. U WASHINGTON	112%
4. U MINNESOTA	109%
5. U CALIFORNIA LOS ANGELES	101%
6. U GEORGIA	118%
7. VANDERBILT	103%
8. U CALIFORNIA AT DAVIS	108%
9. WASHINGTON U	105%
10. EMORY	112%
11. ARIZONA STATE U	147%
12. U IOWA	108%
13. U OREGON	114%
14. U UTAH	121%
15. U WISCONSIN	118%
16. RUTGERS NEWARK	115%
17. U CONNECTICUT	102%
18. VILLANOVA	111%
19. U RICHMOND	102%
20. U KENTUCKY	117%
21. U SAN FRANCISCO	103%
22. CASE WESTERN RESERVE	105%
23. U SEATTLE	132%
24. U NEW MEXICO	104%
25. GEORGIA STATE	107%
26. SANTA CLARA	105%

The Femscore

School	Success Rate
27. U TENNESSEE KNOXVILLE	107%
28. WAYNE STATE	121%
29. U DENVER	114%
30. CATHOLIC U	105%
31. MARQUETTE U	100%
32. U MISSOURI COLUMBIA	104%
33. NEW YORK LAW SCHOOL	110%
34. U MEMPHIS	109%
35. U MIAMI	101%
36. U NEBRASKA LINCOLN	128%
37. ST JOHN'S	108%
38. WILLIAM MITCHELL	100%
39. CHICAGO-KENT	113%
40. DICKINSON	110%
41. U DAYTON	121%
42. U IDAHO	111%
43. U OKLAHOMA	104%
44. DRAKE	105%
45. U NORTH DAKOTA	123%
46. ST MARY'S	131%
47. U MISSOURI KANSAS CITY	126%
48. U ARKANSAS FAYETTEVILLE	125%
49. WASHBURN U	107%
50. U TOLEDO	114%

School	Success Rate
51. CALIFORNIA WESTERN	133%
52. U SOUTH DAKOTA	155%
53. SOUTHWESTERN	122%
54. HOWARD U	112%
55. GOLDEN GATE	109%
56. CREIGHTON	114%
57. PACE	104%
58. U ALBANY	103%
59. GONZAGA	110%
60. SOUTH TEXAS	105%
61. JOHN MARSHALL	104%
62. VALPARAISO	101%
63. SOUTHERN	164%
64. THOMAS COOLEY	144%
65. NOVA SOUTHEASTERN	118%
66. TEXAS WESLEYAN	132%

TABLE #3: THE NIGHT SCHOOLS

Here are the schools with more than 25 percent of their total student population in part-time programs. Once again, I've grouped them by average 1995 LSAT scores. As I noted earlier, the status and success rankings should not be notably different because of the night school numbers, but if there are a lot fewer women in the night than the day school classes eligible for law review, it might raise the success ratio slightly. If you're considering a school with a part-time program, you might want to compare the percentage of females in the part-time classes of 1996 and 1997 to

the percentage of full-time females in the main rankings and give
the school a point or two on the success scale if the night female
numbers are a lot lower than the day numbers. Remember, however, the ultimate Femscore will not be likely to change.

School	Percentage Female in Classes of 1996 and 1997
166+	
GEORGETOWN	43%
162–165	
FORDHAM	40%
161	
U WASHINGTON	39%
160	
U SAN DIEGO	40%
159	
U CONNECTICUT	41%
RUTGERS NEWARK	47%
158	
LOYOLA CHICAGO	45%
157	
U MARYLAND	46%
AMERICAN U	46%
156	
GEORGIA STATE	51%
BROOKLYN	41%
U CALIFORNIA SANTA CLARA	44%
155	
CATHOLIC U	44%
DEPAUL	45%
WAYNE STATE	43%
U DENVER	46%

School	Percentage Female in Classes of 1996 and 1997
154	
U INDIANA INDIANAPOLIS	42%
NEW YORK LAW SCHOOL	39%
SETON HALL	42%
ST LOUIS	36%
ST JOHN'S	31%
WILLIAM MITCHELL	52%
TEMPLE U	44%
153	
DUQUESNE	41%
U ARKANSAS LITTLE ROCK	42%
CHICAGO-KENT	44%
NORTH KENTUCKY	40%
U AKRON	41%
152	
MCGEORGE	45%
SUFFOLK	48%
151	
GOLDEN GATE	44%
LOYOLA NEW ORLEANS	45%
SOUTH TEXAS	29%
SOUTHWESTERN	46%
PACE	43%
U BALTIMORE	47%
150	
CLEVELAND STATE	44%
DETROIT MERCY	47%
QUINNIPIAC	36%
JOHN MARSHALL	33%

School	Percentage Female in Classes of 1996 and 1997
Under 150	
TEXAS WESLEYAN	38%
THOMAS COOLEY	34%
WESTERN NEW ENGLAND	49%
CAPITAL	42%
NEW ENGLAND	44%

The Good, the Bad, and the Ugly: A Closer Look

TABLE #4: THE BEST AND THE WORST

Here is a list of the top and bottom schools in each status group by Femscore. Note: Here and there, there are better and worse law schools around than the ones at the top and bottom of their status group. For instance, Michigan and Harvard, which are exceeded only by the University of Chicago for poor performance by its female students in Status Group #1, have a much worse Femscore at 134 percent than George Washington at 146 percent. GW is the worst school for women, but only in Status Group #3. If GW were in Group #1, it would not be on the bottom—Harvard, Michigan, and Chicago would. I could find no clear pattern as to how women do from one status group to another, although the average Femscore in the lower half of the status hierarchy is a little higher than at the top. Nonetheless, the best and worst of a group is generally representative, and it has the advantage of showing patterns of schools that apply regardless of status. Finally, I've noted where a night program exists, but as I've said, including the night students shouldn't change the ranking for these schools.

Status Group	Best of Group	Worst of Group
#1 LSAT 166+	Duke	University of Chicago
#2 LSAT 162–165	University of Washington	Northwestern
#3 LSAT 161	University of California at Davis	George Washington
#4 LSAT 160	Arizona State University	Brigham Young
#5 LSAT 159	University of Oregon	Tulane
#6 LSAT 158	University of Kentucky	George Mason (night)
#7 LSAT 157	University of Maryland	South Carolina
#8 LSAT 156	Seattle University	University of Montana
#9 LSAT 155	Wayne State University	Campbell
#10 LSAT 154	West Virginia	Mercer
#11 LSAT 153	Chicago Kent (night)	Stetson
#12 LSAT 152	University of North Dakota	McGeorge (night)
#13 LSAT 151	California Western	Cumberland
#14 LSAT 150	John Marshall (night)	Detroit Mercy (night)
#15 LSAT 149 and less	Southern Law School	Ohio Northern

INTERPRETING THE NUMBERS

Twenty-five years after women started attending law school in significant numbers, these rankings represent the first comprehensive analysis of women in law schools. Since this is going to be the world you experience for the next three years—and your performance may continue to affect your life for years thereafter—take a moment and think about what this list shows. Although they span the range of status—from Duke to Ohio Northern—there are real differences between the profiles of the fifteen best success schools for women and the fifteen worst.

Women Do Better at Public Institutions
Ten out of the fifteen top schools for women by Femscore are public, state schools (University of Washington, University of California at Davis, ASU, Oregon, Kentucky, Maryland, Wayne State, West Virginia, University of North Dakota, and Southern). Only three of the fifteen worst schools are public institutions (George Mason, South Carolina, and Montana).

Women Do Better at Integrated Institutions
Eleven of the fifteen best schools are educating minorities as well as women, with minority populations of 15 percent or more (Duke, University of Washington, University of California at Davis, ASU, Maryland, Seattle, Wayne State, Chicago-Kent, California Western, John Marshall, and Southern). Only four of the worst fifteen schools are educating minorities as well as women, with minority student populations of 15 percent or more (Chicago, Northwestern, Tulane, and McGeorge).

Women Do Better at Northern and Western Schools
Thirteen of the fifteen best schools for women are located in the North or West (University of Washington, University of California at Davis, Arizona State University, Oregon, Kentucky, Maryland, Seattle, Wayne State, West Virginia, Chicago-Kent, California Western, University of North Dakota, John Marshall). Only two of the best schools—Duke and Southern in Louisiana—are located in the South, that is, states that were part of the Old Confederacy during the Civil War (Maryland and Kentucky were border states, slave, but Union, and West Virginia broke away from Virginia), and one of the two southern schools, Southern, is more than half African American. The picture is more ambiguous at the bottom. Eight of the worst fifteen schools are in the North or

West (Chicago, Northwestern, George Washington, Brigham Young, Montana, McGeorge, Detroit Mercy, and Ohio Northern). Seven of the worst schools are all in the states of the Old Confederacy (Tulane, George Mason, South Carolina, Campbell, Mercer, Stetson, and Cumberland).

Students Sort of Know If Their School Is Women-Friendly

Many law school guides, such as the Princeton Review's *The Best Law Schools*, are based on surveys of students at the schools. Princeton boasts a survey of "eleven thousand current law students at the 170 law schools profiled." The Princeton survey allowed the students to address what was best and worst about their schools and clearly left room for students to opine about the gender environment and general political environment.

At eight of the fifteen schools where women did worst, the students articulated awareness of gender problems to the Princeton survey. At five schools, students complained. Students at Brigham Young complained that the students were not diverse, Tulane registered a need for more diverse faculty, and Northwestern students complained the faculty was not only "not diverse," but also homogeneous and ideological; when asked about hits and misses, McGeorge students registered "gender bias" in their "miss" column. Some of Campbell's women "complained that condescension directed specifically at minority and female students sometimes hampers their efforts to succeed." Perhaps most interestingly, at three schools where women don't succeed, students expressed some enthusiasm for an environment where women don't succeed. Chicago's students were "all over the map" on Chicago's treatment of women and thought Chicago's reputation was "undeserved." Some students at the University of South Carolina willingly embraced the conservatism of the student body, one first-year student saying, "This is one of the most conservative law schools in America. I like that." According to the Princeton Review, many students at George Mason listed the lack of diversity "*as a positive characteristic* [emphasis added]."

At the seven other failure schools, students at six schools—

George Washington, Mercer, Cumberland, Ohio Northern, Detroit Mercy, and Stetson—had no complaints, and at the seventh—Montana—registered pleasure in the reality of their diverse faculties.

On the other side of things, students at the success schools say almost uniformly positive things to Princeton about the diversity and supportiveness of their institutions. None of the surveys at the success schools reported gender bias. At six of the fifteen success schools, Duke, University of Washington, Oregon, Seattle, ASU, and Southern, the students uniformly praised their diverse classmates. As an Oregon student described it: "You can find a conservative male student sitting comfortably next to a woman with a nose ring in almost every class."

At Washington, Oregon, and Maryland, the students reported progressive administrations and faculty, which in turn generated requests for a little conservatism into the mix! Three surveys at success schools—Chicago-Kent, California Western, and John Marshall—turned up no opinion on issues of gender or diversity.

At Duke, the women-friendliest school in the top group, Princeton reports, "We heard almost nothing but positive remarks."

One Last Thing

As we saw in chapter 4, if you looked at the curriculum in the catalogs for most American law schools, you'd think Gloria Steinem or Catharine MacKinnon was running the world. The inclusion of gender-oriented courses matters. Since women are more than half the population, issues about women come up in all kinds of legal contexts. The issues aren't just the obvious ones like rape and discrimination, either. In civil procedure, a very hot current issue is the extent to which civil discovery can be used to uncover the prior sexual history of a harassment complainant. Remember President Clinton's acquaintance Paula Jones's high school boyfriends? In torts, issues of product liability increasingly include hormonal treatment of all sorts. Property was an historic way to enforce the law of marriage. In contracts, we should be asking why the courts don't enforce contracts for sexual services. If a school offers lots of courses about women in the legal system, chances are those issues will be adequately covered in the general courses as well.

How much curriculum can a school like Harvard, with 15 percent female faculty, manage? Not much, unless Harvard is a hotbed of feminist men. In which case, we'd expect Harvard to find worthy females to hire as colleagues. Maybe you're not interested in how the law works in women's lives. But if such courses and subjects aren't offered, you'll never get the chance to make that choice.

The Dreaded First Year

OKAY, YOU'RE IN. Now what?

First of all, lighten up. You've probably heard the stories about how hard law school is on women, especially the first year. But there's a reason for the rigors of the first year, and it's not just to make childbirth seem painless. Because women report having such a hard time understanding and participating in the first-year exercise, I'm going to take some time to explain why it takes the shape it does, and thus why some of the first year would be hard to change. So, we're going to be talking about ways you female readers can cope with the first year.* The first way is to understand that some of it is not aimed at making you unhappy. That's not to say that the worst excesses are defensible; they aren't. We'll talk about that, too.

* Gender aside, there are two good basic books for everyone: *Law School Basics*, by David Hricik (Los Angeles: Nova Press, 1997), and *The Eight Secrets of Top Exam Performance in Law School*, by Charles Whitebread (San Diego: Harcourt Brace, 1995).

The Secret of the System

A lot of the first year of law school is the product of the American legal system, particularly the common law system, which we got from the English centuries ago. The common law system depends on applying the principles in old decisions to new problems, so lawyers, who are going to run the system, need to think along those lines. Accordingly, the teachers can't just ask you to learn "the law" by memorizing a bunch of information about what the law is. They have to ask you to stretch your thinking to new situations, which is harder than memorizing and often seems scary to people of any gender, and, from all reports, particularly to women.

Although the common law system is an historical accident, most English cultures and colonies like the United States retain it, because it serves valuable political and social purposes. So when you're sitting there trying to figure out what in the world could be in the mind of the scary, Kingsfieldish old man running the place who just called on you out of the blue to tell him what the law would be in a weird situation you never heard of before, you're not just caught in a Kafka novel. You're participating in a completely understandable and quite legitimate historical institution of reasoning from old cases to new ones, which is going to be a lot less scary once you understand how it works.

Statutes: The Legislature's Laws

In the United States and most common law societies, law comes from two places: the judges, who make what we call "common law," and the legislators. You probably remember from American history that the legislatures "make the laws," so let's start there. The legislatures, like the U.S. Congress or the Illinois state legislature, or the Chicago City Council, meet and decide how they want people to act. They then enact what they want done in something called a statute. Regardless of the way the legislative body is selected, the issuance of general commands from a central government authority that people are then all expected to obey is as old as civilization itself. From Egypt to Rome to France to China, whoever governed from the top issued orders to the rest.

So, say the legislature doesn't want business people to get together and agree that everyone will charge the same price, thus eliminating the benefits of competition for the consumer. The legislature says, as the United States Congress said in 1890, that people should not engage in "conspiracies, combinations or agreements in restraint of trade." Nonetheless, and despite the law against combinations, people do all sorts of things: They merge, they wait to see what the competition is charging and snuggle right up behind, they require customers to buy all their products if they want any of their products. It's impossible for the legislature to anticipate all these developments, so, after the statute is enacted, the American (and English) systems assign to judges the task of deciding how to apply the legislature's directions ("no conspiracies in restraint of trade") in any particular case.

There are many techniques for figuring out the legislative will: the language of the statute, what the legislators said while they were considering it, what was happening in the society at the time, and the extent to which the law seems to invite judges to interpret the language to fit a changing society. As the process of interpreting and applying the statute proceeds, a body of cases filling in the meaning of the statute develops.

One of the requirements our legal system imposes on this process is that the applications be consistent, that is, we wish to avoid having the law apply one way to one American and another way to another one. So we don't want to forbid Microsoft, for instance, to insist that you buy its Web browser if you want its dominant operating system while allowing some other software provider to do the same thing. We don't want the First Amendment applied so that Democrats have protected political speech and Republicans do not. Consistency serves two important political values: that citizens are equal before the law and that people, even the people operating through corporations, are able to anticipate what the law requires so they can plan their affairs. How would you like it if there were no signs indicating the permitted speed on the highway or if the police could impose one speed on you and another on your brother?

Accordingly, all democratic societies now have legislatures that set forth general rules in statutory form and some mechanism of interpretation of statutes that aspires to the standards of equality and consistency. As a result, most people's activities in the late twentieth century are governed in large part by statutory law.

Judicial Decisions: The Common Law

Unlike other democracies, however, common law systems not only allow judges to interpret the legislature's laws, they also allow judges to make nonstatutory law, called common law. Common law is not a product of God or nature; it is an inheritance from our English antecedents. The institution of the English common law goes back quite a ways to before the Norman Conquest, when English society was mostly governed by local custom, with its roots in Anglo-Saxon Germanic tribal culture. After the continental William of Normandy conquered England, one of his institutions of governance was the King's Bench, a group of royal judges who roamed the countryside delivering the king's justice to people with disputes all over the place. As there were few statutes, most judicial pronouncements administered justice according to the immemorial custom of the localities. As the national part of the system began to emerge with the unification of the English nation in the early Renaissance, the little local customs began to be merged in a national system of judicial orders declaring the law common to the whole society.

At this point, the English had a king and a Parliament of sorts, so they had the option to adopt the top-down statutory system, where an authoritative legislature or executive told the people what to do about everything. Or they could have taken all the common law decisions together and consolidated them into a code that was then passed by the legislature. But although the English did engage in some legislating, they refused the option of legislative dominance or legislative codification, and much law continued to be made one case at a time by the judges sitting all over England. This was the system as it was transferred to the United States when the first English colonists arrived.

With some exceptions—namely the states like Louisiana, which adopted the civil code from the French before they were bought by the Anglicized United States—the English common law system took root and dominated the developing legal systems here. Even after the American Revolution, when some states declared that they would no longer follow any rules simply because they had prevailed under the English common law, the English system was so powerful that the states abandoned their independence and returned to the lines of cases brought over from England in the years before they parted company with the Mother Country. So common law is judge-made law inherited from England and maintained after the American Revolution and, indeed, to this day.

Judge-made law is a pretty weird idea. As legal historian Lawrence Friedman aptly expressed it, "What [the legislature] can do in a month's intensive work, a court can do only over the years—and never systematically, since the common law does not look kindly on hypothetical or future cases." Instead of the efficient legislative system, over the years, a common law court will decide a series of disputes presenting a legal issue. In the purest case, a court starts from what was customary in Germanic England. The court will say, for example, that a farmer is liable for letting his cow wander out and eat your crops, a kind of bovine trespass. In later cases, the court may say what's liability for the cow is also liability for the pig, and the farmer is responsible for the damage Porky does, too. Slowly, the court will develop from those early recorded cases a larger doctrine of responsibility for damages by animals. As the court confronts each new situation, it is also answerable to the values of consistency, in the interests of equality and foreseeability, that drove the process of statutory interpretation.

Tied by the political commitment to equality and foreseeability, as the doctrine develops, the common law court will try to make the new decision consistent with the old ones. The body of the old cases functions sort of like the statute in our legislative example to limit strictly what the judges can do, although most students of common law admit that common law judges are freer than judges bound by the legislature's expression of its will.

Judges try to tie each common law decision to past decisions for another reason, too. The freedom of the common law judge is problematical, because in a democracy, unelected judges don't have an obvious claim to tell us what to do. As the administrative machinery of the Crown, the English judges in the old days had some claim to participate in whatever made it okay for the king to tell people what to do—over time, a mixture of superior force and divine sanction. In America, the judges are creatures of the states (the common law is much less of a problem on the federal level), and the states try to avoid the "democracy" problem by electing the judges or by having elected officials appoint the judges from a panel of recommendations based on "merit." Still, having only remotely accountable professional judges make or apply a lot of the laws governing our lives is anomalous in a democracy. But both systems exist, and judges try to solve the "democracy" problem in common law cases in part by pretending that they are just discovering and declaring what the law has always been rather than just doing what they think is right. So applying past cases to new situations is very important to the legitimacy of the common law system.

Because of the way the common law develops, and because the process of interpreting statutes resembles the common law process in its obligation to be faithful to the statute, evenhanded, and predictable in applying prior principles to new cases, law school education in the first year especially concentrates on teaching students the skills they need to participate in the common law (and statutory) system. This curriculum consists of presenting the students with a sample of the body of existing cases in different subject matter areas, introducing them to the existing body of law, so to speak, and then pressing them to figure out how that existing body of law might apply to new cases that may come up. All of this is supposed to teach them the method of common law decision making. Usually, a course or two will involve an area, like criminal law, dominated by statute, so the students can learn how the process differs when the foundational authority is a statute, rather than a very old case.

The First Year: An Overview

In some ways, it doesn't matter what subjects the law schools include in the first year, because there only are three generic topics that must be taught in any first year of law school: one, the structure of the American legal system; two, how the common law system develops rules for people; three, how the legal system writes and interprets statutes.

Most first-year curricula imperfectly perform these tasks. The first year of law school is usually the worst at teaching the structure of the American legal system, although they make a pass at it in the basic course on civil procedure. In addition to the blatant failure to inform students of the history and structure of the American legal system, the traditional first-year program also makes the mistake of trying to teach students the statutory and common law methods methods I've just described and the content of the substantive law—of torts or crimes, for example—at the same time. In a third mistake, the traditional first-year program tries to teach the substance of the law, the structure of the legal system, and about a dozen other things lawyers eventually need to know using indiscriminately what law schools call the "Socratic" method.

The Socratic method, loosely defined, is the process whereby the teacher asks the student to answer a question and then engages in a dialogue with the student starting with the student's first answer. Since you will hear Socrates invoked a lot in the first year of law school, you should know that the law school "Socratic" method is a procedure with only the remotest resemblance to the legendary father of Western philosophy. Law teachers often misuse the label "Socratic" when they are asking questions that can only be answered by guessing at the meaning of something completely arbitrary, like the meaning of the numbers following the name of a case (I'll be explaining this in a minute) or asking the student to recite the facts that gave rise to the case. On the other hand, asking people to apply the reasons for the nonenforcement of contracts by minors to the problem of the older-acting sixteen-year-old, as we discussed in an earlier chapter, is closer to the authentic Socrates, because, the teacher is trying to accomplish three legitimate Socratic goals: one, to get the student to probe the reasons underlying the first position the student espouses; two, to get the student to see the limits of the application of the reasons underlying his position; and, three, to get the student to see basic intuitions about the goodness and fairness of the larger enterprise—in my example, the law of contracts.

Although the relatively authentic "Socratic" part of the law school method has its uses in training people for the American legal system, participating in the Socratic dialogue is often painful, so many people have arisen in recent years to criticize this way of doing business, and some schools are trying to move to a more humane system or to limit the use of Socratic method to its appropriate sphere. But, like the old math, the confused and irrational technique of first-year law teaching has lots of support among people who like social arrangements that terrify the powerless and sort people out into hierarchies with rewards for those at the top and pain for those at the bottom, regardless of whether they train people to be lawyers or not. (The real Socrates' students, you may recall, rewarded him with the choice between exile and poison at the end of his life.) Fortunately for you, one response to this nonsense has been the proliferation of a number of books intended to explain the why and how of the first-year experience—and, coincidentally, to explain the structure of the legal system—so that you can succeed despite the evil inclinations of the people defending the Socratic method to the last drop. I hope this book is one of the helpful ones.

The Content of the First Year
in a Nutshell

THE STRUCTURE OF THE AMERICAN LEGAL SYSTEM

A legal system exists to prescribe and enforce rules for behavior to govern the members of a particular society. In the United States, the legal system exists to prescribe and enforce rules of behavior for people living in the United States. A common and influential way to think about the process whereby a bunch of people come to live within a legal system is to imagine them wandering around in some prehistoric time without a legal system, killing and raping each other. Life is, famously, "solitary, poor, nasty, brutish, and short." Either eventually the strongest comes out on top and imposes his will or the people agree somehow they'd be better off with limits on what can be done—or people gradually develop practices of doing things one way and not another, as they see what works. Within some geographical area, the people in power order the others to do some things and forgo others, or the people all agree to do some things and forgo others, usually ungoverned killing, or people just stop doing some things and do others until any other way seems strange. A society of sorts is born, and the legal system develops to produce the official list of things done or forgone (lawmaking) and to be sure the list is made real (law enforcement).

The American legal system is more complex than most, because the Revolution that established the United States separate from England was an alliance of the various colonies, which then became states, and the people who wrote the Constitution setting up the national government were in no position to replace the states. So there is a national legal system, created by the United States Constitution, consisting of the federal legislature (the Congress), the executive (the president), and the federal judiciary (the federal judicial system). There are fifty state legal systems, the creatures of the Colonial charters and eventually of the state constitutions, each of which has its own legislature, executive, and judiciary, and there is the District of Columbia! The federal system is often described as one of "dual sovereignty." Wherever you live, you are subject to two systems—your state system and the federal system. Sitting here in Arizona in January of 1998, I must obey all the traffic laws and criminal and consumer laws of Arizona, as well as the federal laws against racketeering, restraint of trade, and employment discrimination.

Each judicial system has courts to hear and decide disputes, usually called trial courts, which both decide the facts and interpret and apply the law. The systems also include courts to hear appeals from the trial courts, usually only on grounds that the trial court made a mistake of law. Most judicial systems have not one but two levels of appeals courts, the highest being the Supreme Court. Most legal systems make and apply criminal law, which is the law governing relations between the government—representing the whole society—and the individual or company, and civil law, the law governing relations between two private parties. Most criminal law is statutory; much civil law is statutory, but much civil law also remains the province of the judge-made common law. By constitution and statute, many disputes can only be decided by a jury of some number of laymen and -women; other disputes may be decided by a judge or by both.

Much of what trial courts decide is not recorded for public consumption. The opinions of the courts of appeals, intermediate and supreme, are recorded, but, since most appeals are only about law, the recorded opinions include only enough of the facts to explain why the case was decided the way it was. The court opinions are recorded by the agencies of government themselves; for example, Ohio records the opinions of the Ohio courts in the "Ohio Reporters," both appellate and supreme. The opinions also appear in regional reporters maintained by commercial reporting services; Ohio cases appear in the commercial system published by a company called West Publishing, reporters for the northeast part of the country. The "citation" of the cases is nothing more than the name of the parties, the number of its volume in the reporter system, the name of the reporter system, the page of the volume, and the date.

So the most famous of all modern American legal decisions, the Supreme Court ruling in *Brown v. Board of Education of Topeka, Kansas*, desegregating the public schools, has the following citation: 347 U.S. 483 (1954), which tells us that the case involved at least two parties, Brown and the Board of Education, that it was reported in volume 347 of the official reporters the United States government produces for Supreme Court decisions, beginning at page 483, and that it was decided in 1954. The West system reports the case at 74 S. Ct. 686.

The teaching of the notation system is a good example of a misuse of the "Socratic" method. In the printed report of *Brown* in those two volumes, the numbers appear under the title. This probably looks pretty strange to you, although you've doubtless heard the case described dozens of times. This is because the legal system has a set of terms and forms it uses that lay people rarely see. Some traditional first-year teachers abuse the Socratic method by trying to get the student to intuit what these notations mean in an abusive exchange in front of the entire first-year class. I've actually seen professors try to "teach" the notation and reporting system in a travesty of the Socratic method by asking some hapless student during the first few days of class what court decided a particular case. The student says she doesn't know. The teacher asks whether there's anything in the case in the book the student has been assigned that might reveal the name of the court. The student, caught like a deer in the headlights, stares at these meaningless notations, 347 U.S. 483, say, as if the book would talk. The teacher moves to another victim.

In less than one tenth the time it takes for a room full of students to guess at what the notation system means, I've just taught you what it means. If asked to defend their behavior, the offending teachers would say they're teaching the students that nothing in a reported case decision is meaningless or unimportant. Nonsense. Much of what you're assigned in the first year is meaningless or trivial, and much of what you do need to know can be taught directly, rather than by making you guess about what it might mean. Once you know that 347 U.S. 483 (1954) means you're looking at a Supreme Court case from 1954, you'll never pore over the notation again. Ditto with who's the plaintiff and who's the defendant and the fact that on appeal the name of the party appealing usually appears first in the case name regardless of whether they were the moving party in the trial court. This stuff only deserves time-consuming attention because it's strange. Simple instruction makes it familiar.

THE COMMON LAW "CASE" SYSTEM

Because the common law method proceeds from Germanic custom lost in the mists of time (the cases rarely refer to this anymore, but I thought you'd like to know that the common law didn't come to the English directly from God) to cases decided and reported in England to cases decided in the American state courts in the eighteenth and nineteenth centuries after independence to the cases a particular court decided yesterday, a lot of the first-year curriculum consists of reading cases. Remember, once a court—say, the Ohio Supreme Court—says what the common law is on something in Ohio, then that court and all the trial and intermediate appeals courts in Ohio are bound to follow it. The first-year casebooks put together a set of case opinions from the courts of appeals of the various states to sketch a picture of what the current state of the common law is on the core subjects it addresses and a little bit about how it evolved to that point. I'm going to use examples from several fields of law, because the method is the same in any common law course.

In torts (roughly, the law governing civil injuries), for instance, the casebook might contain several chapters. Each chapter would include a sample of opinions on an important aspect of the law of torts. For example, there would be chapters on each of the following subjects: (1) negligence, or the standard we use for tagging someone with responsibility for the harm his acts do to someone else, (2) causation, or the relationship we require between someone's negligent act and the harm that ensues, (3) contributory negligence, or the defense we allow when the victim acted like a

damn fool, too. Instead of just telling you that we consider someone negligent when the risk of harm outweighs the cost of taking
precautions, say, failing to put a biting dog on a leash, the casebooks present actual opinions in appeals from cases where people
failed to leash their dogs, sped in rainy weather, left manholes un-
covered, etc. From these opinions, you are supposed to piece
together a picture of the law of negligence. From the piecing
process, you are supposed to learn how lawyers piece together the
picture of any field of common law from similar case materials.

Since each state is sovereign as to state law, as a technical matter,
the Ohio decisions in the casebook, for example, only govern the
Ohio courts, so the Ohio tort law can be completely different
from the Illinois tort law. Given the common English roots,
the law rarely differs completely from one state to another, so
the casebooks usually contain a sample of cases from around the
country to give you a general view of what the law of torts usually looks like. After all, who knows where you may wind up
practicing? In any event, from the questions after the reported
cases and from the imaginary cases ("hypotheticals") your teachers
ask you about, you are supposed to learn to predict how a court,
faced with these old cases, and bound by the norms of equality
and foreseeability, might act in a new case.

Note that there is no sure answer to how a court would act in a
case it's never seen before. That's why teaching you how to narrow the range of possible future outcomes by thinking beyond
the existing cases through hypothetical questions is legitimate.
On the other hand, there is absolutely only one answer to what
181 U.S. 56 means. There is only one answer to what the highest
court in the state of Ohio is. There is only historical material to
tell us why the court system looks the way it does. That's why using questions and answers to teach you these hard and fast facts is
stupid. That's why all first-year curricula should start with a
straightforward lesson about the legal system, rather than requiring
you to figure it out from a set of case materials. But then you
wouldn't need this chapter!

The casebooks include mostly appeals court opinions, because the "law" doesn't resolve factual disputes, such as whether it was really your dog that bit the plaintiff. Courts need to know the facts, and later courses like Clinic and Trial Advocacy will teach you how to present the facts. For the first year, we're mostly not interested in facts. You're interested in knowing what the law would do if the facts were not in dispute. That is the role of the court of appeals. The trial court decides what the facts are, establishing the record, or story, the law will address, as well as deciding what the law is and how the law applies to that story, but the courts of appeals review only what the law is and how it applies. Such questions include, for instance, whether the "law" should make you responsible for your dog's bite, even if it never bit before. If the victim teased the dog. And so on. By the time you see a court addressing these legal questions in law school, the facts are already decided.

Feminist—and other—critics of the first-year experience criticize this appellate case method for its denatured quality. Where are the people, their stories, their reality? Maybe the court has cast out some fact that might make us feel differently about the rule it announces. Lani Guinier makes a nice point that if you could see the case from the moment the plaintiff walked into your office and told a story, you might see alternative ways that the parties could have resolved their differences. Since this kind of counseling is a lot of what lawyers do, it ill serves the ends of legal education to present the basic material to first-year law students with the facts so limited that only conflict is possible and there has to be one winner and one loser.

While I sympathize with the disconnected feeling the casebooks create, newer and more progressive casebooks often lead you up to the appellate opinion with more background, and Guinier makes the best argument for this approach—to prepare law students to counsel resolution, mediation, compromise.

On the other hand, for purposes of learning what the actual common law rules are, which is a big part of what law school must do, cases, like life, often contain a lot of facts and issues you don't need to know for purposes of the first-year courses, so the editors try to cut them down. You'd go nuts if you had to do all the reading, often twenty or thirty pages of edited cases per class, in the form of hundreds of pages of unedited cases, much less get the factual story from the get-go. Worse still, even if the stories leading to the conflicts were told in all their richness, I think a lot of the denatured quality of the experience results from the assumptions the legal system makes about the interests that matter to women, rather than the fact that we don't know if the biting dog in a dog bite case was a poodle or a Scottie. It's not that they're leaving something out, it's *what* they're leaving out.

What a Case Looks Like

Let's say owner's dog, Fido, allegedly bites victim. Think of yourself as the victim for a moment. You might think the pain of the bite is not the will of God, but the fault of owner, and that the owner should take some of the hurt onto himself, at least by taking some money and giving it to victim. Since owner and victim aren't living in anarchy in some prehistoric world, there is a legal system to decide such claims. Victim resorts to the legal system—in this case, the common law trial court of the state of the incident—to try to share his pain with the owner. Victim becomes a *plaintiff.* As a plaintiff, victim files a complaint against owner, who is thereby transformed into a *defendant.* The complaint tells the story to the court. Defendant then files an answer, denying what defendant thinks isn't true. Think of yourself as a defendant. You might say the dog did not bite the victim, or it wasn't your dog, or assert defenses, like that plaintiff tormented the dog. Or defendant might file a motion to say the facts don't matter—the law doesn't compensate for dog bites, and the case should be dismissed.

If the court denies the motion to dismiss, most civil systems allow the parties to nose around in each other's business to establish the facts, a process called "discovery." After discovery, the defendant or the plaintiff may move the court again, this time for summary judgment, saying, we now know the facts—plaintiff tortured the dog—and, as a legal matter, defendant is not liable for what plaintiff brought on himself, or that plaintiff's conduct doesn't matter, and defendant is still liable. Note that the trial court is deciding a question of law at this point. These decisions usually generate memorandum decisions that in some systems, like the federal system, are collected in the official or regional reporters (and sometimes not), but that are always available in the case file.

If the court decides that discovery has produced an ongoing factual dispute, with defendant continuing to deny that the dog bit the victim or to contend that plaintiff tormented the dog and plaintiff arguing to the contrary (the dog doesn't testify), the court may deny the motion for summary judgment and send the case to a jury or decide the facts itself and decide who should win. The loser can appeal, but except in rare cases, the loser cannot appeal the jury finding that the dog did or did not bite the victim or that plaintiff did or did not torment the dog. The appeals courts don't want to see the witnesses (or the dog) again, so they just leave the facts where the jury found them. Appeal is only from the trial judges' legal decisions, like that it doesn't matter legally whether or not plaintiff tortured the dog. That's why appellate opinions assume facts, include only the facts necessary to present the problem for the law to apply to, and seem oddly removed from life. Despite the abstract quality of appellate opinions, it's interesting to know whether people can be held responsible for what the animals they own do, especially if you might one day represent the dog owner. If this is not interesting to you, I advise you to reconsider your decision to go to law school at all.

Moving from the Cases to the Future

As a technical matter, you don't need to read the dog case to find out if people are liable for their dogs' bites or not. You could just read a summary of existing cases in the form of rules. Such summaries exist; they are called treatises, and they tell you what the law is so far. The law school bookstores and libraries are full of such study aids, in the form of commercial outlines and academic treatises, and some of them are quite helpful to a beginning law student. What the treatises don't teach you is how to put together a picture of the law from the pieces the cases provide; they just hand you the picture already painted. So if you get a legal problem that hasn't been analyzed in any treatise, you're going to have a rough time figuring out what the cases mean. More importantly, the treatises and commercial outlines don't teach you how to try to figure out what the court would do with a case that differed from the existing dog decisions, say a cat case. So the outlines won't help you much when your first client comes in with a ferocious feline. The painful and snail-like process of the first-year classes are intended to teach you both those skills: how to piece together a rule from a lot of case summaries and how to predict how a court will act in a future case.

Now that you know *what* you're going to learn, before you plunge into the crucible of learning these lessons in the traditional first-year curriculum, I'm going to give you a preview of the technique.

Remember our contracts case in chapters 1 and 3, involving the rule that a sixteen-year-old could not conclude a binding contract? There we began by assuming that under the case establishing the rule of eighteen as the age of contract competency, a sixteen-year-old could not make a binding contract. Then we speculated that the court, when confronted with a case of another sixteen-year-old, reached a different result. Since the system requires consistency in the interests of equality and foreseeability, when the same court decided what looked like the *same* case differently, the court had to make a distinction between the two cases. The court did so, focusing on the undisputed evidence in the second case that the sixteen-year-old misrepresented his age to the seller. From this, we learned that the sameness between the two cases was misleading, because the similarity was limited to the fact of chronological age, where there was another area of fact of interest that was different—deliberate wrongdoing on the part of the party trying to get out of the contract. We learned that if the party trying to get out of the contract deliberately misled the other party, the court would not allow a litigant to profit from his own wrongdoing.

Recognizing that the rule had two legs—physical age and innocent behavior—we next asked ourselves what the same court would do when confronted with a case that differed from the first case, in that the party was underage but not completely innocent, but that differed from the second case as well, because his act of misrepresentation was not intentional but circumstantial—say, he lived in a dorm normally occupied by people eighteen or above. Would the court treat the different case the same as the sixteen-year-old case, giving chronology primacy in the decision, or would the court treat the different case the same as the intentional misrepresentation case, allowing the misleading circumstances to trump the chronological factor? Any decision requires the court in the third case to treat different cases the same. If the court put the innocent but misplaced sixteen-year-old case into the underage category, it would mean that contract law defined the category of competent contractors tightly and heavily as a function of chronology. If the court put the sixteen-year-old college dorm case into the intentionally misleading sixteen-year-old category, it would mean that competency to contract is broadly construed, allowing more transactions to take place. Without any act of any legislature, the competency requirements of the law of contract would be changed—or clarified—slightly.

How can a student answer the question about what to do with the dorm-dwelling sixteen-year-old? The underage sixteen-year-old case means we want a role for chronology. The misleading sixteen-year-old case means we don't want formal chronology to exclude any concerns of fairness or specificity regarding particular defendants. Maybe some of the words the court used in one of those cases gives a hint about what it would do with a case that fell in the middle. For instance, maybe the court in the misrepresenting sixteen-year-old case said, "In light of the conscious and strategic behavior of the defendant in intentionally misleading the seller, we find that he is more than mentally competent enough to hold to his contract." In that case, we would know that the court would likely require quite a dose of intentionality before it would suspend the basic eighteen-is-enough rule for contracting. It's important to read the cases carefully to try to find out what the court thinks matters or for direct hints about what the court would do next.

Why the First Year Seems Scary

The first-year classes are scary, even when the reported opinions give you some clue, because it's scary to interpret them with two hundred of your classmates staring at you. But they are really scary, because teachers sometimes ask the "next case" question when little or none of the information available in the casebook tells how the new case should be decided. Either of these versions of the "Socratic" method leaves many women feeling completely buffaloed. They're assigned reading. They do the reading. They're asked questions. The answers aren't in the reading, or if they are in the reading, they are far from obvious. They feel the way you probably do right now—all you want to do is know the answer to the dorm-dwelling sixteen-year-old case and move on to learning the next lesson.

Students often don't even have enough breathing room to ask where the answers are supposed to come from. If they can get their heads above water enough to ask the "where" question, they don't have a clue about the answer to where the answers are supposed to come from. Students, and particularly the women students, feel as if they're being asked to play a game with no rules and for which they cannot prepare.

It is not surprising therefore, that Ms. Gentle was "just devastated by the first year" at Fordham. UCLA's first year said that "such a degrading first year completely devastated me, my sense of self was completely ripped away," and state university's star law student Ms. Editor thinks you're "so scarred after first year, all you can do is damage control."

The sad thing is that most women don't start out like that. They come from their college triumphs ready to try to answer the teachers' questions. Minnesota: "The first three weeks of class I raised my hand every day and after a while I felt extremely pretentious and now there are only men who raise their hands in class." And it's not just Minnesota. A group of second- and third-year students from law schools all over the country whom I interviewed at their summer jobs in Phoenix reported almost unanimously that they didn't talk in class themselves and that women generally volunteered and asked questions much less frequently than men did. Fordham's P. "didn't talk much in class." Nor did J.: "I don't speak in class. I feel slightly intimidated." Fordham's J. J. "was not intimidated in college—once I got to law school I stopped." S.G.: "I tracked it. Women speak in first semester and not in second semester." Minnesota: "I never talk." Fordham's African American T. put it well: "We [women] are newcomers to the legal profession. As a black person, I wouldn't go to a Klan rally looking for support."

How did the first year of law school come to resemble a Klan rally? We have just seen how the first-year curriculum is designed to teach students how to construct a picture of areas of law from a series of common law cases and how to analyze the way a court might approach a new situation. Although this process is unfamiliar to many law students, it's hardly outside the realm of human experience. Philosophy teachers ask their students to reason along until a contradiction is reached; Socrates was a philosopher; that's why it's called the Socratic method. Talmud classes deal with applying ambiguous statutes to new situations. Many of these people had worked as certified public accountants, teachers, actors. As UCLA's Ms. Philosopher told me, "I was a philosophy major and I knew a few people in science and they didn't find the same thing."

And why do women report being silenced while their male classmates are not? Fordham's T: "One or two male gunners challenge [the] professor and have one-to-one with one of our professors." M. J.: "He [the professor] had his guy." At Minnesota: "Who talks?" B.: "The gunners. They raise their hands and say what they feel. I ask myself, 'Did they take a public speaking class or did they already go through law school?' . . . There was this guy who by the second or third class just sat in the front and doesn't even raise his hand; it was just him and the professor. The whole need to be the dominant alpha male with the whole truth all the time. It just takes practice to get your guts up ('I'm going to say it; it may be wrong'), [the men] have been doing it since elementary school." Ms. Editor: "Men here walk in with superiority complexes and [they're] unshaken by humiliation in class. They'll get fried at the beginning of class and by the end of class they'll be raising their hands again . . . women feel that you have to earn it, but men feel that they already have it when they walk into class."

When asked where men get the idea from, Editor thinks it's cultural: "The way you feel is a reflection of how you've been trained and you haven't known disadvantage." Or maybe it's Darwinian. Remember another voice from Minnesota: "There's this guy in my class who always talks. One of his male classmates asked him how he knows so much and he answered, 'I worked for an attorney and I picked up this stuff.' I [the woman speaking to me] had an opportunity to say the same thing to him and his answer to me is not that he worked with an attorney, but was '*Well, that's just the way my mind works.*' "

Like the "natural" lawyer from Minnesota, sometimes the other students act to silence the women. Columbia: "People titter when a woman speaks, younger men, they're awful." "You don't hear the tittering when men speak." Perhaps more destructively, Columbia reports, the men have two categories for their female classmates: "The women are stupid or they are kiss-ass." Male talkers, on the other hand, are "obnoxious." Thus, even smart, high-performing women are categorized as succeeding only by manipulating and pleasing the powerful players in their world ("kiss-ass"), while men get the dignity of being so aggressive as to be "obnoxious."

The people in authority "never, nobody, never" rein it in (Columbia). Editor: "There is no restraint against fellow students. In the faculty's defense, some faculty are so careful, but the best couldn't protect the students from their peers."

I don't know why women report finding the game so much harder to play than men do. I'm not a psychologist. Women report that they don't understand the game and that they don't know the answers. Lani Guinier has been gathering stories from her female students at the University of Pennsylvania that reflect an unwillingness to occupy public space in the classes while they reason their way through the material aloud and in front of hundreds of eyes that they perceive to be hostile. They wait until they have a really good answer all worked out in their heads before they raise their hands or they try to build on what others have said rather than competing with them for the prize of suggesting a "better" answer.

As to the nature of the game, if you've been paying close attention to this chapter, you've already seen that it comes from the nature of the common law and from the problem of statutory interpretation. I can't teach you the answers; it takes three years of law school to even begin the process of learning what all the substantive law is, and even then you need the skills to predict how a new case should come out. I do know that it's a lot easier to play the game if you know where the answers come from and what constitutes a legitimate guess, right or wrong. But, in the end, you will need courage. Until and unless the basic Socratic classroom is restructured to allow students to take their time, to give them some safety net of self-esteem that will encourage them to guess, even if they're wrong, it's going to be a hard game for women, at least as they describe themselves to Lani Guinier. Once you know the game, the source of answers, and the broad scope of reasonable guesses, take your courage and jump in. Even though the cases don't tell you clearly what the court will do next, most of the questions you're being asked have answers, even if the answers are only estimates of the probability that the answer will be a certain way. After we've exhausted the clues in the previous opinions, where should we look for more answers?

ASK YOUR MOTHER

The last time you asked Mother for advice she probably told you never to wear white shoes after Labor Day.

But asking Mother is not as farfetched as it sounds. She's usually giving you her common sense and experience of life, and white

shoes do look silly and would get dirty pretty quickly in a northern winter. In the first-year law class, too, you should look for answers from ordinary common sense and experience of life in
our particular twentieth-century Western culture. In the dorm-
dwelling sixteen-year-old case, our common sense and experience
of life and culture tell us that occasionally people under eighteen
go to college, and just because you find yourself in a place where
older folks reside doesn't make you responsible to tell everyone
who comes along that you're an out-of-place prodigy.

The earlier decision said eighteen, and we presume the reason
the judge picked eighteen is that the judge wanted the defendant
to be as clever as a normal eighteen-year-old to hold him to a
contract. The defendant's strategic misleading of the plaintiff in
the second case makes it possible—and just—to stick him with
the consequences of his obvious mental cleverness. However,
if the standard is that each contracting party must be as competent
as the average eighteen-year-old to understand the consequences
of making a promise in every case, and if, as we know, mental and
chronological ages don't coincide perfectly, we might conclude
that any defendant in a contract case would have to be evaluated
psychologically to see if he had a normal eighteen-year-old capacity to act strategically in his own behalf when contracting. This
is not a stupid rule; we wouldn't try to enforce a contract against
a dog or a two-year-old.

However, if we adopt this rule, the chronological element
would be written out of the law of contracts in this particular jurisdiction, and the first case reference to the age of eighteen
would be rendered meaningless. Similar arguments could be applied to any chronological rule—drinking, driving, serving in
the Armed Services. At this point, a Socratic teacher's game is to
try to force a student to see the weakness in the individual cleverness rule we've just devised by "taking the other side," asking
whether we should test everyone in the country for clever self-
protectiveness before we sell them a beer regardless of what age
they are.

In pursuing this line of questioning, the teacher is trying to force the student to figure out the value of hard-edged objective rules, like chronological age rules, despite the fact that they might work injustice in marginal cases like the strategically misleading sixteen-year-old or, for that matter, the immature eighteen-year-old. As an experienced lawyer and law professor, I know that a good answer to this line of question goes as follows: "We must preserve the chronological test of physical age, because such rules protect people who are mostly too young to tie up with contracts, while allowing commerce to go forward without testing people mostly old enough to tie themselves to contract. This interest is so powerful that the system will not allow you to legally sell stereos to a range of mature sixteen-year-olds but will allow you to sell stereos to a pretty dopey eighteen-year-old. We should make exceptions only in cases of severe injustice, like the sixteen-year-old who showed the merchant an ID he had forged presenting himself as eighteen."

As we will see below, these commitments—to the linkage between competency and promising—are deeply rooted in modern Western political thought. After all, as we already learned, the common law doesn't come from God!

WHAT TO DO WHEN MOM'S NOT AROUND: READ THE LEGAL VERSION OF CLIFFS NOTES

You are unlikely to have these arguments at your fingertips the first few weeks or months of class, but there are other ways to find out what answers generally look like. You can read the commercial course outlines you can buy at the bookstore or the academic treatises on the subject of the day's lesson from the library. You can read the little snippets of cases, called note cases, at the end of the main cases in the casebook. For instance, after the contracts casebook gives you an edited version of the eighteen-year-old decision and the misleading sixteen-year-old decision, the notes will often refer to a case that turns out to be the dorm-dwelling sixteen-year-old case. Go to the library before class and get the note case out of the case reporters (they're all there) and read what the judge said he or she was doing in the dorm-dwelling sixteen-year-old case. That will give you time to think and take some of the element of surprise out of it. Of course, they won't tell you what to do when the professor presses you with the third question and the fourth question (about a home-dwelling sixteen-year-old seen on campus or a seventeen-year-old who shows the merchant a fake driver's license he carried for beer-purchasing purposes by mistake), but the note case may indicate what general problems that particular court thinks it has to address. Why do you think the note cases are there?

The problem is that you're overwhelmed with reading anyway, and one of the best ways to succeed at the first year is to engage in some triage—doing only what you must do and skimming the rest. We're going to review some techniques for figuring out what to do and what to skim shortly. But if you want to go to some classes some of the time with some superior sense of what the answers are, the treatises, outlines, and note cases will point the way.

IF MOM'S NOT HOME, ASK SOCRATES, ARISTOTLE, KANT, BENTHAM, OR CAROL GILLIGAN

Finally, when all else fails, there's Socrates himself, by which I mean one of the many diverse strands in the 2,500-year span of Western philosophy. We saw that one answer to the contracts problem was the assumption that the clever sixteen-year-old has enough capacity to be held to his promises. Now that we've discussed it, this assumption should seem fairly obvious.

But this assumption that responsibility requires capacity is not a fact of nature like the law of gravity: It's the product of a certain set of social, political, and philosophical beliefs. Even Mom only "knew" it because she's a product of the same Western culture as the legal system. But the current thinking is hardly the only way of thinking. There are many issues that can be resolved in different legitimate ways, regardless of the path the law chooses. The idea that responsibility = capacity is a concept of Western moral theory, largely rooted in the work of eighteenth-century German philosophy, although with some roots in ancient teachings. This philosophy was deeply contested almost from the moment of its emergence, and largely supplanted in the West by the later philosophy of utilitarianism, which emphasized consequences, rather than responsibility. If responsibility = capacity was the only touchstone, we would have to test everyone, not just people under eighteen. The argument for holding eighteen-year-olds responsible without investigating their cleverness is that everyone benefits from the smooth functioning of a market economy, which will produce more stuff if sales and purchases can be executed with a minimum of fuss and investigation. This argument, which is not crazy, is a consequential argument, justified because it achieves the good consequences of an efficient market, which, hopefully, makes everyone a little richer.

Even in the century or so that there have been law schools in America, there have been no fewer than six separate schools of thought providing answers to questions like why we hold people to their contracts: that the law has always said so, that it's just because people bound themselves freely, that the productive economy needs reliable contracts, that it's disrespectful to make false promises, that promising is a social practice required in a society in which people live in diverse and far-flung communities, that we should try to mediate between the two promisors rather than hold them strictly to their word. Indeed, each of these historic schools of legal thought has its adherents in the present-day law school. The amazing thing is that with very few exceptions, each school of thought did and does claim to be the only rational one and often each school claims to be the only "natural" one.

Part of the reason law professors defend each separate monolithic system of legal reasoning is that so few of them are educated in the other disciplines from which answers about the law, just like answers about any aspect of the human condition, come from. If they were educated, they would know that all of their answers have roots somewhere in the larger society and they would know that each of these "natural" and monolithic schools of thought has been challenged and superseded, however briefly, over the centuries of Western thought.

Why does the existence of historically conflicting debatable schools of thought matter to a terrified female first-year student? If responsibility = capacity is the only answer human reason could produce, any other answer you suggest is not just wrong, it's irrational or insane. Professors Suzanna Sherry and Daniel Farber of the Minnesota Law School have published a book recently, *Beyond All Reason*, suggesting that feminist and gay and critical race scholars who challenge the dominant way of teaching and thinking about law to include perspectives like Carol Gilligan's relationalism, or who point out that most systems of thought are products of a particular historic time, are "beyond all reason." No wonder women are so fearful of suggesting answers that turn out to be wrong!

What, Me Worry?

The opinions in the prior cases. The note cases, treatises, and commercial outlines. Mom. Socrates and the other schools of philosophical thought. There's enough answer material there for a lifetime. Now that you know that there is often more than one answer and where the answers come from, I'm going to give you a list of techniques to use to overcome any residual hesitation at games in general.

Being an old law professor, let me play the devil's advocate for a moment. One school of thought has it that the lack of female class participation isn't a problem. After all, first-year grades don't usually depend on class participation, but are based on the end of term examination. The guy who was first in my class at Chicago years ago never opened his mouth the first year (or any year).

There are two problems with this answer. First, as Fordham's S. said, "Speaking in class gives you confidence; not speaking loses confidence," and the price of losing confidence is paid "in job interviews" and "in approaching the exam." Our bashful UCLA first year confessed, "Once I got up the courage to ask questions I felt better and my grades went way, way up." J.: "I get more out of my classes because I'm willing to engage in the process." Second, as I've just described, the class experience is designed to teach you something that matters: what the concerns are that will drive a judge to decide a previously undecided case under the common law system. In the words of the inimitable Clara Counselor, "Class participation is like sprinting every day when you're preparing for a twenty-six-mile marathon."

There's another good reason that creeping away from the Socratic class costs women: They don't get to know their professors and they don't get the really good recommendations from them. This is particularly a problem for women at the top of their class or at top law schools, because the next step from law school is a prestigious clerkship, and the professors can open or slam that door for you. Unless you join up in the Federalist Society and win a clerkship based on your political familiarity to the conservative judges, you've got to do it on brains alone.

Several of the women I interviewed had judicial clerkships, and all agreed that letters were the most important, that to get them you had to talk in class and talk to the inaccessible professors. At least one of them, a second-year student at Georgetown, had gotten a good grade on the anonymous exam, but had been refused a letter because the professor did not know her from talking in class and visiting in the office afterward. A student from NYU told a similar story: "I wanted to clerk and didn't know how important it was to my career and therefore I should meet my first-year professors. I didn't realize how connection-oriented things were and how I'd need recommendations. When I came to apply for clerkships, I only knew [a lawyering professor]. My other professors pick names out of a section for recommendations, and a professor I thought should write me a recommendation very much made me feel I was not worthy [even though I got an] A–, [my] best first-year grade." Remember Michele's struggle to get a good letter?

Compare NYU's experiences with Clara Counselor: "I've enjoyed classes and participating and I got good thorough and personal recommendations. Career services advised us to ask professors directly for letters of recommendation and *because of my participation,* I have a good close relationship with my professors.

One [male professor] is like a personal friend and then I did a research project with another professor (a female). I ended up with three good recommendations and I'm interviewing with [several federal appellate judges]." About a month after I interviewed her, Clara called to tell me she'd landed a prime clerkship post. If your teachers don't know you, or if you're only one of a dozen A students they've seen, they can't—and if they're honest, they won't—recommend you *in a way that will get you the job.*

How to Succeed in the First-Year Classroom Dialogue

My interviewees offered several strategies.

1. Just do it.

Fordham's A. advises you to suck it up and deal: "Speak in class! Women tend to be more oblique. If you're going to do anything, bite back. [It] helps to read the material and be prepared. JUST DO IT." As we have seen, there are only a few overarching belief systems that provide the legal system with its answers. All you have to do is figure out how they apply in the particular situation you're trying to analyze in class and suggest the answer.

2. See the professors after class.

Some of my interviewees told themselves they felt "like I got more out of one-on-one with a professor." You can ask questions or pursue points after class or in the office. This is certainly better than nothing. (Of course, you're not going to be the only one pursuing this strategy. As Ms. Public Interest says, "I've been cut in front of when trying to talk to a professor after class; interruptions happen all the time.") Many professors now take and respond to E-mail questions, although the "connections" still seem to rest on some more primitive forms of bonding.

3. Pick your spots.

Ms. Editor advises asking upper-class students about the professors and trying to avoid the ones that will leave "scars." Ms. Rights reports the fruits of that strategy: "I'm really affected teacherwise. Crim law with [Mary Lou] Fellows [provides] a good teacher and good subject matter. Here [I] can talk more freely and I'm not inhibited. She's very open and she lets everybody talk. In that class, our opinions count more." Rights compares her criminal law class to "con[stitutional] law, where it's very arbitrary and all made up. The professor lectures a lot and he's very intimidating. It's tough to raise your hand, because you answer and then he's in your face. He's very smart but he just can't . . . And he's just going to make you look bad." Perhaps coincidentally, another Minnesota woman picked the same teacher as her negative example: "Con law was interesting in the beginning, because I had never taken an American history class and it was the foundation of our system. But when we got into the commerce clause. . . . I got a B and I was happy, because I really didn't understand what was going on." By contrast, "In torts, like criminal law, we could speak our minds."

Lani Guinier always makes the point that an abusive teaching system hurts men as well as women, so I asked my Minnesota women how the "gunners" acted in con law, and one said some men spoke less in con law as well. "In con law we're so terrified he's going to make us look bad in front of the other students." When asked how, considering the shared level of fear, the professor achieved this undesirable state of affairs, she described a relatively mainstream Socratic experience: "He'll take the other side and you have to say something about what he just said." By now, you should recognize this process, because I gave you an example of this technique when I described the contracts case above. To repeat, in teaching the cases about competency to contract, a professor expects a student to propose that the case may mean each contracting party must be examined for mental fitness separately. The teacher shows the student that they must always test the validity of their position by posing hypotheticals from the "other side," like how such a system would make it impossible to sell beer. Thus, the dreaded con law teacher at Minnesota is acting right in the mainstream of law teaching in "taking the other side" and asking you "to say something about what he just said." What could be going wrong?

One of my UCLA interviewees spent her first year at the University of California at Berkeley's Boalt Hall School of Law, which she described as a place where "law is taught by people who think it's a hazing ritual to teach," and she and a lot of the women at UCLA had picked up the fact that torture is not a necessary aspect of teaching law. Here's one of her UCLA classmates: "I was a law and public policy major and I was used to law courses [where] they just throw you in," concluding that her undergraduate experience had not taught her to be silent or afraid. It is true that the external understandings that supply the students with the answers in con law have a lot to do specifically with American history and politics, which is hard for students to dream up unless they've had some college classes in American constitutional history. However, a good teacher should be able to help them through this process even in con law without terrifying the students, by asking them to address small problems at the edges of their positions or even coaching them a little bit as they start to think along the right lines.

Minnesota actually unwittingly told me where her con law teacher went astray. "He makes you feel you should be able to get it like [snaps fingers]." Another interviewee made a similar point about another school: "One professor will let the men go on and on but he'll cut me off. I need a second or two to gather my thoughts, but I have to raise my hand before I'm ready." But, another added, "the longer you wait, the more you think you have to be precise." A law student with a master's degree described her experience by detailing the difference between law school and graduate school: "[In grad school], if you raise your hand, it's over. Here they keep coming back to you until they get you to a question that you can't answer . . . even if it takes them five questions, they are going to leave you feeling like a piece of shit."

So it's not the questions. Don't be afraid of the questions. It's the lack of "openness." It's not letting the students feel that their "opinions count." It's the failure to recognize that dragging some sort of answer from the ether, when the answers are not in the reading, takes most people some time. It's asking the fifth question in a way that makes the student feel like a piece of shit, instead of letting them know they're great for having made four successful moves in a very tough game.

One solution is to stay away from the teachers who do these things, rather than adopting an across-the-board policy of silence. Although you can't pick your first-year teachers, the usual mixture of four courses will turn up some people like the con law teacher, but also some Mary Lou Fellowses. Practice your speaking skills with them.

4. Make alliances.

Many of the students I interviewed recommended working with other students throughout the first year or at the end near finals. A good example comes from the University of Arizona and involves the outlines of the law that students produce for themselves as study aids. (More about outlines in chapter 7, "Studying for Class and Taking Exams.) The Arizona women knew that the first-year men networked with the older students and got their outlines, and the women did not. So they started their own women's caucus, open to everyone, to change the outline exchange system. Pretty soon, the open outline exchange replaced the covert one. An ASU student participated in a tutoring program for disadvantaged students and said she thought there were ways to learn how to succeed in the first year, and she wished she had learned them.

As we will see in chapter 8 ("Making Law Review"), nothing works as well as a success network. Share notes to save each other time, study together, using the case notes to throw hypotheticals like the dorm-dwelling sixteen-year-old example at one another, go over old exams together. If you are fearful of speaking in class, have your study group run a model class once a week. Let one person play teacher (you never learn anything as thoroughly as you do in preparing to teach it) and grill the other study group members as hard as you can. The Mills College conference on Women and Legal Education turned up a simple technique for circumventing an abusive teacher who wouldn't let female students finish their sentences or ask follow-up questions in class. Get one buddy, then have them raise their hand after you've been ignored or cut off and say, "I was wondering what Linda had to say. Could she tell us what she was about to say?" or "I think Linda was going to ask a question I've been wondering about, too. What was it you were asking, Linda?" The coeditors of the *University of Chicago Law Review* in 1998-99 are two women best friends. When interviewed, they said their friendship was the most important factor in getting them through law school.

If your school has an academic support program, visit it early in the first semester and get all the tips about different ways to learn: orally, written, alone, in concert, by doing, by reading. Then, if you feel one way is not working for you, you can try other paths before you pay the price with less good first-year grades.

5. Just don't do it.

Some of my California group recommended bypassing the law school procedure altogether. "Don't think about the law," one recommended, "just memorize the doctrine from hornbooks [premade treatises] and [the commercial] Emmanuel law outline." Others heavily recommended that you "make sure you have a life out of law school, like extracurricular activities." J.: "Make sure law school is not your whole life. Take weekends off." L.: "Give yourself rewards."

These sound like ways of numbing yourself while you pass through a painful experience you don't understand. I vastly prefer to have you understand what's going on, be able to do it for what it's worth, and recognize the bullshit and especially the stuff that's designed to hit a female target, like the "kiss-ass or stupid" dichotomy or the "how fast can you think with a hundred pairs of eyes trained on you." Take a deep breath, take your time, don't be afraid to express your thinking as it evolves around the problem the professor has just posed, and don't be afraid to be wrong. Winston Churchill was dismissed from the British government several times before he saved the Western world from the Nazis.

6. Seek out women professors.

One Minnesota student suggested, "The women professors try to help you participate: 'That's right, you're on the right track.' They take what you give them and do something with it instead of squashing it." The numbers show that, statistically speaking, women are more likely to do well in schools with a larger number of women faculty. The correlation is not exact, and there are many causal explanations. Barbara Black, the former Columbia dean, who brought many feminist theorists to that prestigious law school, thinks there is a role for women in the classroom: "I believe that it's very important to have women in the classroom. The One Ls [first-year law students] have at least one woman teacher. Women in the classroom affect both the men and the women."

In my interviews, the strategy of seeking out female professors got mixed reviews. A student from Arizona State complained that "the woman who taught feminist law was always running to a plane and didn't have time to talk to me, either." The Minnesota group uniformly rejected the idea that *any* woman professor, regardless of politics, was better than none, and it is a fact that one of their women faculty, Suzanna Sherry, has been a vociferous defender of the existing law school system and method on the grounds that "there are unrepentant bigots everywhere, and [no one has shown] the legal profession has any more than its share." Fordham's female professor Maxine ("Marc") Arkin was quoted a year ago in an article in a story about how the evolving persecution complex in many female students can make teaching difficult, asserting, "If you call on them, you're imposing hierarchy; if you don't call on them, you're overlooking them. Either way, they're upset."

So unless faculty are in the habit of talking to reporters, it's hard to know whether they'll be a better bet for female students just because they themselves are female. Arkin certainly wasn't eager to share her views for this guidebook. When I called her at Fordham to ask her to expand on her position regarding women law students, she at first denied she had said any such thing, and then, when I quoted the title and date of the article in the *City Journal*, she responded, "I won't expand on what I said. I had an off-the-record conversation with [author and conservative think tank member] Heather MacDonald, and I'm furious with her for quoting me. I won't confirm or deny that I said anything." "You won't confirm that you said what she quotes you as saying?" I asked. "No," she replied, "and if you quote me, I'll deny ever having this telephone conversation." "You'll deny having the telephone conversation we're having right now?" I asked. "Yes," she replied, "and I'm going to hang up on you now. Thank you for calling my attention to the fact that I've been quoted by Heather MacDonald."

Despite the presence of unsympathetic women, however, many of the women felt that having women faculty was more important for forcing their male classmates to confront a woman in power than for its direct effect on the female students. As Ms. Interest said, "I think there should be more women faculty, because the men need to see more women in authority, more than women law students."

Students and faculty alike report that a lot of male students and even some female students treat their female professors differently, especially if they try to break the mold of the strict Socratic dialogue leading to resolution of uncertainty in future cases. "I had two women professors the first year; one led a small discussion-oriented class with no memorization and the students were constantly going to her office and complaining. They can't live with uncertainty. The other woman professor was very pedagogically conservative." Regardless of gender, "If the teacher lacks authority or seems uncertain, the students hate it and it falls heavier on the women teachers."

Mary Lou Fellows believes that "the existence of a significant number of women faculty makes no difference at all. . . . There is a struggle to get each section of the first-year class to have *one* woman teacher and there is no question that that lack has a dramatic effect on both women and men students who feel completely free to challenge everything. It's a very hostile class. When you're trying to teach them critical thinking, what passes at Minnesota Law School for critical thinking is the notion of law as an autonomous discipline with a narrow range of answers." By identifying the damage done by limiting the range of legitimate answers, Fellows is a living rebuttal of the argument that having a woman teacher makes no difference. Remember how liberating it was to realize that even a wrong answer to the underage contract case is not crazy?

7. Know that law is not an autonomous discipline.

In looking at the competency = responsibility problem of the contracts case, we've seen that law is not an "autonomous discipline" but the product of historical, philosophical, and social forces at any given time. The "law as an autonomous discipline" crowd try to take the current set of answers these forces have embedded in the law and make them the universal rational answers to any question a legal system may ask. This may sound like an obscure academic debate that has nothing to do with your desire to get your degree and start representing the Widget Company as a $90,000-a-year associate at a big secure law firm. It doesn't even sound like something Legal Aid lawyers need to know. Maybe it's a dumb idea, but it's not obvious that this should be any harder on women than on male law students.

In fact, if you care about getting through the first year of law school with your ego intact, you'd better listen up. The notion of law as an autonomous discipline is one of the most dangerous barriers to women succeeding in law school. Remember Fordham's tough-minded African American student I call T., who compared law school to a Klan meeting? Insofar as women have concerns that are different from men's concerns, the centuries-old mixture of philosophy and history that actually provides the content of American law often doesn't recognize women's concerns. Rape is just misunderstanding no for yes; marital agreements are just like contracts to buy widgets; laws against sexual harassment interfere with the perfect market. The participants in the Mills College conference on legal education recommended time and again that materials outside law be brought into the curriculum—film, literature. I'm guessing that the pressure for outside materials would be a lot less if the ordinary case law had been built up by a society that recognized women as people and citizens with just claims to be treated properly by their cultures.

This is not the fault of the dead white males who missed

women's humanity for centuries. Women are latecomers. The fault lies in circling the wagons of "right" answers derived from the historical, philosophical, and social theories of the past just at the moment before women started making claims and then calling the resulting discipline "autonomous" or "reason" or "natural."

The students at Minnesota—and at the University of Chicago, too, as it happens—reported that when the teacher tried to dig beneath the details of application of the law as a freestanding natural system to show the role of rape law in redressing the natural physical inequality between males and females, the students clamored for "black letter law" and characterized the discussions of underlying theory as "irrelevant" to their ambitions to become attorneys for Widgets, Inc. This refusal to look at what larger purpose the law serves, rather than just what the rules are, is interestingly strange, because legal education is filled with such theory. We resort to assumptions about human values and behavior every time we confront a common law case—to reprise our earlier discussion, how else do we know why we don't tag a sixteen-year-old with responsibility for his contracts? We discuss issues of political and economic importance when we decide what we think about tort reform or the flat tax or the exclusion of confessions coerced by the police or the problem of antidemocratic constitutions.

So it can't be that the theory of what the law of rape can legitimately prohibit is different from the theory of tort reform just because it's theory. The difference between discussions of rape theory and discussions of tort theory is that in most law school classrooms, the interests of the middle class or aspiring middle-class propertied law students are in most areas of law essentially the same regardless of gender. No one wants to be murdered, and no one with any property wants to be robbed or have their contracts broken, etc. However, women being on the whole smaller, physically weaker, and vulnerable to rape and vulnerable in childbirth and nursing, as well as socially poorer and less powerful, also have many interests in the legal system that are different from men's. When it comes to the law of rape, then, the unadorned self-interest of the males and females are not the same. They are different. *Not only are they different, they're in conflict.*

The generic male, whether he is inclined to rape or not, as most men are not, has little interest in a very protective law of rape and an interest in a narrow law that doesn't reach ambiguous cases like the drunks. The generic female, whether she will ever be a rape victim or not, and most are not, has an interest in living in a world where rape is highly restrained and where the marginal actors are punished to protect against hard-core wrongdoing.

Worse, still, the handful of "legitimate" theories the law school establishment allows seems to justify women's exclusion from the benefits of the law on "autonomous," "natural," and "rational" grounds. On the subject of rape, for example, a lot of traditional Western political theory that created the various legal doctrines would have it that the natural order of things is that people have as much range of action as they wish. In systems that privilege individual free action, the burden of proof is always on the side of those who try to stop an individual from doing what he wants to do. If this is the natural order, then only the most compelling reasons or only fully consensual transactions, like written contracts they sign of their own free will, can justify restraining anyone from doing anything he wants to. (This is why ensuring capacity to contract is so important to justify enforcement in our contract example.)

In rape law, this would mean that only the use of levels of force that threaten the whole social order would violate the norms of freedom for the strong and only a resounding "NO!" can justify a woman in invoking the criminal law against a sexual attacker. Otherwise, free action by the strong is unjustifiably restrained. Under this strict standard, silence is considered nonresistance, so silence means yes. More important, for our purposes, the Antioch College rules construing silence as resistance and requiring an explicit consent to sex (silence means no) are not just bad policy, they're irrational and a fit subject for mockery.

Similarly, the theoretical tilt toward free action has it that "Better ten thousand guilty men go free than one innocent one be wrongfully convicted." If this is the natural order, then only the highest standards of proof can convict a rapist. Rape shield laws directed at enabling a sexually active woman to successfully pursue a rape charge by excluding evidence of her other, desired sexual experiences are violations of the core values of a free society and the natural order. Likewise, the admissibility of prior rapes, which are designed to make it easier to prove rape, violate core political norms favoring the defendant. Here's what happens when these assumptions meet the subject of rape. Ms. Rights: "We had a very intense class in rape with Professor Fellows . . . it was mainstream dominant men versus nonmainstream dominant view." LH: "What is the mainstream dominant view these days?" Rights: "Why should a male be burdened with proving that it isn't rape? Why should a male have to restrain himself?"

The male students in Fellows's class, Rights reported, just kept coming up with ever more fanciful hypotheticals to prove that the standard of requiring men to restrain themselves was silly and unworkable. "What if he was drunk?" "What if they were both drunk?" "What if she were a two hundred pound lady wrestler?" And so on.

The first thing to note here is that there will always be hard cases at the margins of any rule. We saw that with our age and contract example. The students were really arguing about whether the rule should be drawn closer to the men's interests in free action or closer to the women's interest in security.

Now there are answers to why a people should have to restrain themselves, even in marginal cases. For one thing, it is the function of the law to cause people to restrain themselves. We continue to rein in the strong with laws against murder, because no one wants to live in a world where they're afraid to go to sleep. In other words, if anything is irrational in a legal class, the presumption of free action by the strong is irrational! These insights were adequate to support the laws against murder, before women came to the legal system with their particular claims for protection, such as for protection against rape.

The reason these age-old insights seem so remote to a discussion of rape is that men are fundamentally not afraid of women when it comes to rape. So some other reason to rein in the strong besides the universal fear of murder must come into play. Indeed, the skepticism about "restraining yourself" if you're not afraid of the other person would actually argue against any prohibition on rape at all. For centuries, the prohibitions against rape were justified on the same grounds as murder—to avoid provoking the fury and retribution not of weak women but of the men whose females had been violated and whose children's legitimacy had been called into question. Once women began to be considered independent of their fathers' and husbands' interest in their virginity, however, that reason disappeared. Some theory relating to respect for the personhood of the individual female had to be found if the rape law, which manifestly reins in the free action of the strong, was to continue to be justified. The presumption that only free action is legitimate makes that a hard task. If such a presumption is natural, or if it is the only rational assumption in a world of freestanding legal doctrine, there is no justification for anything but the most minimal prohibition of rape.

But contrary to the assumption of law as an autonomous discipline, there are lots of justifications for a protective rape law. Just to cite four strands of theory, treating some people with concern and respect regardless of their physical strength has roots all the way back to Socrates, who made a pretty convincing argument that it was better for the soul to suffer evil than to do evil. Ancient Judaism used men's responsibility not to rape their wives as a measure of their entitlement to God's mercy. Treating all other people as if they were entitled to concern and respect by virtue of their personhood goes back at least to early Christianity and is a big part of the reason we require someone's capable consent before we hold him to a contract. In terms of consequences, one can argue that the pain caused by an unwanted sexual act exceeds the pain of the lost opportunity for a sex act that a rigorous rape law discourages.

A protective rape law, like the one Mary Lou Fellows's crim law class was discussing, invokes these theories about justice and personhood to draw the line closer to the claims of the weak. Maybe there are reasons to resist the development of protective rape law. But those reasons do not occupy the whole world of reason. Every argument for a protective rape law is not "against all reason." It's sad to think that in a law school classroom the argument that the strong must restrain themselves because the weak are human persons, too, would be "out of the mainstream." But, as Fordham's T. reminds us, "Women are newcomers to the legal profession."

There are similar answers to why it may not be better to let ten thousand guilty men go free, etc. But the students in Professor Fellows's criminal law class didn't want to discuss the underlying theory. All they wanted to do was show that any ambitiously protective law of rape was ridiculous because it was inconsistent with the received wisdom about free action and the fear of the state. It's sad to think that in a legal classroom, of all places, the assumptions of where the power lies are not allowed to be examined.

Every school I interviewed at reported some such flare-up over the subject of rape, which the women students experienced as horrifying. *The more demanding the law of rape is of male self-restraint, the more power is shifted from the stronger males to the weaker females.* It's scary for women to confront the fact that they are members of a group that needs something from the more powerful men in their world, namely, consent to sexual self-restraint. Women hate head-on confrontation with men, and no wonder. And it's galling for men raised to believe in the constitutive political sanctity of the right of the strong individual to be forced by a formally empowered female teacher to confront the claims of their weaker classmates. Even though they would never force themselves on an unwilling female, suddenly the sexual rights of the drunken frat boy look terribly important to them. And nothing makes the frat boy easier to defend than the assumption that his behavior is the only reasonable way to run a legal system.

You may not enjoy being confronted head-on with the desire of the stronger players in your world to act as they please when you encounter it in your law school education. But at least you know now that there's plenty of theory on your side. Even in law school.

8. "Tell students that often there is no answer" (UCLA).

Let's assume you've come to the answer that the lying sixteen-year-old can be held to his contract, but the dorm-dwelling sixteen-year-old cannot. You've guessed that dorm dwelling is innocent enough, so that the preference for hard-and-fast standards for capacity leaves the youngster without responsibility. The professor then asks you about a freshman who hangs out at an upper-class dorm when he knows the man who sells computers on credit is coming by or the youngster who doesn't say anything when the salesperson says, "I assume you're old enough to have a credit record." The purpose of this exercise should not be to make you look foolish. The purpose should be to teach you that at some point almost any legal line is going to be arbitrary. (This is also the answer to the more fanciful hypotheticals the students were pressing on Professor Fellows.) In philosophy, we ask, With the loss of which individual hair does a man "go bald"?, to illustrate that there are always going to be cases indistinguishable in principle at the edge of any rule. When you get that far down the questioning, it's legitimate to say just that. But notice that before you "yield" in that way, you've helped the teacher and the class sort out a lot of important things about contracting: that we require capacity, that chronological age is a marker but not a complete answer, that we prefer hard lines, that we're willing to make exceptions in cases of gross injustice. You're a star! Now say, "When does a man go bald?" and sit down.

Studying for Class and Taking Exams

As Men Have Always Known, Small Differences in Measurements Can Make Big Differences in Life

Like the first-year classes, which commingle teaching the substance of important bodies of law with the technique for making or resisting novel legal arguments, first-year exams test for the ability to identify the legal questions and recite the body of law you've learned, as well as to spot and argue about novel legal issues in an imaginary case. These skills are not unrelated to the business of being a lawyer. If you're going to advise people and argue on their behalf, you have to know if what they're doing is forbidden, permitted, or required in most of the areas where law applies at all. So you'll need to know the rules about crimes, injuries, agreements, wills, and all the rest. You'll need to know when their behavior invokes different applications of law, so you'll need to be able to see a contract problem or whatever in the story they tell you. After all, clients' stories rarely come in neatly labeled "tort problem" or "potential criminal liability." Finally, much of life is undecided by law, so you'll need to be able to predict what the law will do when your client's novel situation is before it.

This being said, legal problems rarely require lawyers to answer these hard questions in three hours after they are presented without ever being able to open a lawbook or consult with a more experienced colleague. So traditional law school exams only weirdly imitate life. Moreover, almost every law school requires its first-year teachers to grade on a curve. If you look at the grids for who gets into various law schools, you will see that all first-year law classes cluster at the middle on both grades and scores. So law schools take several hundred people whose grades and admissions test scores are almost identical to one another. For example, UCLA's 1996 admits were almost all between 160 and 169 on their LSATs and 3.5 and 3.75+ on their undergraduate grade point averages. Then the schools give them their first-year exams and they redistribute them according to their performance on the exam along a scale of A to D.

In separating you from the sources of answers and forcing most people to fail, it's no wonder the first year of law school feels like the societies we envisioned before there was a legal system. It sort of is a war of all against all. A Minnesota student who is also a trained accountant picked up the essential arbitrariness of law school life. "There's a scant difference between a twelve answer and a thirteen answer, but it makes a big difference [in your class rank]." The University of Chicago's Dean of Students made the same point to me in an interview: "The grading system by exact numbers exaggerates small differences." The difference between the sexes, according to Dean Crozen, however, is that "men are angry and think the professor was stupid. Women think *they're* stupid. *And they give up.*" Over a point difference.

But not all of them give up, and they're the ones you want to keep your eye on. The indomitable Ms. Daughter didn't give up: "I got mediocre grades the first year and [when] interviewing the second year they never got past the first-year GPA. [But thereafter] I ended up writing onto law review and being coordinating articles editor and getting amazing grades." Studies of women's success reflect Daughter's story; they conclude that women close the grade gap with men a lot in the second and third years. By the time Daughter graduated, she had beaten thousands of other law graduates for one of the most prestigious placements in the legal profession. As she put it, "Rapidity is rewarded and rapidity is a function of how much you need to unlearn." Many women, like Ms. Daughter, do better after three years than after one.

Here, too, first-year exams are harder than the actual act of practicing law. As you will see in chapter 9 ("Compared to Law School, Life Is Easy: How to Succeed at Firm Job Interviews"), even the fiercest law firms give people more of a chance to succeed than the first year does. In practice, lawyers assume that complex problems take time to analyze and express, that people work better in teams than alone, and that much of law practice is getting people to work out their problems rather than kill each other. Sure you have to work hard and give the impression that you're working hard, and make human connections that will enable you to bring business to what is an increasingly business-oriented profession. And your partners would rather pocket the profits than share them with each other or with their associates. But law firms have no structural investment in redistributing 80 percent of their associates to the bottom of the barrel, to "lick their psychic wounds." Ultimately, the more you rise, the more the firm benefits, and even the most rapacious firm has to reward its bottom sufficiently so the people won't quit and go to work for legal aid. The profession is replete with data on how hard it is for women to practice law, especially in firms, and do the domestic work (the "second shift") at home. But as a matter of purely practicing law, just as women do better after three years in law school than after one, women have the opportunity in the legal profession to do better after thirty years than after three.

Ms. Editor found a different way around the system than Ms. Daughter did, by emphasizing her strengths—writing and arguing: "I had a very strong education and good writing coming in, and I use writing as an alternative to speaking." She sought out seminars and courses with papers as often as possible. First year success is almost always determined on the basis of formal exams, however. When asked how she did on her exams, she repeated,

"[A]gain, writing ability; I don't know how to score on tests." But while writing ability is hard to learn, if you don't already have it in plentiful supply, there are ways to score well on tests. Remember all the techniques you learned from the Princeton and Kaplan people for scoring on the Law School Admission Test? Studies have shown that the LSAT predicts nothing as well as it predicts success in the narrow world of closed-book exams in common law classes the first year in law school. So it stands to reason that there are methods for raising your scores on those exams, too. Fortuitously, some of the ways of doing well on the exams also serve you during the first-year class preparation.

The Material of the First-Year Class

The typical law school class will likely involve a casebook and some supplementary materials. More progressive teachers often have their students read material beyond the casebook to remind them that the cases come from the outside world. For example, for years I gave my civil procedure classes the story of the multi-party action following the terrible flood in the Appalachian town of Buffalo Creek as a way to put meat on the bones of appellate opinions about how cases are tried. There is a set of trial situation films in evidence class. My legal ethics class watched *The Verdict*, *A Few Good Men*, and some other courtroom dramas. But mostly you're going to be reading casebooks, collections of appellate opinions that, among them, describe an area of the law, and that include notes to point you to the other directions in which the law was or might be developing.

I was amazed as I went around the country interviewing at how inarticulate the students were about the all-important art of studying in the first year. When asked how they had succeeded, for example, no one in my group of Arizona interviewees had much of an answer. An older woman from the University of Arizona said, "I just put my buns on this chair and sat there. I never dreamed it would be so hard or that they would care so much about tiny differences. My husband never saw me and my kids had to study in the same room with me and leave messages on my answering machine. At the end of the first year, he [the husband] said he hoped the second and third years would be easier." (They are.) The Arizona woman wasn't wrong about how time-consuming it is. If you do as I say below and brief the cases and go back and annotate them with your class notes and do the reading for the next class and so on, you are not going to have much time for regular manicures or barhopping.

It turns out that study styles and reporting differ depending on the area of the country. Almost without exception, the University of Arizona students reported that despite the seriousness of the older students, among most students there was an overt contest for who studied less, the "didn't break a sweat" school of one-upmanship. And remember the Arizona State students reciting "P = JD" for passing means you're a lawyer. But a Georgetown student reported the opposite: In her school, the guys boasted about hours of booking it, perhaps, she speculated, in anticipation of the norms of the workplace where hours billed are a big part of success and esteem. One woman—an extremely self-confident and very expensively dressed woman from the University of Arizona—volunteered that she thought the top students in her class were guys, that indeed they studied all the time (failing the no-sweat contest), and were geeks and nerds. Although they got first interviews at the firms, she reported, they "never" got invited back. Her theory was that women were "more well rounded" and "had other interests" so they made more pleasant interviews and were seen as business getters, which mattered more in their eyes. So she got a good job, even though she didn't have top grades.

I suggested that maybe the guys had the right ideas—study all the time, impress the professors, get good clerkships, and work in New York for $100,000 a year rather than get jobs in Phoenix based on charm. (By the way, the people from the hiring offices at a couple of Phoenix law firms vehemently disagreed with Miss Congeniality. They said that you had to do really well in law school to get jobs—even summer jobs—with their firms.) The University of Arizona woman just looked blank, but the woman from Georgetown picked my description right up, and said that was the guy strategy at Georgetown for sure.

So maybe there might be different styles of successful law student behavior in different parts of the country. Certainly, my interviewees Carol Counselor, Ivy League Law Review, Ms. Too Good for Harvard, Midwestern Law Review, and Ms. Fordham Law Review, all chose not to rely on charm. Instead, they chose to "go to class and . . . participate," "work very hard your first year," and "use [study guides] throughout the semester and not just at the end. Read the case, then read the study guide, big picture as you go."

If you decide not to rest on your "well-roundedness," there are three steps to learning the law first year. Almost all my successful women followed this routine, and although it will come to seem obvious, you're a lot better off knowing the routine in advance. One, make summaries of the cases, called "briefs," from the reading. Second, start to develop an outline of the substance of the law as it emerges as you come to the end of each section of the casebook. Third, join and stay in a study group, especially at the end.

Briefing the Cases for Class

David Hricik, a practicing lawyer and legal writing teacher in Houston, whose book I have recommended for the dreaded first year, sets out the two purposes of case briefs: "(a) I never had to reread the case again, and (b) if I were called on in class I could answer likely questions without having to pour [sic] over the case." As you can see from this statement, briefing the cases is instrumental to these two completely respectable goals: learning the law well with the minimum of effort and not looking like a fool in front of your peers.

The brief should look something like this:

(1) Case title: say, *Brown* (plaintiff) *v. Board of Education of Topeka, Kansas* (defendant), United States Supreme Court, 1954.

(2) Facts: say, Topeka maintained two separate public school systems, one for black students and one for white ones, but they were (arguably) equally well funded and maintained.

(3) Law: The Fourteenth Amendment to the U.S. Constitution prohibits the states to "deny to any person the equal protection of the laws."

(4) Hard issue the teacher is likely to be interested in and why it's hard: Do separate, but equal, school systems violate the Constitution? This is a hard question, because the only technical argument for inequality is that separation is inherently unequal and the connection between pure separation and inequality is hotly contested; for this reason, old precedent approved the constitutionality of racially separate but equal facilities.

(5) Holding: The Topeka school system is unconstitutional.

(6) Opinion: Separate is inherently unequal. Among other things, segregation hurts the self-esteem of the people from the excluded group, which was historically on the bottom of the social structure.

(7) Dissent: none.

Hricik recommends the admirable practice of typing in class notes regarding what was said in class about this case, figuring that's what the teacher is likely to care about on the exam, and he's usually correct. At the University of Chicago in the sixties, we learned that *Brown* was an inferior decision made by an overreaching court that had no intellectual pride in its work, and that any politically "neutral" interpretation of the Constitution would conclude that equal is equal, regardless of the history of slavery and racial caste, and segregated schools are fine.

As nauseating as that opinion was (even in 1967, when I first encountered it), at least typing the class notes alongside the brief of *Brown* would alert me to the fact that the teacher would be looking for a problem in the source of inequality in a similar case on the exam. For instance, an exam question might ask what if the school segregation were an unintentional by-product of housing patterns? By noting the teacher's opinion that *Brown* rested on a very fragile interpretation of constitutional "equality," I would know the teacher would be looking for me to spot how easily *Brown* could be limited in its scope. On the exam, I might argue that if humiliation were the source of the low self-esteem, which was in turn the source of the inequality, the Constitution might not forbid segregation, absent the humiliating factor of the city deliberately setting up "white" schools from which black students were excluded.

As to avoiding humiliation in class, the bold form of who's the plaintiff and who's the defendant, etc., is designed to get you through the first part of the so-called "Socratic" ritual with which you are now familiar, in which the teacher asks you to tell the class what the case is about. Just use large-size typeface and print each case brief on a separate sheet of paper, stack them in your notebook and turn to the one the teacher is asking about.

What the briefs won't do is help you answer the real Socratic question, such as whether the unintentionally segregating school district violated the Constitution. For that, you'd need to know whether you thought the Constitution could be invoked to dismantle a society-wide system of racial caste with its roots in chattel slavery, or whether it just does the minimum to avoid the unseemliness of the intentional "whites only" high school. As I said in chapter 6, the only hint you have that this is the direction of the class discussion is in the language of the case itself, the contents of the note cases following the main case, and your newly acquired familiarity with the basic philosophical premises underlying the legal system described in chapter 6.

By the time you're done with the reading and briefing of all the cases for any section, you've got the raw material for an outline. I'd add a P. S. after the briefs for a whole section of the casebook for the note cases, noting very quickly the issues they raise, as follows: "Note cases [if they do] raise issues of unintentional school segregation, segregation outside the school context, and private school segregation." These follow-up issues are a natural for the exam, and, as I said, if you note them—or even read a few—before class they may help you anticipate what the teacher is going to ask.

Making the Outline

The strange thing about studying for the first year is that essentially you re-create the common law in the areas of the first-year courses. Using your case briefs and following generally the pattern in which each course has unfolded, you will create a little treatise on, say, torts. But you won't just write about torts. If you were to do that, you might just as well buy the canned commercial outlines that are available in the bookstores everywhere or borrow a relatively up-to-date treatise or restatement of the law of torts from the library. You are going to write about your teacher's versions of the law of torts, contracts, etc. Thus, your first-year outline at Minnesota, for example, would consist of Fellows on Criminal Law (which is not a common law course technically), at Wisconsin you would outline Larson on Property, at Chicago you might have Richard Epstein on Torts. Once upon a time somewhere you would have had Hirshman on Civil Procedure.

If you look at your casebook, you will see that after some sort of introduction, the book includes a series of cases for each of the elements of the area of the law in question. In torts, the casebook might have sections on liability, special duties, causation, damages, defenses like contributory and comparative negligence, collective, or enterprise, liability and insurance. These mean, in English, how bad you have to act before the harm you do gets redistributed from the victim back to you (liability), do we owe special duties to anyone or is tort law to regulate everyone's conduct regarding everyone (duty), how close does your dumb act have to be to the harm (causation), how do we measure the harm (damages), was the victim a dope, too (contributory or comparative negligence), and were you a member of the tobacco industry (enterprise liability)? (I don't have to teach you torts, and it's a good thing, too.

This is just a rough example to teach you the lesson I am interested in—how to score on your first-year exams.)

As you brief your way through the cases and notes that comprise each section, rules of law will emerge. In one first-year torts class at Columbia, the teacher taught the students torts in the following way. First, he introduced them to the idea that you should be responsible for your negligent acts. This is interesting, because it teaches the students that the idea that anyone should be responsible for damaging a victim is not a law of nature, after all. Maybe the victim just has bad luck and they have to live with it. After all, every time you drive, you put someone in danger. A big question in this part of the course on torts is whether we will hold you responsible whenever you drive, when you drive without your glasses, when you drive on a rainy day, or only when you speed. Then the casebook covered the competing theories of standards of care—for example, before the legal system shifts the victim's bad experience to the offender, how harmful does the conduct have to be, how likely and how expensive to take care against, what is the person like who makes these assessments, and how can it be proved?

Then he or she digressed to some relationships where the law of torts requires special levels of care or allows an unusual level of neglect. Such areas of increased or decreased liability include obligations not as obvious as the obligation to drive carefully, which every driver owes everyone. They include the obligation to control others—for example, whether doctors are liable when the nut cases they're treating actually do kill their wives, or the duties of landowners, and the emerging issue of causation of emotional injury. Next, the course covered causation, which asks how close the connection is between the defendant's act and the plaintiff's injuries; for example, did an electric failure that put out a light cause a fall down a dark staircase? Causation involves a lot of interesting issues, like the responsibility of any drug company that was one of several manufacturers of a harmful drug for the damage to a plaintiff who can't remember which brand he took. Then the Columbia course turned to the defendant: Was he or she negligent, say, bicycling on a dark road without a reflector, or did they ask for it by buying seats in the end zone of a football field? Finally, torts addressed the hotly contested issue of holding people liable regardless of how many precautions they took, which is a kind of insurance issue. The last issue was damages—how to use money to make a plaintiff whole, punish a defendant, or allocate unexpected things if, for instance, the victim of your myopic driving turns out to be The Artist Formerly Known As Prince.

The Nature of the Standard Law School Exam

The best book I've seen on law school exams is Charles Whitebread's *Eight Secrets of Top Exam Performance in Law School*. I can't tell you what they are or he'd probably sue me, but I can tell you what the exams are like, and I was certainly amused to see Whitebread recommending the method for doing pretty well that I learned from my legal writing tutor at Chicago in the Dark Ages thirty years ago.

A classic first-year law school exam would consist of one humongous essay question, usually in the form of an imaginary case, like my case of the computer-buying sixteen-year-old, which is so complicated that it contains almost all the issues you've learned about all term. The teacher would ask essentially how the case should be decided. You would sit over this essay for three solid hours, with no books or notes to assist you, trying to answer from what you learned and hastily memorized in the three days prior to the exam.

Mercifully, very few exams are this pure anymore. Usually, a teacher will ask several questions, and you will be able to identify roughly which subject matter of the law you learned is the particular focus of the question. For example, the teacher in torts might ask a question that focuses closely on liability for behavior that seems negligent. An example might be a lawsuit by The Artist Formerly, etc., against a chartered bus driver who drove with a broken windshield wiper on the passenger side of the windshield in a rainstorm. Note that the question includes behavior that might be just on the other side of the negligence line and thus only be illegal under a standard of strict liability (such as if we have a higher standard of driving for common carriers like bus drivers than for drivers in general, and whether a chartered bus is a common carrier), and that would come out differently depending on whether the defendant had any special duties to the plaintiff, who, in our question, was not a passenger in the bus.

Another question might focus heavily on causation, with all kinds of crazy intervening things happening after the defendant set out with the broken wiper and before he ran into Prince, like paparazzi chasing Prince (intervening third parties) and Prince's driver falling asleep at the wheel (intervening defendant's own agent), and so forth.

Usually, the exam includes a question about a currently disputed issue of policy, like whether it's a desirable development in the law to tag a drug company with damages to pay for Mr. X's ruined liver when all they did was make some pills, which Mr. X may never have taken, since all we know is that Mr. X took somebody's bad medicine. Current hot policy issues change from year to year; when I was in school, the question was whether the Warren Court had violated the norms of good lawyering by striking down school segregation; tort "reform" limiting the way the society distributes bad luck and loss seems hot these days.

The Safety Net: Things You Must Never Fail to Do

KEEP AN EYE ON YOUR TEACHER'S PROFESSIONAL LIFE

A good way to anticipate the policy question is to see what your teacher is writing about in the course in your field. You can find this out by chatting the teacher up after class ("So, what are you working on these days?"), searching for his or her name in the computerized legal research database you're going to learn about in your course on legal research. In the LEXIS database, the library to find your professor in is called "LAWREV" (meaning law review) and the file is called "ALLREV." Search for your teacher's name, "linda w/3 [meaning within three words of] hirshman," and you will get everything she wrote and everyone who referred to her. The first is usually the most important.

The second way to figure out what your teachers are likely to ask about is to pay attention to what they emphasize in class and in supplementary materials. What do you think I'd ask about on a contracts exam or a criminal law exam, now that you've read this book? Might it be theories of competency and responsibility in Contracts? Might it be theories of restraining the violent impulses of the strong in Criminal Law?

It's probably prudent to check up on what your teacher has been up to anyway. If a teacher is really irresponsible, he or she will just ask you an exam question that exactly duplicates his or her most recent law review article. Given the mandatory curve we talked about earlier, if your classmates know about your teacher's areas of current interest and you don't, they may scope out some of the exam questions in advance and your grades on the curve will be lower than theirs. My contracts teacher did that—asked a big question on secured transactions that he had just written about in an obscure law review. In those Dark Ages before there was LEXIS, I just got the article by chance.

The best way to find out what the exam is going to look like is to look at the teacher's old exams. Law professors hate writing and grading exams, so the temptation to reuse old material is almost irresistible. The odds of repeat questions or question types go up if he or she is still using the same casebook year after year. Better still are the practice exams the teacher gives you, because they reflect the teacher's absolutely most recent thinking, unless, of course, the teacher uses an old exam as a practice exam, in which case it's all the same.

TWO HEADS ARE BETTER THAN ONE

Everyone I talked to participated in a study group at the end of the first and second semesters of the first year to go over possible exams. An even better way is to get the old exams and go over the questions directed at a subset of the material after you've finished studying it in class. Carol Counselor puts her head together with others when it comes to practice exams, because "three or four heads are better." Together they issue-spot, rule-state, analyze, and discuss where the law might go next. Going over the torts teacher's old exam question on negligence after finishing the section on liability and negligence, for example, gets you used to thinking in law school mode.

It's probably helpful but not critical to establish a study group during the semester and before exams. A very young and shy woman I interviewed at the end of her first year at a big D.C. school graphically described how her shyness made the pressure to find and participate in a study group very hard on her. Like many women, she needed to see what the social rules were before she took a social chance (needless to say, the experience of participating in class discussion did not fill her with feelings of unmixed delight either). But by the end of the semester even Ms. Shy had found a group. She describes her study group technique. "We would do monster study sessions and sit for ten to twelve hours and go through the entire semester [for each course] and say what we knew out loud and explain it to someone else." The bad news is that the study group is probably necessary for most people's success, but not sufficient to guarantee a good outcome. Although Shy did brilliantly, scoring in the top of her class, others in her study group did "well" but "didn't get the grades [Ms. Shy] did." However, when Shy got behind in her contracts outline, she blew off the study group in order to finish her outline before the exam and her grades really suffered.

The IRAC

Regardless of the form of the exam, its purpose is twofold: first, to allow you to show off that you know the basic rules that have evolved to govern particular issues in each area of the law; second, to allow you to show off that you've mastered the disputes that have arisen at the new places where issues in the law are still evolving. In order to do these two things, you must be able to spot the issues. So, Hirshman's 1-2-3 of examsmanship:

(1) Spot the issues.
(2) Show off that you know what the settled law looks like up to the point where it became unsettled over the particular issue.
(3) Show off that you know the hard arguments on all sides of the particular issue that's unsettled.

Then go for a beer (okay, Rule 4).

Whitebread tells you that the secret to this process is the IRAC: issue recognition, rule in general, applied to the point you recognized, conclusion of how it should be resolved. Here's how it works. You read over the exam question once quickly to see what the teacher is asking at the end. Then you go back over it slowly and look for the issues of law buried in it. As you spot each one, draw a circle around it.

Here's how your outline comes in handy. After you make your outline, memorize around ten of the categories of legal issues you've identified. A torts list might be: (1) standard of liability, (2) proof of liability, (3) duty, (4) nonphysical harm, (5) causation, (6) defenses, (7) strict liability, (8) damages, (9) insurance, and (10) alternatives. As soon as you walk into the torts exam, write the ten or eleven categories of issues down on the inside cover of your blue book. This is your blue book list or BBL. That way you won't forget anything major. As you go through the question looking for issues, keep the categories of issues in mind.

Although you can't bring a forty-page outline into the exam unless the exam is open book, with the categories of issue in mind, the particular version of the issues buried in the question will jump out at you because they will *resemble* although not be identical to the issues in the cases you read and discussed in the various categories you've just written down. So as you read the exam, BBL category 1, standard of liability, should alert you to the question of whether driving with one broken wiper is negligent; standard 3, duty, will alert you to the issue of whether the driver has an elevated duty to everyone or only passengers on a common carriage; and so forth down the line.

Once you've spotted the issue, you have to remember without much more help in the exam what the rule is for the issue. In negligence, for example, a common rule is that the risk of the harm times the severity of the harm must exceed the cost of taking precautions. So when you spot the issue of negligence in the form of the broken windshield wiper, write down the rule as quickly as you can. Then you ask how the rule applies to a passenger-side wiper, and if your teacher is doing her stuff, the issue will be right at the edge of the clear application of the rule, so you must say so: How likely is it that the driver would have to see out the passenger side (after all, we don't have wipers on side windows) to avoid a big accident (probably any auto accident is big)? It wouldn't cost much to fix it, but maybe he just discovered it was broken. Then you may take a stab at asserting a conclusion about the issue—for instance, that the driver would be liable, because, after all, we have a custom of putting wipers on rear windows, so we must think collateral windows matter, or whatever. You don't have to reach a conclusion; actually, most issues in the marathon of first-year exams are actually springboards to the next level of analysis, which in this case would be that the driver might be a common carrier with a heightened duty of care. (State common carrier rule, apply it to charter bus, conclude that it does or does not apply, and spring on to next issue: Does the heightened duty apply to nonpassengers?) When you finish the question, go over your BBL to be sure you haven't forgotten anything.

A word of caution here. Just because it appears on your BBL doesn't mean it's in each question. I just told you teachers tend to break the course down into a series of exam questions covering subsets of the course material. If you write about something in the course that is completely irrelevant to the question—that Prince could afford insurance or whether he assumed the risk of being hit when he got into the car, for example—most teachers will just glide right past it and you will have wasted your time. But the BBL does exist as a check on exam panic, because it suggests the categories if your mind freezes and it ensures that nothing major will escape.

Just Memorize the Body of Law and Spit It Back

A substantial minority of my interviewees filed a dissenting opinion on the brief, outline, IRAC strategy. They said, "Don't think about the law; just memorize the doctrine from hornbooks and Emmanuel law outline" (Columbia). Most compellingly, UCLA invoked her mom: "My mother [a lawyer] went through exactly what needed to be done and I did really well." UCLA's mom advises, "Don't brief the cases; buy the canned briefs." This elicited some nods in the group. "We wasted so much time fishing, and it helps you not look like a fool in class." The canned briefs definitely have their place. Even Carol and other semipurists "dip into Emmanuel [the most common of the commercial outlines for sale in the bookstore] around exam time."

Most professional law school strategists advise you to outline your answer for five minutes before you start issue spotting, rule reciting, applying, and concluding. UCLA's mom says not to bother—it just takes time and teachers don't care about a well-organized answer. Ms. NYU agrees. She thinks you should know what you want to say before you go into the exam and then just use the exam as an opportunity to write what you've memorized. In other words, in response to my hypothetical question about the windshield wiper, just write a one-hour treatise on the law of negligence without paying much attention to the actual question. I regard this as a high roll, but pretty useful if it's a course you feel insecure about. If you can't understand the material well enough to distribute your learning around in an elaborate question, then memorizing and reciting is much better than freezing in the exam room. Just check the question to see what general areas of the course are reflected there (Is this a question about negligence? Is this a question about negligence and causation?) and then recite your outline or the commercial outlines on those areas.

Carol also emphasized speed: "Perfectionists in law school and on the exam have to learn to let go and cover issues however imperfectly." In other words, the teacher is looking as much for you to see there's an issue as to decide what the outcome will be—to note "It's a bus line and therefore may have a heightened obligation" than to say "In *Smith v. Jones*, the Ohio supreme court held that bus lines have an extra duty to their passengers, but that was a city bus, and this is a charter bus." "You need courage and confidence to be imperfect," she concluded, and that's why you mustn't bail out on the class hazing if you can possibly avoid it. Unless the atmosphere is ruinously hostile, with students hazing any woman who tries to answer and visibly sexist professors, try to keep playing the game. You need courage to be imperfect.

The UCLA group had some other easy, clever ideas: Underline key words or cases in the question and in your answer, so the teacher grading as quickly as he or she can will see you've remembered the applicable concepts; start with the last question, because you'll stand out because everyone else is out of time, and start with the shortest questions; it builds your self-esteem. Whitebread's book has some invaluable suggestions for these technical aspects of exam taking.

8

Making Law Review

MS. INSTRUMENTAL GOT such good grades her first year of law school that she obtained a place on the *University of Chicago Law Review*. When she interviewed with firms the next year for a job for the coming summer, the interviewers would glance at her résumé. "Oh, you made law review?" they would say. "What can we tell you about our firm?" The offers came rolling in.

Midwestern Law Review's Ms. Daughter did not get grades that qualified her for law review her first year. When she started interviewing for jobs with firms for a summer job, the big, prestigious firms she started interviewing would not give her the time of day, so she canceled the rest of her interviews to concentrate on trying to get onto law review another way.

Carol Counselor had grades good enough for *Ivy League Law Review*, but she also had a sensational summer job and didn't have time to stick around to do the requisite work. So she turned it down. Because of her fabulous grades and references, she obtained a prestigious judicial clerkship without being on law review, so obviously grades alone are sufficient in most circumstances. Indeed, one reason law review matters is that judges and employers simply treat it as a quick way to find out what your first-year grades were, and, of course, the actual grades would also be proof of that! (As we will see in chapter 10, employers use the grades to screen the résumés for big firm interviews.) However, now Carol's thinking about going into law teaching, and she's wondering if she didn't make a mistake not doing law review after all.

What is law review, that $90,000 law firm jobs or access to the prestigious legal academy seems to ride on it?

The catalog of Rutgers (Camden), the State University of New Jersey, describes the "journal" as follows:

> The Rutgers Law Journal is a professional publication devoted to critical discussions of current legal problems. . . . Participation in the work of the Rutgers Law Journal affords students a unique opportunity for intellectual and professional growth. . . .
>
> Invitations for staff positions are extended to a limited number of first-year students on the basis of their academic achievement in the first year of law school and a writing competition. Other students are encouraged to compete for Rutgers Law Journal membership through subsequent open writing competitions.

Although this is a fairly neutral-sounding statement, the author of Rutgers Camden's catalog gives the careful reader a hint about what's really going on: "a unique opportunity for . . . professional growth." With a few exceptions for people like Carol, the staff and editors of the named law review, in this case the *Rutgers Law Journal*, are the 20 percent who don't have psychic wounds to lick. The people not on the law review are the rest.

As I said in chapter 6, I don't think all the benefits of a law school diploma—or many law school diplomas—are exhausted by students in the top 20 percent. There are down-to-earth human beings who believe that well-paid jobs in pleasant surroundings with interesting clients are quite a large benefit of obtaining a law degree, and the University of Chicago, for example, has the highest rate of big-firm job placement in the country. There are even people who believe that moving into the professional middle class that such jobs represent is a benefit not to be scoffed at. After law school, many things can happen. Bill Clinton didn't make law review.

However, scoring big on law school grades and making law review can certainly set the stage for a lifelong career. My favorite example of this is Joel Klein, the hotshot head of the Justice Department Antitrust Division—in other words, the United States' point man in the big suit against Microsoft. Klein, around fifty, emerged from the Bronx to attend Columbia University, was articles editor of the *Harvard Law Review,* and graduated magna cum laude, which fewer than 5 percent of law students achieve. As day follows night, he moved right up from the *Harvard Law Review* to a clerkship for federal appeals court judge David Bazelon, followed in lockstep by the highest honor—a Supreme Court clerkship with Lewis Powell. After clerking, Klein held a variety of prestigious law firm jobs, at his own firm and with others, specializing in appellate argument, which is the closest thing the practice has to offer to the experience of being a successful first-year law student. As a grown-up successful law student, he represented a variety of interests, arguing in the Supreme Court an awesome ten times, lending his talents along the way to such movements for social change as the effort to make educational institutions answerable for sexual harassment and the movement to increase minority representation in the U.S. Congress. He came to know President Clinton. He joined the administration in the summer of 1993 in the office of White House Counsel and thereafter at Justice. By all reports, Klein is a brilliant and gifted man, but, reading his résumé, there is no question in my mind that his success as a first-year law student at Harvard in 1968 was a big piece of the springboard from which his career was launched.

Law review is by no means a guarantee that you'll be Joel Klein in thirty years. One study revealed that law review at Case Western Reserve School of Law actually *reduced* women's lifetime earnings! The perverse explanation for this may be that women on law review actually had a better shot at the low-paying, but very competitive, public interest jobs. If so, women got more of what they wanted, even though money was not a priority for them. It remains the case, then, that if you want to squeeze the maximum career advantage out of your three years at law school, it is usually better to be on law review than not to be. You will be more likely to get a good-paying firm job during the summer and after graduation, as Instrumental and Daughter learned. You will be more likely to get a prestigious clerkship with a high-status judge. You will be more likely to wind up as the head of the Antitrust Division of the Justice Department when the moment comes to take on Microsoft and earn a place in history, or infamy. You are now well ahead of your fellow first-year students, because you know what lies behind the "unique professional opportunity" of law review, and you know what the goal of a substantial number of first-year students is. The goal is membership on law review. One of our criteria for ranking the schools according to women-friendliness is whether women make law review in proportion to their proportion in the class.

There is another reason why women should strive to make law review. It is indeed "a unique tradition in the legal world to accept as authoritative professional journals that are written, edited, and published by" students. What Rutgers Camden's catalog doesn't tell you is that most of what law reviews publish are articles from faculty at other law schools. Because of this setup, which is the result of a bizarre history in the legal profession and in the legal academy, the students get to pick which of their teachers' articles get published and where. And, believe me, it makes a big difference to the teachers if their articles are published in the *Harvard Law Review* or the *Crummy Law Review*.

Since the system is so irrational, many faculty members bail out and do different things like write books for professional editors and publishers. But one very important group doesn't have that option: the untenured members of the faculty. *Accordingly, the mostly white male editorial boards of the high-status law reviews are essentially picking the future teachers of the legal profession.* In 1995, only Stanford and Iowa, of all the top twenty *U.S. News* elite law schools, had a law review membership that was more than half female, and most of the elite law reviews were under 40 percent female.

Considering what an opportunity for abuse this position is, the student editors of the past few decades have a pretty good record of trying to select articles of merit, rather than playing politics. However, I have certainly seen young faculty sucking up to the conservative law review editors who gather every year at the national meeting of the Federalist Society and heard stories of other political influences on article selection. In case you think the law review editors don't take their politics seriously, the legendary attack on the recently murdered Mary Jo Frug at the *Harvard Law Review* banquet in 1992 actually sprang from two conservative white editors who had opposed publishing an article she had written. I know a young law teacher who didn't show up anywhere as a professional scholar in the database of published law review articles for many, many years after graduating law school, at which point she produced an antifeminist tract and landed in the pages of the *Harvard Law Review*. Maybe her antifeminist article was just a terrific piece of legal analysis, but somehow the "merit" of her other writing just never got noticed. Certainly, her chances of tenure went way up as a result of this student decision to publish her work.

Not only do the law reviews play a role in shaping the membership of the future faculties, the law reviews remain a place where important social ideas sometimes get launched. The Legal Services Corporation was the product of a law review article in the early 1960s. Robert Bork's expressed opposition to the Supreme Court decision defending birth control was a law review gem; so were the words that defeated Lani Guinier, President Clinton's nominee for civil rights chief. The battle over gun control is being fought out in the pages of law reviews right now, and so is the argument over the morality of African Americans engaging in jury nullification in response to an allegedly racist criminal justice system. The politics of law review articles matter. The only people who say they don't are the ones who don't want to give up control of what gets published.

So politics is hardly an unknown quantity in the law review process. There are certainly white men of good faith in these dominant positions. I am going to write about one of them in this chapter. And everyone knows women who get onto editorial boards and pull the drawbridge up behind them, advancing no female-oriented political agenda. Nonetheless, the chances of white male editors selecting articles advocating serious social change are just a little less than they would be if the beneficiaries of social change were present during the process when articles are selected. Remember the difference between the expressed beliefs and priorities of female voters and male voters. Remember the rape discussion in Mary Lou Fellows's crim law class.

Selection Criteria

Different institutions have different law review selection processes. Almost without exception, the student-run journals themselves set the policy, although the policy usually reflects the political atmosphere of the institution. Since journals are for writing and editing scholarly articles about the law, most of them require some sort of performance on a uniformly administered writing test at the end of the first year. At the less women-friendly end are the admissions based strictly or mostly on first-year grades. As we have seen, a tiny difference in first-year grades can keep you off law review. Women do less well than men the first year, and then pretty much catch up the second and third years. So using first-year grades as the entrance test to law review has the effect, if not the intent, of reducing the representation of women. (Coincidentally, this policy also serves to keep many minorities off the law review.) At the University of Chicago, grades count heavily, because anyone in the top 10 percent of the class, fifteen people, are entitled to membership if they did no more than a good-faith effort at the writing test.

Other schools administer a job-related entrance test based on the students' ability to analyze a problem, write up their analysis, and put documents into the weird form law reviews have traditionally demanded. This is called the writing competition. Most schools use a mixture of grades and writing ability. In some of such mixed competitions, anyone in some top percentage of the class on first-year grades can compete, and half of the contestants will be chosen based on their success in the writing competition.

Mixed qualification systems are a mixed blessing. Northwestern law review editor Michele Landis analyzed the selection process there and she found that the grades requirement eliminates most minorities, while she found women having a worse time getting through the writing competition. The Northwestern law review study, Landis says, found that male readers evaluated women's writing in the competition poorly. In 1995, Northwestern's law review was only 33 percent women from an applicant pool of 43 percent women, tied for a low fifteen out of the twenty schools I examined. On the other hand, Ms. Persistence benefited greatly from the emphasis on writing. She describes herself as having the lowest grades of anyone on law review because she barely made the cut to compete in the writing contest, ranking approximately number fifty in her class of two hundred. Nonetheless, because Persistence scored above many of her higher-ranking classmates on the writing contest, she is a fully functioning member of law review. Even the heavily grade-oriented Chicago system is actually a mixed system, allowing the 130 or so students in the "bottom" 90 percent of the class to compete in the writing contest for the ten or so spots remaining after selecting the top fifteen first-year students for easy entry.

Finally, after any formal writing competition, many law reviews allow any high-rolling class member a second chance to use his writing skills by trying to write a publishable student article during their second year, a process called "writing on" to law review. The write-on process is not to be confused with the writing competition, which takes place at the end of the first year. In writing on, the risk-embracing second-year student just takes a chance that her piece will be good enough, writing a student note along with carrying a full load of academic classes, and submitting the piece to the editorial board. This was the strategy of the student I'll call Ms. Risk, and it worked.

Despite these alternative ways of making law review, "making" law review is more of a symbol of getting high first-year grades than doing the actual work of law review in many places. Chapters 6 and 7 are about getting grades that will catapult you into competition in the majority of schools where grades are a factor, so in this chapter I will concentrate on the other pieces of your law review strategy. First, unless, like Carol Counselor, you have an irresistible opportunity after your first year, if you qualify for the writing competition, you should try out. Like cramming for the LSAT, time invested in doing well on the writing contest for three days after the end of your first year bears a disproportionate weight in your future.

How to Succeed in the Writing Competition

The writing competition is essentially the first-year exam, but it takes three days, usually right at the end of the first year, rather than three hours. A uniform problem is devised by the law review or, in some schools, by all the journals, who then share in the results. At some schools, the problem is "closed book," that is, the editors devise a problem, like the eighteen-/sixteen-year-old problem we've been addressing, and they provide the contestants with copies of all the relevant precedents, cases, statutes, etc., that apply. They hand out the problem and the contestants have three days to produce a short written analysis of the problem. The competition consists of analyzing the problem sharply from the cases already decided, writing up the analysis clearly, and using the weird and complex citation form the law reviews require. (The citation process involves, in most places, the *Blue Book*, a manual of citation published by a consortium of top law reviews.) Since all the relevant authorities are provided, research skill does not enter into the closed-book example.

I'm going to describe the typical student law review note in the section on writing onto law review later, but it's useful to know what the finished notes look like even for the abbreviated writing competition. The most obvious way to find out what a student note looks like is to read the student notes from the last few years of your school's law review, information readily available in the law school library. Do this before the writing competition opens, so you don't waste precious time during the competition learning something you could have done months earlier. The typical law review note, as you will see later, has a different form from the papers you used to write. It's more redundant and it's more rigid. You will not have time to write a fully formed note during the three-day competition, but reading existing notes will give you a model.

You will probably see that the writing competition, like most law school problems, follows the issue, rule, analysis, conclusion routine I've already described for test taking. Most analyses of a particular rule involve sorting through a line of cases, like the age of competency cases, as the rule developed chronologically, and seeing what each court did, what it said it did, and what issues were left undecided in prior precedents. Most cases ambiguous enough to be law review problems involve differing lines of analysis from courts of different jurisdiction, so there is room in the analysis for a few lines about which courts are more persuasive. Finally, the problems are likely to involve at least a few simple policy considerations, like the demands of a market system consideration we looked at in the age of contracting cases.

Like everything in this book, the first rule of succeeding at the writing competition is *Just do it*. Someone ahead of Persistence told her the writing competition was really important in the selection process. "Otherwise," Persistence confided, "I would have thought it was out of reach." Instead, Persistence thought, "I'd try really hard." Someone else told her that *"Blue Booking"* was really important, so Persistence devoted a large percentage of her time and effort being sure her entry was properly cited. As we will see, putting all the references to authorities in the very stylized format required by the *Blue Book of Uniform Citation* also plays a role in writing on.

Since law reviews seem to put such a premium on it, let us take a moment to acquaint ourselves with the *Blue Book*, although that is a skill you will learn in your legal writing course, so I'm not going to go into any detail here. The *Blue Book* is a manual of style published by a consortium of prestigious law schools. As the title indicates, its ostensible purpose is to ensure that the forms of reference in legal scholarship are uniform. In theory, this enables the reader to find references from any law review article easily, once she masters the basic system. Here's the way you might alert your reader to the source and meaning of the references you're relying on. If you want to cite *Brown v. the Board of Education of Topeka, Kansas*, perhaps the most famous Supreme Court decision of the twentieth century, you would think you'd just write: "Brown versus the Board of Education of Topeka, Kansas, Supreme Court, 1954." But you would be wrong. The *Blue Book* tells us that the proper way to cite to *Brown* is as follows: *Brown* v. *Board of Education* 347 U.S. 483 (1954). And so on. There are 365 pages in the *Blue Book*, which tell you how to refer to every imaginable legal document and many nonlegal documents. Cases, statutes, law review articles, administrative regulations—all have special names and forms in the *Blue Book*.

Putting your writing into *Blue Book* form is like translating it into another language. Every time you refer to something, you have to locate its proper form in the *Blue Book* and conform your reference to it. To make matters worse, the University of Chicago, disgusted with the clumsiness and artificiality of the *Blue Book*, published some years ago the *Maroon Book* (maroon is the University of Chicago's school color), which sets forth a simplified citation system, and some law reviews now prefer *Maroon Book* style.

You may wonder why the law reviews, gatekeepers to the clerkships, etc., of the high-flying legal world, would care whether someone said 347 U.S. 483 (1954), or 74 S. Ct. 686, or 354 U.S. 543 and so on every time she referred to *Brown*. Someone told Persistence that the problem was that the writing contest included so many more cases than the students could really use that it was hard to judge the entries. With *Blue Booking*, however, "you either did it correctly or you did not." If this were the criterion, the law review might as well run a footrace as a writing contest (you either cross the finish line first or you do not), but, as Persistence hastened to add, proper Blue Booking "also shows attention to detail and that you finished your writing enough in advance." In selecting participants in a publishing venture, these are not trivial matters. Pay attention to detail and finish your writing in advance.

When pressed to share her writing secrets, Persistence told a telling story from her experience in public relations. She had a good and attentive legal writing teacher, she said, but also she was willing to bend, to do what her legal writing teacher was asking, rather than "getting mad because of what they said about your writing." In addition to the ordinary skills of good writing—using topic sentences to introduce your content, sticking to short paragraphs, and the like—Persistence treated legal writing as a "house style," just like the styles for different businesses she had to learn in her public relations job. So when your first-year legal writing teacher corrects your college style and tries to teach you law school "house style," don't get mad. Get on law review.

How to Succeed in Writing On

In examining why a low percentage of its minority students winds up on one of the many journals at Georgetown law school, administrators learned that a large number of them didn't try out. An administrator at McGeorge School of Law in Sacramento speculated that their law reviews might be overwhelmingly male, as we saw in chapter 2, because the women who are eligible choose not to serve, preferring to make money at a part-time job or do other personal things. Also, remember Claude Steele and the "stereotype threat" that makes people defeat themselves because they lack self-confidence? Don't do that. Do what Persistence did. Or you could do what Risk did.

After Risk learned that she had achieved only a mediocre average her first year, she knew that the law review judges wouldn't even read her writing sample in the grade-based competition, so she didn't waste her time on the competition. Instead, cannily advised by one of her female professors, she decided to devote the summer after her first year to finding a topic of her own to write about in the later, write-on competition.

Student notes are most often about very constrained subjects, so the student with only one year of legal training can master them in a limited time and express them in a limited space. A good self-selected topic usually involves a question of law on which the federal courts of appeals are split. Splits occur because there are twelve federal appeals courts, each with jurisdiction over several states or the District of Columbia. Like the different state courts, the different federal circuits are not bound by each other's rulings, so one circuit may decide a legal issue one way and another a different way. Unlike the different states, the United States is ultimately one nation, so the Supreme Court regards these splits as undesirable and will usually take a case to resolve the split and impose a uniform nationwide rule.

As of this writing, the circuits are split, for example, on the subject of whether the interest on accounts lawyers hold for their clients for various brief periods of time (called lawyer "trust accounts") can be allocated by the bar association into a fund for legal services to the needy. Challengers argued that the clients have a constitutionally protected property interest in the interest on the accounts, which the bar associations can't take. The United States Court of Appeals for the Fifth Circuit held that the state bar programs are an unconstitutional taking, but the First and Eleventh Circuits upheld similar programs. The Supreme Court correctly dislikes having clients in the Fifth Circuit's Texas keeping the interest on their accounts while clients in the First Circuit's Massachusetts are supporting legal services with their money, so a timely student note that addressed this split would be focused on a subject likely to be of national import. Indeed, the Supreme Court has now exercised its discretionary review power over this case presumably to resolve the split.

In addition to its import, the student writing on a circuit split can focus on the issue dividing the courts and use the courts' conflicting analyses, adding only a narrow argument for why to choose one outcome over the other, rather than having to do a sweeping amount of original research. All you have to do is anticipate what the Supreme Court will do, an exercise most of the first year is devoted to teaching you how to address.

United States Law Week, a publication of West Publishing, the same people who bring you the commercial versions of the court reporters, contains short summaries of noteworthy decisions that come out every week. Since a circuit split is usually noteworthy, an efficient way to find a good topic is to read the *United States Law Week* every week, watching for splits on interesting subjects. This is what Risk did, all summer. As it turned out, she didn't see anything that interested her, so she took a second good route to finding a voluntary note—she got an idea from a professor she was working for, for a topic involving a sex tort case.

Over the summer, Risk called the relevant editor from the editorial board in the third-year class and told him she was interested in writing for the law review. There were six spots left, and twenty-six people originally started down the process, but she "knew it would drop." (In the end, thirteen voluntary pieces were turned in.) After strategizing with her professor, Risk stopped interviewing for jobs for the summer after her second year, as she reported it, went to "no" classes, and "devoted herself" to law review. Note the risks involved here: She had a little less than one chance in four of making it at the beginning and she was risking having no summer job. Moreover, she was willing to use feminist theory to make a case in her piece for an outcome favoring the almost inevitably female plaintiff, an approach that she had heard "was death at her school." All in the interests of her long term résumé.

Risk was shamelessly willing to cozy up to the white men in

power. Two of the six white men on the executive board of the law review lived nearby, so she "went over and hung out with them and chitchatted with them, which ended up paying off" even more later, as we will see.

Sometimes white men can be really good friends. The editor Risk called in D.C. turned out to be an incredible mentor to her, forward-looking politically, believing in her. When the law review asked the marginal "write on" candidates to do voluntary grunt work, checking sources in existing articles and making sure they were in the correct *(Blue Book!)* format (called "source and cite"), Risk's mentor advised her to do it, even though it took more time from her classes, interviews, and, most important, working on her own article. The white male editorial board took this, she later learned, as evidence that she was willing to work incredibly hard.

"How did you get chosen?" I asked Risk again after I heard her whole story. "The editors could read the piece and understand that I was smart enough to be part of the club." When I pressed her, she said, "I knew from grad school [Risk has a master's degree] how to write a piece when I have long enough to think about it."

It turns out that you don't need a master's to master the task of writing your piece, either. The year after the editors defeated the effort to open up Northwestern's law review to more minority candidates by emphasizing the writing over the first-year grades, a handful of editors, including the irrepressible Michele Landis, ran a mentoring program to encourage Northwestern's minority students to try to write on. At the end of the fall semester, six of the nine minority students Michele's group had mentored (and one from outside the program) succeeded in writing on to the Northwestern law review, more minority members than in the previous ten years altogether. Just in case you think this stuff can't be learned, Michele's group got it down to a science. Here's what Michele's group did.

MICHELE LANDIS'S WAY

First, they called a meeting of all the minority second-year students interested in writing on to law review. They all went to a "fancy restaurant" off campus, thereby kicking off the process by showing the minority students that they deserved to be well treated. (Remember "stereotype threat"?) Michele asked the students to describe what they wanted to write about, why they wanted to be on law review, and how their topic was something that a white male would be unlikely to pursue, thereby allowing them to realize how important it was for them to penetrate the law review not just for their career ambitions but also to change the institution.

Then, following the basic sociological literature about how networks succeed, they did the following things. Note that none of them involves getting a master's degree. Every single one of them is something you can now do for yourselves.

GET A BUDDY

Pair off with someone else who's also trying to write on to law review. We know from chapter 6 that where everyone else is going at it alone in the war-of-all-against-all image that law school presents, the smart strategy is actually cooperation. Michele encouraged the students to pair off on the basis of similarity of topic, but that's not so important. What's important is what they did for each other: They cut the work almost in half. They did each other's classwork, freeing each other up to work on their would-be articles. First one would go to class and take notes, copy them, and share them with the other, who was writing away. Then the second buddy would do the same. It only takes a minute to Xerox a week's worth of class notes and give them to the other buddy, but it frees her up from a week of classes. At the end, the group established an outline bank, so they didn't each have to make four outlines for all of their classes and could spend the time working on their articles.

GET A MENTOR

Michele asked the potential mentors to do three things: discuss prospective topics at the outset, meet along the way as the students developed the drafts, and read and comment on the drafts. When you pick a mentor, be sure to ask her or him to commit to doing these three tasks.

Faculty members are the most obvious mentors. Look for sympathetic faculty members. Northwestern had people around—visitors, nonacademic faculty like clinicians—who were willing to help Michele's group: Professor Mary Becker was visiting from Chicago, and she mentored a civil rights act project, which is her area of expertise; family clinic lawyer Bernadine Dohrn acted as a resource on a paper about female genital mutilation as a problem of family law.

Faculty are not the only source of mentorship. Do you know any successful alums of your law school? Some of the Latino students at Northwestern linked up with a very successful Latina woman alum, still bitter years later about her lack of access to *Northwestern Law Review*, but, most important, happy to help other Latino students make up for it.

Law review itself may hold some mentors for you, as it did for Risk. Are there any sympathetic editors, particularly people who wrote their own way on, who will help? The year after Risk wrote on, she came to Northwestern and spoke to Michele's group about how to succeed in writing on, and some of the students even adopted her as their helper.

USE THE MENTOR

Michele again: "Some people took advantage of the process and met with a mentor every week and they were the ones who made it. Those who didn't, didn't make it." Michele strongly encouraged the students to produce the drafts of their articles one week before the competition closed, so that she and the faculty mentor could subject it to an edit before it was turned in. Among other things, the mentors told the contestants "who to avoid and who to suck up to." This political advice is perhaps the most important product of networking—finding out where the bodies are buried.

PICK A SUITABLE TOPIC

Topics are critical. If you want to increase your chances of getting on, get together with the other women trying to write on and try not to write on the same topics. Also, try not to take opposite sides of the same topic, so the editors won't use that to eliminate one of you as making the law review look silly. Get together with a group and get feedback about your topic.

Just like the secrets of the LSAT and the "Ten Commandments of First-Year Exam Taking," there are secrets as to what a successful student note looks like. You actually can see what the current editors wrote when they were staffers, because their student notes should be published by the time they begin serving as editors. After all, they're the ones who are going to be judging you! You obviously can't write the same topic, but you can pick a topic with a similar structure. If they wrote about a tiny proposed change in the tax code, you can write about a tiny proposed change in the occupational health and safety code, using the same materials of legislative history they used; if they wrote about the split in the circuits over whether taking interest on trust accounts for legal services is constitutional, you can write about the split in the circuits over whether zoning regulations for beach access is an unconstitutional taking or whatever is current.

Pick a *narrow* topic. You don't know much after only one year of law school. This is not the moment to propose a revision of the entire criminal law to substitute monetary penalties for jail sentences in a sweeping libertarian revision of all Western jurisprudence. Risk's note analyzing the state decisions about a procedural aspect of sex torts is a good example of a narrow topic, especially since, mercifully, there weren't fifty state decisions on the subject.

Law practice often generates nice narrow topics. I wrote my first law review article about an issue that had arisen in my practice, before I went into teaching—whether an action to enforce a contract mandated by federal law belongs in federal court or state court. This may not sound like a world-altering subject to you, but as I made my way to the United States Supreme Court with it (I lost), it was all-consuming in my eyes. More important, it was manageable. There were only a handful of cases on the subject, and a few things that applied by analogy. For her student note, Persistence was directed to an intellectual property lawyer who had just gotten a decision in a case of his from the famed legal academic and appeals court judge Richard Posner. As he is notorious for doing, Posner generated what some people would consider a completely new doctrine for the occasion. Presto! If it's not a circuit split, it's almost as good as one: all prior precedent on one side and Posner on the other. All Persistence had to do was analyze how the new Posner case could have been resolved under current doctrine, which she could get from the lawyer involved.

Pick a topic that hasn't been done to death. You have to check and see if someone else has already published something directly on your topic anyway (this is known as the dreaded "preemption"). Circuit splits, which are nationally visible in the pages of the *U.S. Law Week*, are likely to involve the danger of preemption. But many topics have that problem. One of Michele's group wanted to write about female genital mutilation. A glance at the computerized legal database, LEXIS, would tell you that there are a million articles on the immigration law aspect of that problem— mostly whether the practice entitles women from cultures that practice genital mutilation to refugee status in the United States. Most editors will not think you can add much to the existing wealth of analysis already published.

However, the existing writings did not exhaust the possibilities in the subject. There are large colonies of immigrants from such cultures already here. A good article would focus on whether such an act would amount to child abuse and neglect as a matter of family law or whether family law, as the immigration articles sometimes argue, should defer to claims of "cultural relativism."

You can find such a crossover approach by proposing a general subject matter to sympathetic teachers in several areas and see if they see what interests you as having a place in their area of expertise. I'm particularly high on looking at familial or criminal behavior through the lens of civil law these days. Some betrayed wife just sued the other woman for tort recently. I think there are real possibilities in treating adultery as a breach of contract. State law cases on the cutting edge in these areas would make a good note.

IF IT LOOKS LIKE A LAW REVIEW NOTE, IT IS A LAW REVIEW NOTE

Michele Landis says, "All first drafts of law review notes [whether from grade-selected staffers or would-be write-ons] look like papers for class." The editor's job is to put them into law review note form. If you want to succeed at writing on to law review, you will make your note for the competition look as much like a law review note as possible. It almost doesn't matter what you say, as long as it looks like a law review note.

Law review notes have the following characteristics. One, they are extremely redundant. First the writer tells you what she's going to tell you, then she tells you, then she tells you what she told you. So you have to know what you're going to say before you start to write. Second, the author gives the reader a clear diagram of the development of the legal doctrine being analyzed. So she usually starts with a statement of the subject in dispute, opens with a literature and precedent search (what's been said by others), makes an argument for why one approach is superior to the others, and discusses what will happen if the author's approach is used. Third, nothing, absolutely nothing, is said without a reference to some other authority. This both relieves the ignorant student author of responsibility for knowing anything and demonstrates her commitment to thorough research. Finally, the note is in impeccable *Blue Book* form.

If I were using law review note form for the paragraph you just read, it would look something like this:

Aspiring law review members want to know what the characteristics of law review notes are. In this paragraph, I'm going to analyze what the characteristics of a law review note[1] are. *Northwestern Law Review* editor Michele Landis has said the characteristics of a successful law review note are: redundancy,[2] road map,[3] footnote heaviness,[4] impeccable *Blue Book* form.[5] Although there are a minority of law review editors who believe that law review notes should be an original effort to say something creative about a developing legal doctrine,[6] very few of student notes of this sort ever see the light of day, much less get aspiring members onto the law review. So if you want your note to have the proper characteristics, you will be sure it's redundant, lays out a clear map to the topic, uses more footnotes than text, and is carefully conformed to the *Blue Book*.[7]

1. Notes 1–7 herein are imaginary footnotes to the law review note above. A law review note is a student-written article, published in the student's second year, etc.
2. Redundancy is the characteristic of superabundance, superfluous excess. Webster, *New International Dictionary*, p. 2089, G. 42. Merriam Co. 1935.
3. A road map is a map showing roads. Id., at p. 2156.
4. See, supra and infra. One way to produce more footnotes is to include in footnotes material that in any normal publication would be included in the text. See, infra, note 5.
5. *Blue Book*, a publication of the Association of Law Reviews, sets forth the mechanical rules for the citation of authority in law review articles. Probably the hardest job of the aspiring law review member is to master the arcana of the *Blue Book* and make her article look as if she's one of the in-group. Association of Law Reviews, *Blue Book*, Introduction at publisher, date.
6. Note: "Letitallhangout," 12 Crummy University Law Review 125 (1994).
7. Telephone interview with Michele Landis, 12/29/97.

I've given myself a pass on the perfect *Blue Book* form, but you get the idea. For some reason, this format is not natural to the English-speaking world. Accordingly, *you cannot just turn your computer on and write a note in law review form for the competition.* Like anything unnatural—ballet dancing, softball catching, cross-examining—writing a law review note takes practice and review. Write your note at least a week before it's due, check it to be sure it's redundant, clearly laid out, overly cited, and *Blue Book* perfect and then take it to your mentor to be sure you were right when you thought you were sure.

IF IT LOOKS LIKE A LAW REVIEW MEMBER, IT IS A LAW REVIEW MEMBER

Like Risk, Michele counseled her aspiring candidates to do the voluntary source and cite work when offered in the fall. Remember, they were helping each other with their classwork, so they could generate some extra time. The advantage of the source and cite work is that it made them look hardworking to the editors who were going to be judging them. When I told her my story about the big-firm associate who left his jacket over the chair while he sneaked home for a life, she roared. "Exactly," she said. "Looking hardworking is almost as important as doing the work."

JUST DO IT: FINISH THE ARTICLE

As one law review editor confided: "The most important thing is finishing. Law reviews are full of mediocre people who finished."

How to Succeed in Becoming a Hotshot Editor Your Third Year

Joel Klein didn't just make it onto the *Harvard Law Review*; he was articles editor. Here the pyramid steepens again. Of the thirty-some staff members chosen from the two hundred first-year students, only six become executive board members. Chicago's Instrumental reported that the jockeying for the next cut at the *University of Chicago Law Review* began within weeks after the people came back to their staff jobs the fall of their second year. When I first spoke to her, she contended that she wasn't going to be part of it, having had doubts about doing law review at all (before she saw how it transformed the interview process). But for those who are interested, they're hanging around the law review suite in the law school library elbowing one another to be the ones to carry the existing editors' coffee. Being able to sit in your carrel in the law review suite until the last editor has gone home is good practice for making it in the early years of firm politics, too. P.S. As this book was going to press, Ms. Instrumental was named co-editor of the law review.

The year Risk wrote her way on to law review, all six big shots were white males. The next year Risk became one of three women on the executive board.

The selection process for editorial board is pretty typical: The staff members interested fill out a questionnaire regarding the things they've done and they each have an interview with the executive board and the people who stuck it out to become third-year editors. The editors included only two women Risk's year; as she put it, "It was a sea of white men with disembodied voices." Risk claims she was uncharacteristically nonstrategic at this stage of the process because it's all "so subjective." But she did note that her hard work to get on and her unflagging sense of humor in schmoozing the men on the board probably carried her a long way. As to the interview, she said, "They smell you, and if they don't smell fear they put their heads down and submit." Risk is the first write-on ever to have a position on the executive board better than managing editor, who is the one who pays the bills and turns out the lights.

Finally, Risk was doubtless assisted by the radical upward slope of her grades—the first semester of her second year, her grades rose to the top 15–20 percent. A lot of data confirm that women don't catch on as quickly as men to law school. Risk's story is a living lesson in why you do not have to take that toxic first year as the last word. Next year, she's going to hold one of the most sought-after fellowships in the country, having been chosen from thousands of students in a national competition. Although she says she's spent the last two years overcoming her first-year handicap, I fully expect to see Risk sitting on the opposite side of the courtroom from some Microsoft heavies someday.

9

Compared to Law School, Life Is Easy: How to Succeed at Firm Job Interviews

Question: *"How do you decide which students to interview for jobs?"*

Answer: "If the grades meet the cutoff, it's almost automatic for an interview."

—Hiring partner, medium-sized Southwest law firm

"We give the law school a set of criteria based on the law schools' grading system."

—Hiring partner, medium-sized Northeast law firm

"We use a minimum GPA and class rank."

—Hiring partner, large national law firm

ARE YOU GOING to law school to get a job practicing law? Almost 70 percent of all law school graduates are. If you are one of the 70 percent, chances are you'll get your first job right out of law school. Fifty-six percent of 1995 law grads and slightly fewer women grads started practicing in private practice (as opposed to being directly in business, government, or the like). A big avenue for getting that important first job is the on-campus law firm interview at the beginning of your second year. Almost all law schools have on-campus interviews by prospective employers. I asked a lot of employers how they decide which students to see, if the law schools allow them to choose whom to see. The first answer in all cases was grades.

How the System Works

The law school placement offices are supposed to help the students get jobs when they get out of school, and, to a lesser extent, during the summers or even during the school year. Recruiting can take many different forms, but the placement offices are usually the administrators of all the different aspects of job placement. The University of Houston (Femscore 153, fourth out of seven in Status Group #4) has an exemplary placement office, so I asked its placement director, Deborah Hirsch, to describe its program.

The placement office at Houston regards its job as to "teach students job search skills and to partner with them as they look for jobs." Beginning with the first-year initiative, the placement office breaks its first-year students into small groups to introduce them to the placement services, go over résumé preparation, and have second-year students talk about their summer experience. First years have excursions to the legal community, networking breakfasts with the law school alumni, a partnering program to match students with alumni for introducing them to the lawyering process, brown bag lunches on "a day in the life" of different lawyers, and personal appointments with the placement directors to review their goals.

In addition to the standard on campus recruiting, which I will describe in a moment, Houston participates in a number of consortium efforts with other law schools, for example, the Texas Off-Campus Recruitment Program, in which nine law schools and the Texas Young Lawyers' Association hold interviews with legal employers at hotels or schools in Dallas and Houston. Since the Off-Campus Recruitment Program occurs in the spring, it captures firms that usually don't participate in the standard interview program, smaller firms from the larger areas, firms from smaller towns, places with sporadic hiring needs or without the resources to go around to schools recruiting, government agencies. Houston organizes on-site interviews with firms in five Texas cities that have small clerkship programs or lack resources to travel, the students go for twenty- to thirty-minute interviews in the employers' conference room. Finally, Houston, which has a special Intellectual Property Program, prepares a résumé book for employers that specialize in that subject.

Since Houston is "a very active legal marketplace," Hirsch says, "some students do get paying law-related jobs in their first summers." The office runs a job listing service, where the office posts job opportunities electronically and in writing, usually as lawyers from the community contact them for law students during the year and for summer research and writing. I begin with this description of a broad and diverse recruiting program because most American lawyers aren't employed at the one-hundred-plus member law firms. When picking your school, ask about the placement office. Ask the students you meet in particular and the ones who didn't make it into the top 10 percent especially. An active placement office can increase your chances of getting a good job by a lot.

The Ten-Thousand-Pound Gorillas

There are scores of firms of over one hundred lawyers in America today. These large institutions are not the stable, socially rigid partnerships of the period before the explosion in the size and importance of the legal profession. Getting a job at a big law firm is no longer a guarantee of life tenure. Many firms hire a lot more associates than they intend to—or financially can—promote to partnership. Their clients merge, or are merged, mutate, metamorphize, or otherwise move around. Many firms decay, disintegrate, divide, or otherwise disappear.

Large firms, however, are stable enough so that in most years they can anticipate with some certainty in the fall what their hiring needs will be the following spring. Usually, before the hiring season begins, the big firms appoint a hiring committee, chaired by a hiring partner, which determines approximately what the firm's needs for associates the following summer will be. Typically, the hiring committee also decides which of the previous summer's associates should be extended offers to return as full-time employees after graduation at the end of their third year in law school. The hiring committee, or some such body, also determines which law schools the firm will recruit from and how many lawyers they will send to interview students. Typically, the firms send someone from the hiring committee, a younger associate with whom they feel the students can relate, or an alum of the school. The firms are most interested in interviewing students at the beginning of the second year in law school for employment the summer between the second and third years. Some interviewing of third-year students for permanent employment also takes place at the fall season. In the case of the big firms, most firms hire as full-time starting associates people they liked in the summer program between the second and third years of law school.

At the same time the firms are gearing up, so are the placement offices. They arrange to schedule the firms into interview rooms at the law school for however long the firms wish to come and they make the interview list available to the students to choose whom the students wish to see. Then the placement offices either send the students' résumés to the firms for the firms to decide whom they want to interview or they run a lottery at the school to determine whom the students will get to see or some combination of both sorting techniques. Columbia and NYU start early by participating in a big hiring fair in a public space in New York in August, before school starts.

Once the hiring season begins everywhere else, second-year students interested in firm jobs begin rounds of twenty- to thirty-minute interviews at their schools followed by "callbacks" from the firms interested in them after the interviews. Most firms that bother calling someone back will bring her to wherever the firm is located for a day of interviews with more of the lawyers and some serious wining and dining. From the interview and callback process, the firms will decide whom to hire for the second summer and also which graduating students to add as full-time associates, if they haven't filled their full-time needs from the previous summer's class.

Recently, *American Lawyer* magazine did a survey of the Am Law 100—the one hundred highest-grossing law firms in America—to see where their starting associate classes of 1996 and 1997 came from. Eighty-nine firms responded. Then the magazine corrected for the size of the classes in each school and ranked the schools according to what percentage of their graduates found work at one of the Am Law 100 high-rolling firms. The list contained few surprises. Yale, Harvard, and Stanford, *U.S. News*'s top three, did not place in the *American Lawyer* top three, I suspect because they are schools that also feed clerkships and academic jobs, whereas the top three, Chicago, NYU, and Columbia, are traditionally more corporate feeder schools.

Some interesting information did emerge, however. First, no school placed more than 55 percent of its graduates in the top one hundred firms. In light of the emphasis the firms put on grades, the value of making it to or near the top half of the first-year class is clear, even in the top-placing schools. Once you get to the fifth-ranked school and below, the percentage placed in Am Law 100 firms goes below 50 percent, raising the value of making it into the top half even higher. Put another way, if women underperform their numbers in making top half of the first year class as the little public data we have suggest, there is a real job cost.

Second, the list of top-performing schools includes the schools where women succeed, as well as those where they fail. Thus, the number-one-ranking law school for getting its students hot firm jobs, the University of Chicago, placed 54 percent of its 1996 and 1997 students, while NYU came in number two for placement, at 52 percent. What's the difference for women? At Chicago, women made law review in only 69 percent of their presence in the classes of '96 and '97, while NYU women outperformed themselves at 122 percent of their presence in the class. Since most law schools (including NYU and Chicago) refused to answer my survey requests, I don't know how the top half breaks down along the same lines as law review, but chances are the outcomes will be similar. Using law review as a rough stand-in for grades, women stand a much greater chance of being in the target group of the fancy-firm employers at NYU than at Chicago.

In addition to choosing a law school where women succeed as opposed to one where women don't succeed, if the prospects are otherwise similar, there are other things you need to know to succeed at the interviewing process. Accordingly, I interviewed the hiring partners and some administrators at several different firms. They spoke frankly with me, and I promised them their privacy. I'll call them Midwest National, Midwest Regional, Southwest Medium, and Northeast Medium. But rest assured that they are real firms, and that none of them is peculiar in any important way.

1. Midwest National. Midwest National is a several-hundred-lawyer firm, with offices in all major American legal centers as well as in Europe. Midwest National interviews at more than thirty schools firmwide, but not all schools for all offices. The firm interviews at what it calls "national" schools for all its offices, but at "regional" schools for its regional offices only. So, in 1997, the firm interviewed at Harvard, Yale, NYU, Columbia, the University of Chicago, Georgetown, Michigan, Berkeley, Northwestern, Penn, Stanford, UCLA, USC, Virginia, and Wisconsin for all offices. Their interview list also includes Cardozo, Fordham, and Brooklyn in New York, and places like DePaul and Chicago-Kent in Chicago and University of Missouri in the Kansas City region, but the latter group probably was expected to provide lawyers only for the particular local offices.

2. Midwest Regional. Midwest Regional is a several-hundred-lawyer firm with most of its lawyers in two neighboring midwestern states, but with small offices in several other American cities

and abroad. Midwest Regional does not distinguish between whom it gets for which office, but it interviews at only a handful of national schools—Harvard, Michigan, the University of Virginia, Duke, Texas, and Georgetown, and intensively at the top and secondary schools around the cities in the mid-South, South, and Midwest, where it has its local offices, for a total of twenty-five schools at present. Midwest Regional does a lot of interviewing at the midwestern universities of Missouri, Kansas, Iowa, Minnesota, and the like, and at southern law schools like Emory, the University of North Carolina, Tulane, and South Texas.

3. Northeast Medium. Northeast Medium is a several-hundred-lawyer firm with offices in a big northeastern city and D.C. Northeast Medium interviews at seventeen different schools. Being smaller than Midwest National and Midwest Regional, Northeast Medium concentrates on national schools like Harvard, Yale, Chicago, and Georgetown, adding schools where they hope to attract people with a genuine interest in living in the Northeast. Northeast Medium voiced a concern that probably a lot of law firms share. They didn't want to send their recruiters to places from which people were unlikely to come. Thus, they do not go to Stanford, even though Stanford is one of the two or three most prestigious law schools in the country. Recruiting, after all, is time-consuming and expensive. Why should they send a partner whose time is worth $500 an hour all the way to Palo Alto, California, if most Stanford grads don't want to be more than five hundred yards from the surf?

4. Southwest Medium. Southwest Medium is a hundred-lawyer firm with offices in its state's two main cities. Southwest Medium has only two offices, so, like Northeast Medium, all its recruiting is for all its offices. Like all the rest, Southwest Medium starts at Harvard; its national schools include Virginia, Duke, Northwestern, and Chicago. Southwest's selection of the other national law schools reflects its southwestern orientation: Texas, UCLA, and USC. Like all the rest, Southwest adds a number of regional schools in its geographical or cultural area—Arizona State, the

University of Arizona, Iowa, and Brigham Young—as well as a couple of Washington area schools: Howard and George Washington.

These lists actually reveal more about the firms than they realize. Midwest National is a big city firm, with its headquarters in one of America's largest and most sophisticated cities. Its choices beyond the obvious Harvard or Yale are law schools that are mostly in big cities—New York, Los Angeles, Chicago. Midwest Regional is a medium heartland city firm. Its choices beyond the obvious are concentrated in Midwest or mid-South cities often of a medium size—New Orleans, Atlanta, Minneapolis. Northeast Medium is a very elite firm. Its choices beyond the obvious are concentrated in East Coast cities of a national intellectual elite population. Southwest Medium is a frontier town firm. Its choices beyond the obvious are concentrated in frontier cities— Chicago, Salt Lake City, Phoenix, Tucson, Los Angeles.

Why does this information matter to you? If you don't get into Harvard, where you choose to go to law school will affect the choices you have when it comes to getting a job. Your chances of getting a job with a firm that has identified your school to recruit from are greater than they would be if you had to apply to the firm on your own (see page 265, "The Guerrilla Girls."). So give it some heavy thought. Do you like to shovel snow? Minneapolis firms recruit more at the University of Minnesota than at Texas. Do you hate to shovel snow? Texas firms recruit more at Texas schools than in Minneapolis.

Let's be strategic. Say, your LSAT score isn't high enough to get you into a law school in Status Group #1 or #2. Or say you only get into a school in the high-status group where women don't succeed very well, like Michigan or George Washington. If you want to work in California, you can go to University of California at Davis, where women succeed very well. Firms from California that will interview at Davis won't even go to Michigan or George Washington. Or if you want to work in Arizona, you can go to ASU. Southwest Medium interviews at ASU every year. And it's not going to places like Georgetown or Stanford, which are actually harder to get into. If you want to work in a New York firm and you can't get into NYU, where women succeed, you might be better off at Rutgers Newark, where women succeed, or Cardozo, where they do pretty well, than at higher-ranked Notre Dame or Texas, where New York employers just don't bother to recruit.

The First Year Is No Moment to Examine Your Life

One drawback of the big-fish-in-a-small-pond approach is that you'd better be sure you'll be a big fish. All four firms indicated that they insist on prescreening the résumés of the students who want to meet them to screen out students whose first-year grades are below a certain level when they interview at the lower-status regional schools. Thus, Northeast Medium looks for "strong undergraduate and graduate records," for example, "honors for undergraduates and top 10 percent to top 50 percent" in law school depending on the law school. The scrutiny goes down "the more rigorous the process of getting into law school . . . the résumés at Yale all look somewhat alike, for example." (This is not a criticism!)

Although Southwest started the interview with me by contending that her firm only interviews the "top five to ten percent" of the first-year class, going "down" to "fifteen to twenty percent at Harvard or Yale," upon close examination she admitted that they see everyone from Harvard and Yale. "If they're from Harvard and Yale, we just *see* them. There's no such thing as the bottom." This conforms to what other firms report as the practice at the most elite schools—they won't allow the firms to prescreen the résumés of their students. The most common practice is for the elite schools to run a lottery if more students sign up for a particular firm than the firm has time for. Midwest National and Midwest Regional also screen the résumés for top students at all but the most elite schools.

The screening is often done by an administrator, who isn't even a lawyer, much less a partner in the firm. At Northeast Medium, the administrator will go to a partner if there's a question, but the firm doesn't want to spend any more resources on hiring than it must. What this means is that screening is a pretty mechanical sorting for grades. When screening, Midwest National looks for "GPAs or class rank." When grades meet the cutoff, an interview is "almost automatic" at Southwest Medium. If you haven't gotten the message, here it is: If you want to work in a big corporate firm, *don't engage in civil disobedience in your first year of law school.* As the hiring partner at Northeast Medium put it, "Think of it like the bar exam. You know this is an important year." Buy the commercial outlines, brief the cases in your casebooks, study alone or in a group, practice on the old exams.

Despite the firm's tough talk, there is always wiggle room at the edges. If grades are near the cutoff at Southwest Medium, they will look at other factors, like well-roundedness that bodes well for business development or expertise in substantive areas of interest to the firm, like intellectual property or health care. Indeed, Southwest Medium even admittedly looks for evidence of management skills or community development work that involves business contacts. Business contacts are more and more a criterion. Southwest Medium aspires to hire lawyers who can "mind and bind clients."

Northeast looks for credible connections with its headquarters city. Since, like most big firms, they hire permanent employees mostly from the second-year class, they don't want to waste a slot on someone who's just having a "flyer." Sometimes Northeast will take outstanding undergraduate grades into account; an accounting or an MBA degree or someone who wants to do corporate work is a plus, and a challenging job between college and law school is also a plus.

All the firms treated law review as we have done—as a symbol. Midwest National was frank. If you got on by grades, it's a big plus. If you wrote on, you go in the pile behind the people who graded on. It's still a plus, however, because it shows the person has high energy and is a "go-getter."

Looks and Charm

Remember—at many places, you never get to strut your looks and charm in interviews unless your first-year grades are pretty good. When you get into the actual interview process, however, the dynamic changes. Now you have to be sociable. The interviewer from Midwest National had a good tip. Make your résumé "short," so the interviewer can work from it, and "put a couple of things in it that are conversation starters, an interesting or unusual hobby, for example, or an interesting job after college or the subject of your senior thesis."

The interviewer from Northeast Medium described the interview best: "I administer an 'in front of the client test.' Can I see this person advising a client and instilling confidence in a client?" When pressed for more specificity, he said something quite easy for you to do. "Don't look at my shoes, rather than my eyes. And don't say 'Like,' 'Ya know,' and 'Sorta.'" When being interviewed by this gentleman, expect some "structured silence" and expect him to pick something from your résumé to discuss. Be prepared to make it interesting.

The longtime hiring chair at Midwest National asserts that you could not meaningfully discern someone's intellect in twenty minutes. She looks for four things: "Who is the person? How comfortable? How articulate? How motivated?" The Southwest interviewer asks whether the person is "comfortable talking substance, comfortable in conversation, and grabs my confidence level with solid knowledge, intellect, and demeanor." These sound hard, and they're a lot more obscure than not looking at your feet! Midwest National strongly suggests taking advantage of the mock interviews the schools' placement offices often run.

Female Problems

Perhaps the most interesting thing to know about the interviewing process is that when asked to describe their needs in greater depth, the firms all describe a person with a lot more of the stereotypical "female" traits than most law schools seem to reward. Southwest Medium actually has the traits reduced to a list: "quality, people skills, team spirit, pro bono public service, education and training, practice development, and 1,800 billable hours a year." "We've had experiences with very bright people," Southwest went on. "We really want a harmonious work force. We don't want morale-busting divisiveness. We want people to fit in the team and fit in with the program." Midwest National explained its reputation as a good place for women by a poignant analogy. "A lot of people started this firm who couldn't get jobs at other law firms regardless of their skills, so there is traditionally less resistance to diversity." Midwest Regional actually specified a "well-rounded person."

All four firms purported to have close to fifty-fifty gender breakdowns in their entering classes. This is probably an overstatement, because the law schools are rarely more than 44 percent female, and a smaller percentage of the already smaller number of women go to work in firms at all. Northeast Medium refused to acknowledge any difference in qualifications, prospects, or hiring. When pressed on the subject of work and family, the hiring partner said he'd take a flier on someone who only wanted to work nine to five if "the academics and intellect" were okay, but that he doubted the person would succeed in limiting their hours that way. The interviewer at Midwest National, a female, said she had a preference for people with oddball hobbies and brightly colored clothing, but that she doubted that was the best strategy. "Go with the lowest common denominator," she advised; be conservative until you get the lay of the land. An overwhelming interest in doing good doesn't do *you* any good at Southwest Medium. "We represent a lot of companies with environmental problems," the interviewer told me. "I ask people with a lot of public interest stuff on their résumé if they'll be comfortable doing our work for our clients. This isn't the ACLU."

In the course of interviewing firms for this chapter, I ran across a highly placed female interviewer whom I won't identify, but she had a tip you need to know. "Men," she told me, "tend to be a little more sure of themselves, a little cockier, that they're interviewing us as much as we're interviewing them. Women are more into pleasing the interviewer." When asked how she reacted to this difference, she said, "Occasionally, a man is too cocky or too arrogant, and I worry about the clients. My male colleagues," she confessed, "see it as self-confidence and commanding. In order to make partner these days, you must have the self-assurance that you're going to be able to stand up to a judge on [clients'] behalf no matter what. Timid women will not survive and make partnership."

The Guerrilla Girls

Remember the woman from UCLA who hung around the interview rooms snaffling off the interviewers from any firms she didn't get to see? All the hiring partners loved that story. Midwest National shared with me that an enterprising student at the University of Minnesota showed up to drive their interviewer to the airport after his day there, got a job, and was a great success. Several firms said that people called them the summer between their first and second years in law school and said they were from law schools far away and had occasion to be in the firm's city and asked to send a résumé in advance of an early interview while they were in town. Northeast Medium was delighted to hear from the Stanford first-year student between his first and second years. They took his résumé and interviewed him before he went back to California.

A little-noticed tactic is to make friends in your first year or at the very beginning of your second year with the second-year students who are going to firms where you think you would like to work. Then when they come back from their summer jobs, if *they've* succeeded, they are little ambassadors for the firm, scouting the newly advanced second-year class for prospects for the firm. If they have a friend to recommend to the firm, chances are the firm will at least do them the courtesy of meeting you. Once your foot is in the door, who knows? Maybe your macho self-confidence, relational teamwork skills, interesting hobbies, and technical engineering skills will boost you right over the line.

You Can Succeed
in Law School

THIS BOOK IS *your springboard, not your ladder.*
Now that you've seen what the landscape looks like from a distance, you need to take over. Make yourself a success in law school. First of all, do as Carol Counselor did: Look up the rules. Every subject I discussed in this book is the subject of more extensive treatment elsewhere. There are books that describe the locations, course offerings, student opinions, etc., of all the schools, although not from a gender standpoint. Still, they contain much information I didn't have space for here, including an overview of the sources of funding. Such books include

LSAC, *The Official Guide to U.S. Law Schools, 1998* (Broadway Books).

Harry Castleman and Christopher Niewoehner, *Going to Law School?* (John Wiley and Sons, 1997).

The Princeton Review, *Student Advantage Guide to the Best Law Schools* (Random House, 1996).

American Bar Association, *The Official Guide to Approved Law Schools, 1998* (Macmillan, 1997).

Ruth Lammerts Reeves, *Kaplan: Getting into Law School* (Simon & Schuster, 1997).

Most law students fund their educations from a combination of their or their family's resources; federal work-study, which allows you to work for the law school as well as in community service after the first year; federal loans; and institutional loans and scholarships. For a first overview, the Law School Admission Council publishes *Financial Aid for Law School: A Preliminary Guide* (Publication Code 003), obtainable from Law School Admission Council, Box 2400, Newtown, PA 18940-0977. Once you've zeroed in on a number of law schools, the most efficient way to assemble your financial aid plan is to gather materials from all the schools you'd like to attend.

Most programs, federal or not, rely on the Free Application for Federal Student Aid, a form that requires you to reveal your income and assets, as well as the assets of your family and spouse if any. Although you can get the FAFSA from lots of places, here again the best procedure is to use the financial aid resources and information available through the admissions procedure at the schools you are considering. Almost every application for admissions includes information about the resources available at the particular school and about the national programs like federal loans.

LSAT cram books are probably responsible for the deforesting of Brazil. I discussed the two main ones in chapter 3. In addition to the Hricik and the Whitebread, there are a handful of other success guides, including books about how to study. Many of them can be found in the same section of your local bookstore where you found me.

Many of the people I interviewed learned a lot about their law school options from caring and more experienced people in their lives. If you aren't related to a lawyer or living near one in your hometown, call the local bar association and ask if there's a committee on women and the law. Once you've found it, ask if they can put you in touch with someone to talk about the pros and cons of law school. Your college probably has a prelaw adviser. My favorite prelaw adviser hung a copy of my *Glamour* magazine article on the bulletin board outside his office. Knowing about law school is their job. Take advantage of it.

If you live near a local law school, or if you attend a university with a law school, go to the admissions department and ask to sit in on a whole day of classes. Have a woman student take you around and ask her about her experience.

Other people evaluate law schools. The most famous one is the annual *U.S. News & World Report* issue on law schools, usually published in March. The *U.S. News* survey is the subject of some controversy, because it allows deans and other people to rank all the law schools according to what they think of them, and this is an awfully fuzzy measure. You will notice that the only aspect of the *U.S. News* ranking I thought was useful was the hard numerical data about the median LSATs in the entering class of 1995 (graduating '98). The other stuff is too vulnerable to manipulation for my taste. Still, you can get up-to-date info on the selectivity and placement rates, as well as the median scores, from the *U.S. News* report, which should be reliable.

The computer is a valuable resource. Go into the library or someplace that offers the LEXIS/NEXIS database and look up the names of the law schools you're interested in. The search format is Library "NEWS," file "CURNWS," or "ARCNWS" for older info. If a scandal has broken, it may be reported there. If one or more of their faculty have written opinion pieces, a search for the school name will tell you what some of the faculty are thinking. Use the Internet. The Web sites of the law schools have a wealth of information about the faculty and the courses, and now you know how to use it. Many newspapers and magazines are on the Internet, and you can look up the name of your prospective schools there if you can't find the easier LEXIS/NEXIS service available anywhere.

Inquiring TPUs Want to Know

Appendix A of this book contains all the questions I've asked of deans—and which you can now ask, too. As a prospective tuition-paying unit (TPU), you can ask again. You don't have to make a pest of yourself—I was trying to write this book for you, after all—but pick two or three things and ask for answers.

Ask for real answers. I was surprised at how often a dean would write or call (or I'd ask) about their law review and be assured it was "half women" when the numbers were much, much lower. If you don't think you're getting the straight scoop from admissions or you don't want to be a pest, go to the law review office and ask whoever is there to give you a copy of the list of editors and staff and do your own up-to-date analysis. You can even call and ask if law review participants with names like Glenn or Alex are male or female. You're not looking into 160 schools!

Be My Best Friend

E-mail me or visit me on my Web site, www.lawwomen.com. Do you know something I missed? When you went to follow up on something I said, did it turn out that someplace where women didn't succeed in 1996 and 1997 had turned itself around? What did you want to know that I didn't provide? If you're thinking about a decision and you'd like to talk it over before you sign on the dotted line, give me a digital jingle.

Would you like to go to prelaw summer camp? I'm thinking about offering young women a short course in law school before they start the first year, so that the first-year classroom won't be so surprising. We'll conduct mock classes, pull the curtain away from the many intimidating techniques of Socratic teaching, and give you a grounding in the way the system works. After all, by the time they're in their second and third years, women seem to do much better than in the first year, or at least the first semester. We're speculating that you can learn 90 percent of what you need to know to be at full speed by September in a few weeks before the semester starts. Let me know if you'd be interested in signing up.

Wanna Change the World?

At the Mills College conference, the several hundred participants—lawyers, judges, law professors, law students—broke up into groups, with the assignment to create an agenda to change law school for women. After a day of conferring, they met in a plenary session to give their recommendations. Some of them were quite far-reaching—abolish tenure, create a Portia law school for women, etc. But a lot of them were very practical and achievable. When you get to law school, you may want to work to make some of these changes. Some of them you can even make yourself.

The Mills College recommenders again and again hit on the same ideas.

1. Teach teachers how to run the Socratic method to help students learn, not scare the shy and encourage the bullies. What this means for you is that the whole structure of law school teaching is not your adversary. You can focus your learning in classes where the teachers do that already.

2. Make the process transparent. What this means for you is that the mysterious game is really not impenetrable and it's not just an arbitrary exercise. The Mills conferees thought if law students understood what was basically going on, they would be more comfortable with their role in the process. I hope this book has started that process in motion for you.

3. Teach other things. The people at Mills College weren't explicit about what they wanted taught, but I'm sure they meant to teach law as if women mattered, as if their freedom to reproduce when they desired to do so mattered, as if their security from rape and violence mattered, as if their touching faith in romantic love mattered, as if their commitment to childbearing and child rearing

mattered. If you learn nothing else, take from this book that a curriculum that excludes women's claims and hopes is not natural or an "autonomous discipline." It's as old-fashioned as hoop skirts and garters.

4. Law school is not an autonomous institution. The conferees revealed their exasperation with the dug-in world of law school and its "autonomous discipline" by recommending reaching out—to prospective students who will demand better treatment in exchange for their tuition payments, as well as to members of the bar who will exemplify the more humane values of the firms we saw, and to alumni, who will reform the schools from a safe distance. What this means for you is that although you have to retool yourself, you are also entitled to demand that the schools retool themselves and provide you with a better deal. Once you're accepted, you're in as strong a position as you'll ever be in. Make demands. Ask for a schedule that has at least one woman teacher before you accept their offer. Ask for a schedule that doesn't include teachers your research has revealed will demand that you become your own worst enemy.

Appendix

QUESTIONNAIRE FOR DEANS

I. Questions About Your Students

1. What is the size of the student body?_____

2. What percentage of the entire student body is female?_____

II. Questions About the Class Entering This Fall (Class of 2002)

3. What is the size of the class?_____

4. What percentage of the class of 2002 is female?_____

5. What are the entering statistical test qualifications of the class of 2002?
   a. What is the mean LSAT for all students?_____
   b. What is the median LSAT for all students?_____
   c. What is the mean LSAT for all women students?_____
   d. What is the median LSAT for all women students?_____
   e. What is the mean LSAT for all men students?_____
   f. What is the median LSAT for all men students?_____

6. What are the entering statistical grade qualifications of the class of 2002?
   a. What is the mean UGPA for all students?_____
   b. What is the median UGPA for all students?_____
   c. What is the mean UGPA for all women students?_____
   d. What is the median UGPA for all women students?_____
   e. What is the mean UGPA for all men students?_____
   f. What is the median UGPA for all men students?_____

7. If you have an automatic admit category for admissions, what percentage of your auto admits for the class of 2002 were women?_____
   a. What percentage of the auto admits actually enrolled?_____
   b. What percentage of the enrolled auto admits were women?_____

III. Questions About the Current Second-Year Students (hereafter, the class of 2001)

8. What is the percentage of women in the class of 2001?_____

9. What were the entering statistical test qualifications of the class of 2001?
   a. What is the mean LSAT for all students?_____
   b. What is the median LSAT for all students?_____
   c. What is the mean LSAT for all women students?_____
   d. What is the median LSAT for all women students?_____
   e. What is the mean LSAT for all men students?_____
   f. What is the median LSAT for all men students?_____

10. What were the entering statistical grade qualifications of the class of 2001?
    a. What is the mean UGPA for all students?_____
    b. What is the median UGPA for all students?_____
    c. What is the mean UGPA for all women students?_____
    d. What is the median UGPA for all women students?_____
    e. What is the mean UGPA for all men students?_____
    f. What is the median UGPA for all men students?_____

11. What was the GPA of the class of 2001 at the end of the first year, spring of '99?
    a. What is the mean LGPA for all students?_____
    b. What is the median LGPA for all students?_____
    c. What is the mean LGPA for all women students?_____
    d. What is the median LGPA for all women students?_____
    e. What is the mean LGPA for all men students?_____
    f. What is the median LGPA for all men students?_____

12. What is the percentage of women in the top 10 percent of the class at the end of the first year?_____

13. What is the percentage of women in the top 50 percent of the class at the end of the first year?_____

IV. Questions About the Graduating Class (Class of 2000)

14. What is the percentage of women in the graduating class?_____

15. What were the entering statistical test qualifications of the class of 2000?
    a. What is the mean LSAT for all students?_____
    b. What is the median LSAT for all students?_____
    c. What is the mean LSAT for all women students?_____
    d. What is the median LSAT for all women students?_____
    e. What is the mean LSAT for all men students?_____
    f. What is the median LSAT for all men students?_____

16. What were the entering statistical grade qualifications of the class of 2000?
    a. What is the mean UGPA for all students?_____
    b. What is the median UGPA for all students?_____
    c. What is the mean UGPA for all women students?_____
    d. What is the median UGPA for all women students?_____
    e. What is the mean UGPA for all men students?_____
    f. What is the median UGPA for all men students?_____

17. What is the LGPA of the class of 2000 as of the end of their second year, spring of '99?
    a. What is the mean LGPA for all students?_____
    b. What is the median LGPA for all students?_____
    c. What is the mean LGPA for all women students?_____
    d. What is the median LGPA for all women students?_____
    e. What is the mean LGPA for all men students?_____
    f. What is the median LGPA for all men students?_____

18. In June 2000, please update the class of 2000 to take into account the third-year grades._____

V. Questions About Law Review and Honors

19. What is the number and percentage of women writers on the law review staff of the named law school review (like the *University of Chicago Law Review*, usually general in subject matter) from the class of 2000?   Number_____   Percentage_____

20. What is the number and percentage of women editors on the law review of your named law school review from the class of 2000?   Number_____   Percentage_____

21. What is the number and percentage of women on the managing board of your named law school review from the class of 2000?   Number_____   Percentage_____

22. How is membership on law review determined?_____
    _____

23. How is editorship of law review determined?_____
    _____

24. If there is a diversity procedure for law review membership, what are the categories to which diversity procedures apply?
    _____

25. What percentage of the class of 1999 graduated with honors (Coif, cum laude, magna, summa, honors, high honors, and similar honors)?_____ (You may aggregate all the categories of honors)

26. What percentage of the class of 1999 was female?_____

VI. Questions About the Academic Tenured or Tenure-Track Faculty*

27. Who was the first woman to be hired in an academic tenured or tenure-track position?_____

28. When was the first woman hired?_____

29. Who was the first woman to be tenured as a tenured academic faculty member?_____

30. When was she tenured?_____

31. Since 1988, how many women have been hired as tenure-track academic faculty?_____

32. How many of the women hired as tenure-track academic faculty have received tenure since hiring?_____

33. How many women faculty have visited your school teaching a subject normally taught by tenured or tenure-track academic faculty since 1988?_____

34. Of the academic women visitors, how many have been hired since visiting?_____

    Of those hired, how many visitors were hired as laterals?_____

*Academic tenure or tenure track means full-time teachers of academic legal subjects but not including visiting professors, unless indicated, clinical or legal writing instructors or professors, regardless of tenure, adjuncts, lecturers, or guests from other parts of the university.

35. How many women other than visitors have been hired as tenured (lateral) academic faculty since 1988?_____

36. What percentage of academic tenured or tenure-track women are officially employed by your law school as of the school year 1999–2000?_____

37. What percentage of the academic tenured or tenure-track women officially employed by your law school are actually going to be teaching three or more academic law school classes during the school year 1999–2000?_____

38. How many women visitors are officially employed by your law school to teach three or more academic law school classes during the school year 1999–2000?_____

39. Since 1988, has your appointments committee been chaired by a woman? If so, how many years?_____

40. What is the percentage of tenured women on your appointments committee for the current academic year 1999–2000?_____

VII. Zeitgeist Questions

41. How many tenured or tenure-track academic faculty are scheduled to teach a course in the mandatory or optional academic (not legal writing or clinical) first-year curriculum during the school year 1999–2000?_____

42. What percentage of the faculty described in Question 41 are women?_____

43. What percentage of your first-year class has no women teaching any of their courses in the curriculum described in Question 41?_____

44. What percentage of your first-year class has one woman teaching any of their courses in the curriculum described in Question 41?_____

45. What percentage of your first-year class has more than one woman teaching any of their courses in the curriculum described in Question 41?_____

46. How many portraits of actual living or dead human beings (*not* Daumier prints, for example) are hanging in your law school?_____

47. What percentage of those portraits are women?_____

48. Does your school offer an orientation program for students?_____

49. Does your orientation include discussion of gender issues?_____

50. Does your school offer academic support during the first year?_____

51. Does your academic support include small-group or one-on-one tutoring?_____

VIII. Classroom Questions

52. What is the casebook assigned in each of your first-year torts courses?_____

53. During school year 1999–2000, will you require first-year students to take criminal law?_____

54. If the answer to Question 53 is affirmative, will—or did—the criminal law curriculum include lessons about the crime of rape?_____ If less than all classes will or did so, what percentage of the criminal law classes included lessons about the crime of rape?_____

55. Does your first-year core (not writing, not clinical) curriculum include any assignments other than exams at the end of the academic term, whatever it is?_____

56. Do any of the assignments described in Question 55 affect the first-year students' grades?_____

57. Do you have a policy regarding the types of examination professors may use to determine the students' grades?_____ If so, please include it.

Finally

58. Have you done any studies of gender at your school? If so, please describe the nature and administration of the study.

_____

Please attach a copy of the study.

Index

Index

Index

Index

Index

lawyers:
  clients of, 15
  in private practice, 14–16
  in public interest jobs, 15, 16–18, 29–30
  respect commanded by, 19–20
  salaries of, 13–14, 17–18, 46, 47
  trust accounts and, 242–43
  working hours of, 15, 46
legal reasoning (legal process), 11, 12
Legal Services Corporation, 235
legal system, 177, 179–82
legislatures, 172–73
LEXIS/NEXIS database, 158–59, 224–25, 248, 269
Littleton, Chris, 36
logical reasoning, in LSAT, 56, 68–71
Los Angeles, University of California at (UCLA), 32, 36, 160
  in Femscore table, 140
Louisiana, University of, at Baton Rouge, 151
Louisiana State, 110
Loyola Chicago, 144
Loyola Los Angeles, 143
Loyola New Orleans, 152

McGeorge School of Law, 23, 41–42, 54, 168
  in Femscore table, 151
  law review at, 241
  women faculty at, 42
MacKinnon, Catharine, 95, 104, 108, 119
Maine, University of, 109
  in Femscore table, 147
Manne, Henry, 36–37, 38, 39, 40, 41
Maroon Book, 240
Marquette University, 161
  in Femscore table, 147
Marsh, Heather, 128, 138
Maryland, University of, 144
Memphis, University of, 107–8, 109, 161
  in Femscore table, 148

mentors, law review and, 246–47
Mercer University, 107
  in Femscore table, 149
Miami, University of, 112, 161
  in Femscore table, 148
Michigan, University of, 107
  in Femscore table, 140
Mills College conference on women in legal education, 2, 202, 206, 271–72
Minnesota, University of, 111, 160
  in Femscore table, 140
Mississippi, University of, 151
Missouri, University of, at Columbia, 61
  in Femscore table, 147
Missouri, University of, at Kansas City, 161
  in Femscore table, 150
Montana, University of, 146
moot court, 33, 35–36
Morgan, Richard, 33

National Association of Law Placement, 7, 14
National Jurist, 129, 133
National Law Journal, 18, 124
Nebraska, University of, at Lincoln, 112, 161
  in Femscore table, 148
New England School of Law, 154
New Mexico, University of, 160
  in Femscore table, 145
New York Law School
  in Femscore tables, 148, 161
New York University (NYU) School of Law, 23, 28–34, 36, 54, 78
  in Femscore tables, 139, 159
  job placement from, 257–58
  public interest careers and, 29–30
  Root-Tilden Public Interest Fellowships at, 29, 30
  women faculty at, 3, 34
night schools, 135–36, 162–65
North Carolina, University of, 142
North Carolina Central, 129

Index